Japan Discovered

A Guide to Culture, Traditions, Society and Etiquette —
From Zen Gardens and Cherry Blossoms to the Hidden
Logic, Ancient Rituals, and Modern Paradoxes That Define
Japan

Annie Atlas

Contents

Chapter One

Introduction

Why Japan Remains Misunderstood Introduction

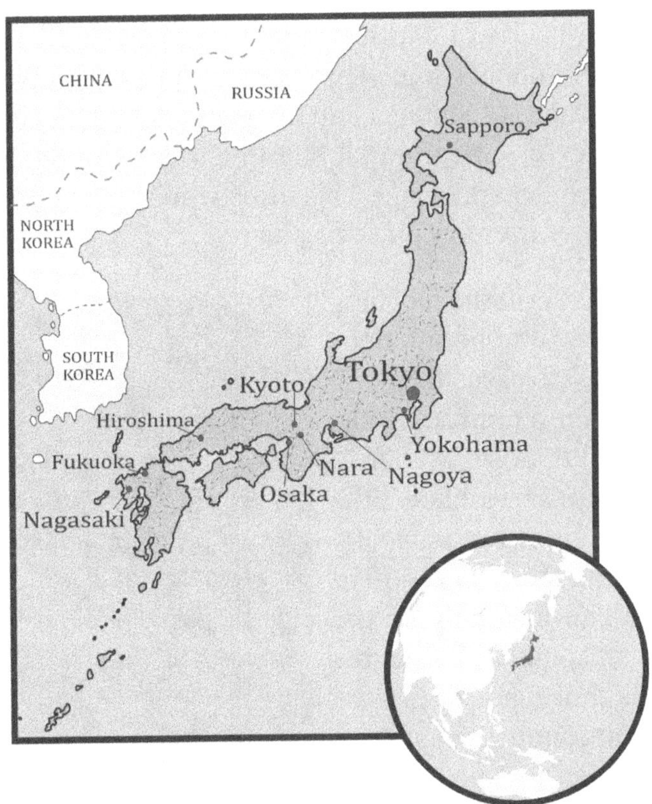

M ANY PEOPLE ENVISION JAPAN'S history as one of isolated uniformity, a polished tableau of samurai and geisha, untouched by external influences. The arrival of Yasuke, a towering African man, on Japan's shores in the sixteenth century challenges this perception directly. Yasuke quickly became the first documented foreign samurai, serving the legendary Oda Nobunaga. This singular historical detail disrupts the common narrative, proving a more complex and dynamic history than most people acknowledge.

Overlooked stories like Yasuke's act as crucial gateways to understanding the true depth of Japanese culture. Consider the ancient belief that a household tool develops a soul after a hundred years of use, transforming into a tsukumogami. Now place that alongside the modern phenomenon of millions of Japanese families celebrating Christmas Eve with buckets of Kentucky Fried Chicken. Japan is a nation built on layers of captivating contradictions. Each of these details hints at a deeper logic that eludes the casual observer. The vibrant streetscapes of Shibuya, bustling with neon and cutting-edge technology, coexist with tranquil Shinto shrines where rituals echo those performed millennia ago. This intertwining of the timeless and the timely defines the very pulse of Japan.

Picture this: it is six in the morning in Kyoto. A street sweeper meticulously clears fallen leaves from the pavement outside a temple. Inside, a monk begins his morning chants. They do not speak to each other, yet their actions are perfectly synchronized, a silent agreement to maintain the harmony of the space. This unspoken choreography happens thousands of times a day across the country, invisible to anyone who does not know how to look for it.

For many visitors, and even long-term residents, this underlying rhythm remains frustratingly opaque. You might learn the language, master the train system, and memorize the etiquette of exchanging business cards, yet still feel an invisible barrier separating you from the true core of the culture. You observe the impeccable service, the pristine streets, and the seamless public order, but the underlying mechanisms—the unwritten rules governing these behaviors—remain hidden. The desire to move beyond the role of a perpetual outsider, to genuinely comprehend the why behind the what, is a common and profound frustration.

I understand this frustration intimately. My name is Annie Atlas. I lived in Japan for over fifteen years, arriving initially as an English teacher before being recruited as a cultural analyst for a boutique risk-assessment firm in Roppongi. During that time, I immersed myself in the culture in ways few foreigners experience. I lived for six months in a Buddhist monastery, delving into the disciplined rhythms of monastic life. I meticulously documented the underground vintage denim trade in Kojima, navigating a fascinating intersection of global trends and local craftsmanship. I even had the unique privilege of discreetly guiding visiting diplomats through the unspoken rules of Japanese society, translating the delicate currents of honor and hierarchy. These varied, intensely personal engagements provided an unparalleled lens through which to decode Japan's inner workings and its often-unseen values. It was this rich, immersive background that solidified my conviction: Japan is one of the most misunderstood countries, simply because most narratives merely skim its surface.

My move from consulting to full-time writing was born from a desire to share these hard-won insights. My aim is to explore the fascinating friction points where Japan's ancient traditions robustly collide with its hyper-modern present, offering a perspective shaped by direct experience and rigorous analysis.

This book is designed to be your guide through those friction points. We will navigate the country's historical currents, delve into its philosophical depths, and examine the intricate dance between tradition and innovation. I will not give you a checklist of temples to visit or a phonetic guide to ordering sushi. Instead, I will give you a lens — one shaped by fifteen years of living inside the culture, not observing it from outside. Let us begin.

Chapter Two

The Story of Japan

From Ancient Times to Modern Nation

Mythical Origins and Early Societies

M OST NATIONS TRACE THEIR legitimacy to conquest, revolution, or treaties. Japan claims descent from the sun.

The Kojiki, compiled in 712 CE, recounts how the deities Izanagi and Izanami stirred the primordial ocean with a jeweled spear, creating the Japanese archipelago from droplets of brine. Their daughter,

Amaterasu, the radiant sun goddess, became the divine ancestor of Japan's imperial line — a genealogy that linked emperors directly to the heavens. Until 1945, these myths were taught in schools as literal historical fact, underwriting the emperor's sacred status and anchoring national identity in celestial authority.

Their influence extends far beyond political legitimacy. The Kojiki established the foundational grammar of Japanese life: that nature is alive and listening, something to be revered rather than subdued. A mountain, a waterfall, or an ancient tree carries presence and agency in the Japanese worldview. This is the operating system beneath every Shinto shrine, every seasonal festival, every garden raked into deliberate stillness.

The story begins even earlier, in the clay.

The Jōmon people, spanning roughly 14,000 BCE to 300 BCE, created some of the world's earliest ceramics — vessels adorned with distinctive flame-like cord patterns that still feel oddly modern in their elegance. They lived as hunter-gatherers, harvesting chestnuts and salmon, with settlements across forested islands. Burial practices, including carefully arranged stone circles, reveal nascent beliefs in an afterlife and ritualistic intent. Their society remained egalitarian, without the rigid hierarchies that would later define Japan.

Everything changed with the Yayoi period, beginning around 300 BCE. Migrants from the Korean Peninsula introduced wet-rice cultivation and bronze tools. Fields required coordination; coordination demanded hierarchy. Social stratification emerged alongside granaries and irrigation channels. With rice came surplus, and with surplus came the architecture of power. The Yayoi period likely saw the earliest stirrings of the imperial line — a dynasty that still exists today, making Japan's monarchy the oldest continuous one in the world.

By the fourth century CE, the Yamato clan had consolidated control across the fertile Nara Basin, absorbing rival clans and asserting divine authority as descendants of Amaterasu. This was not merely political conquest — it was the fusion of religion and governance into a single, self-reinforcing structure. The emperor ruled because the emperor was divine. Questioning the throne meant questioning the cosmos.

The consolidation accelerated in the seventh century when Chinese bureaucratic models arrived alongside Buddhism. The Taika Reforms of 645 CE centralized imperial land ownership, dismantled clan holdings, established a national tax system, and remodeled the imperial court on Tang China's capital. Governance was no longer a matter of personal loyalty to a warlord — it became a system of written law, census records, and administrative hierarchy. Without this centralization, Japan would have remained a patchwork of competing tribes. With it, the country developed the cultural continuity that would define it for the next fourteen centuries.

Then came the Kofun period, named for its enormous keyhole-shaped burial mounds. The Daisen Kofun, built for Emperor Nintoku in the fifth century, stretches nearly half a kilometer in length — larger in footprint than the Great Pyramid of Giza. By the time the Asuka and Nara periods arrived, Buddhism had entered from the Korean peninsula, mingling with native animist beliefs to shape what we now call Shinto: not a codified religion, but a way of seeing the world, one built on reverence for nature, spirits in everything, and ritual over doctrine.

By the Heian era (794–1185), Japan was writing itself into history. The imperial court moved to Kyoto. Poetry flourished. Aristocrats refined aesthetics that still define Japan today — seasonal awareness, layered clothing, and the subtlety of gesture. This was the age of The Tale of Genji, written by court lady Murasaki Shikibu around 1000 CE and widely regarded as the world's first novel. Art, politics, and spirituality were inseparable in Heian court life, and beauty was treated not as a luxury but as a form of virtue.

The Rise of the Samurai and the Shogunate

Behind the refined poetry of the Heian court, cracks were forming. Local clans grew stronger, armed with private militias and family loyalties that stretched farther than imperial edicts. Out of this shifting landscape rose the figure who would come to define Japanese history for centuries: the samurai.

The samurai were never defined by a single written code. Bushido, the Way of the Warrior, emerged from lived practice — shaped by Zen meditation, Confucian loyalty, and an intimate relationship with mortality. A samurai's morning might begin with calligraphy. Calligraphy demanded the same mastery as swordsmanship: balance, breath, and unwavering intention. The brush and the blade were parallel exercises in presence, training mind and body as one instrument.

Loyalty superseded survival. When a lord died, his retainers often followed through seppuku — ritual disembowelment performed with ceremonial precision. How do you convince an entire class of elite warriors that their lives are worth less than their duty? The answer lies in a worldview where personal identity did not exist in isolation. A samurai was only as real as his relationship to his master. Remove the master, and the self had no anchor.

The samurai ethos permeated Japan's cultural architecture: tea ceremony aesthetics, spatial design, linguistic formality. Modern corporate hierarchies still echo their structures of discipline and collective obligation — remnants of a warrior class whose influence outlived the sword by centuries.

By the late 1100s, the Kamakura shogunate emerged — Japan's first real military government, headed by a shogun, or commander-in-chief. The emperor remained, but only as a symbol. Real power was now held by warriors. During the Muromachi and Sengoku periods that followed, Japan became a land of near-constant warfare. Lords, known as daimyō, built castles on mountaintops and plains, vying for control with shifting armies. It was a time of upheaval, but also of unexpected creativity. Noh theater, ink painting, the tea ceremony, and Zen Buddhism all took deeper root during this era of violence and introspection — as if the proximity of death sharpened the Japanese appetite for beauty.

The chaos finally gave way under Tokugawa Ieyasu, who emerged victorious at the Battle of Sekigahara in 1600 and unified the country. His consolidation was meticulously engineered through administrative architecture that would define Japan for the next two and a half centuries.

The Tokugawa Shogunate and the Locked Country

Picture two thousand people moving in procession along a mountain road. Retainers in formal dress. Lacquered palanquins. Prescribed rest stops at government-approved inns. This was not a military march or a royal celebration — it was a tax. The Tokugawa shogunate's sankin-kōtai policy required each daimyō to spend every other year in Edo, the shogun's capital, traveling with elaborate processions that bled their treasuries dry with mandated spectacle. Their families remained in Edo year-round, hostages in all but name. What does it mean to govern a nation not through force, but through ceremony? The Tokugawa answered that question for two hundred and fifty years.

The policy achieved what armies could not: it bankrupted potential rebels, kept them moving rather than plotting, and ensured loyalty through proximity and financial exhaustion. The Kaga domain's annual journey regularly involved over two thousand people. Governance was disguised as ceremony, and it worked.

Edo swelled into the world's largest city by 1700, housing over one million people. The shogunate mapped every domain, standardized road systems, and regulated commerce down to which merchants could sell silk. Power was woven into geography, economics, and daily routine. Society became a carefully arranged pyramid: samurai at the top, followed by farmers, artisans, and merchants — whose growing wealth often outpaced their official status. Movement was restricted. Social roles were inherited. Yet beneath the surface, urban culture bloomed. Kabuki theater drew crowds. Woodblock prints, known as ukiyo-e, captured the fleeting pleasures of Edo's pleasure quarters. A new middle-class aesthetic was forming — stylish, witty, and acutely aware of its own impermanence.

Between 1633 and 1639, the shogunate issued a series of calculated edicts that sealed Japan from the world for over two centuries. Sakoku — the "locked country" — banned Portuguese traders, outlawed Christianity as a subversive force, and made it a capital crime for Japanese citizens to leave the archipelago. Only a tightly controlled opening remained: Dutch and Chinese merchants confined to Dejima, an artificial island in Nagasaki harbor barely larger than a city block. The shogunate had watched Christianity spread rapidly through Kyushu, seen rival feudal lords convert to secure European firearms, and recognized that foreign ideology could fracture their newly won centralized power. Sealing the borders was a calculated act of political survival.

The result was cultural distillation. Cut off from external influence,

Japan turned inward with remarkable intensity. Kabuki evolved into elaborate spectacle. Haiku crystallized into seventeen syllables of precision. Artisans refined metalwork, ceramics, and textile techniques across generations, uninterrupted by foreign competition. When Commodore Perry's black ships appeared in Edo Bay in 1853, many Japanese had never seen a Westerner. Japan had become something unprecedented: a nation that chose complete solitude and emerged with an identity entirely its own.

The Meiji Restoration and Industrial Transformation

The Meiji Restoration began not with a grand proclamation but with a bureaucratic coup. On January 3, 1868, forces aligned with Emperor Meiji seized Kyoto's imperial palace and issued a single declaration: the shogunate no longer existed. What followed was systematic reinvention. The new government inherited Tokugawa administrative structures and repurposed them with startling efficiency. Samurai stipends were abolished in 1876, liquidating an entire class overnight. Former warriors became policemen, teachers, and bureaucrats — their swords exchanged for fountain pens.

The changes were fast and they were everywhere. Steam trains cut across the countryside. Telegraph lines stitched distant cities together. Children studied in classrooms built on a Western model, while factories rose along the rivers. Western ideas, dress, and technology were adopted with breathtaking speed — not because Japan wished to imitate, but because it intended to compete. Japan studied Prussian military doctrine, British naval strategy, and French civil law, then synthesized them into something distinctly Japanese. By 1889, Japan had a constitution. By 1895, it had defeated China in war. A feudal archipelago had become an industrial power in a single generation.

Textile mills demonstrated this transformation most clearly. When the Tomioka Silk Mill opened in 1872 with French machinery, it needed a disciplined, educated workforce. It found one in an unexpected place: the daughters of the newly abolished samurai class.

Families who had spent centuries defined by martial pride and strict social standing suddenly had no income. Sending their daughters to operate steam-powered looms was a matter of survival. The hum of those machines did more than produce export goods — it dismantled a feudal hierarchy in real time, placing the descendants of warriors onto the factory floor.

The Shimbashi-Yokohama railway line — eighteen miles of British-engineered track — officially opened in October 1872. Within twenty years, the country operated nearly two thousand miles of rail, reshaping commerce, communication, and mobility across the archipelago. Industrial capacity prepared the ground, but political insecurity sparked territorial expansion. After centuries of sakoku, Japan entered a world already carved into colonial spheres, where military weakness invited subjugation. The First Sino-Japanese War of 1894–1895 demonstrated this logic: Japan defeated Qing China, seized Taiwan, and established dominance over Korea. The Russo-Japanese War of 1904–1905 confirmed Japan's arrival as a regional power — the first modern instance of an Asian nation defeating a European empire.

War, Devastation, and the Economic Miracle

Military success concealed deepening contradictions. Expansion required resources Japan lacked: oil, rubber, and iron. Each territorial gain increased dependency rather than resolving it, trapping the nation in a cycle where conquest became the only perceived solution to scarcity. The years leading up to World War II were marked by imperial ambition, culminating in the occupation of Korea, incursions into China, and ultimately, war with the Allied powers. The atomic bombings of Hiroshima and Nagasaki brought Japan to its knees. Cities were flattened. Over three million dead. The imperial dream lay in ruins.

In Hiroshima's Peace Memorial Museum, a watch remains frozen at 8:15. A carbonized bento box sits in its case. A shadow, burned permanently into stone steps, marks the exact spot where a person stood when the bomb fell. Step outside the museum. Department stores line the streets. Trams glide through intersections. Schoolchildren laugh near the river. This contrast between remembrance and renewal reveals Japan's post-war philosophy more clearly than any economic statistic: complete acknowledgment of catastrophe, paired with an unwavering commitment to rebuilding.

The 1947 Constitution, imposed during American occupation, became the cornerstone of renewal. Article 9 renounced war, redirecting national resources from military ambitions toward industrial reconstruction. The zaibatsu conglomerates were dismantled, then quietly reassembled as keiretsu — interconnected networks of banks, manufacturers, and trading companies that would drive Japan's export economy for decades. By 1955, industrial output surpassed pre-war levels. By 1968, Japan was the world's second-largest economy.

The recovery was engineered, not miraculous. Early transistor radios crackled. The first Japanese cars rattled and leaked. Factories ran on repurposed American machinery and sheer improvisation. What emerged from this was kaizen — the philosophy of continuous improvement. Make something functional. Then make it better. Then make it better still. Progress compounded through relentless, incremental refinement embedded in every assembly line, every clerical procedure, every design iteration. From Sony radios to Toyota sedans, quality became Japan's calling card. Behind that success was a workforce that believed in collective effort, precision, and pride in the smallest details.

Culture did not disappear beneath industrial expansion. Tea ceremonies found new life in corporate boardrooms. Shrine festivals wound through concrete neighborhoods. Calligraphy schools opened beside electronics retailers. Tradition did not retreat into museums — it discovered fresh contexts, new spaces to inhabit. Japan rose from devastation by rejecting entirely the notion that heritage and progress must cancel each other out. The nation forged a third path: synthesis.

Today, Japan remains a country shaped by its past but not imprisoned by it. It rebuilt itself not by forgetting, but by remembering — and then choosing to begin again with extraordinary care. What emerges when a society holds catastrophe and beauty in the same hand, and refuses to drop either?

The Hangover

The miracle had a ceiling, and Japan hit it in 1991.

For four decades, the economy had expanded with a momentum that seemed self-sustaining. Land prices in Tokyo's Ginza district reached a point where the theoretical value of the Imperial Palace grounds exceeded the entire real estate value of California. Golf club memberships traded like securities. Companies borrowed against inflated asset values to fund further expansion, and banks lent freely because collateral appeared inexhaustible. The system worked until it did not.

When the asset bubble burst, it did so slowly — not in a single crash but in a long, grinding deflation that would consume the following decade and a half. The Nikkei index, which had peaked at nearly 39,000 in December 1989, fell to a third of that value within two years and kept falling. Land prices collapsed. Banks, carrying enormous portfolios of non-performing loans secured against assets now worth a fraction of their stated value, stopped lending. Companies that had borrowed against those assets found themselves technically insolvent. The government, reluctant to force the reckoning that restructuring would require, extended credit and delayed resolution. The result was not recovery. It was stagnation.

The Lost Decades — a phrase that eventually required a plural — lasted from the early 1990s through the mid-2000s, with aftershocks extending well beyond. The human cost was not measured in unemployment statistics alone. Japan's corporate culture had been built on a specific promise: join a major company, commit your working life to it, and the company will commit to you. Lifetime employment was not merely a contract. It was a social architecture. Seniority-based promotion, company housing, corporate health insurance, retirement bonuses calculated across decades of service — these were the pillars of a system that had delivered middle-class stability to an entire generation.

The bubble's collapse cracked those pillars. Companies that could not restructure through redundancies — because the social contract made mass layoffs culturally catastrophic — instead stopped hiring. The generation that graduated in the 1990s and early 2000s entered a labor market that had quietly closed its doors. Unable to secure the permanent positions that the system was designed to provide, many took temporary or part-time work instead. These workers became known as freeters — a portmanteau of the English "free" and the German Arbeiter, meaning worker — and their numbers grew into the millions. The term carried a stigma that the individuals themselves had done nothing to earn. The system had simply run out of room for them.

The consequences compounded across generations. Workers who entered the labor market as freeters found it nearly impossible to transition into permanent employment later, because Japanese hiring culture treats career gaps and non-standard work histories as disqualifying signals. Many remained in precarious employment into their thirties and forties, unable to afford the housing, marriage, and children that the previous generation had treated as default milestones. The declining birth rate — a demographic crisis now discussed with genuine alarm — has roots that extend directly into this economic soil. When stability is uncertain, the decision to start a family becomes a calculation rather than an assumption.

Understanding this history is essential for reading modern Japan clearly. The work culture described in later chapters — the karoshi overwork, the hikikomori withdrawal, the quiet exhaustion visible in late-night commuters — did not emerge from cultural pathology. It emerged from a specific economic rupture and the social structures that formed in response to it. The miracle generation built a system of extraordinary collective achievement. The generations that followed inherited the architecture of that system without the conditions that made it function. They are still negotiating the terms.

Beneath the Surface

The Philosophical Foundations That Still Rule Japan

Shintoism and the Native Way of Kami

BEFORE BUDDHISM ARRIVED FROM China, before Confucian ethics structured social relations, before emperors claimed divine mandate through continental philosophy, Japanese religious practice already existed.

Shintoism lacks the defining features of a Western religion. It has no founder, no sacred text commanding obedience, and no theology debating the nature of divinity. What it possesses instead are stories. The Kojiki and Nihon Shoki, compiled in the eighth century CE, codified myths that had circulated orally for generations. They described how the deity Izanagi thrust his spear into primordial waters to create islands from the dripping brine, and how his children became mountains and rivers. These texts described the literal origins of Japan's landscape, encoding the radical belief that every element of the natural world — waterfalls, ancient trees, oddly shaped rocks — contained kami.

Kami defies direct translation. Words like gods, spirits, or sacred presences fail to capture the concept entirely. A kami could be an ancestor, a mountain peak, or the force animating a particular grove of cedars. Early Shinto practice involved purification rituals, offerings of rice and sake, and rhythmic clapping to signal one's presence. No sin required absolution because purity and pollution operated as physical states, not moral categories. You did not confess wrongdoing; you rinsed it away.

This framework still governs Japan in ways most visitors never recognize. Purity remains the organizing principle of daily life. Removing shoes before entering a home is the physical enactment of leaving outside pollution at the threshold — hygiene is incidental. The interior space is preserved as purified territory, and the act of crossing that threshold barefoot is a ritual acknowledgment of the boundary between the contaminated outside world and the protected space within. This boundary consciousness appears everywhere. Public baths require meticulous washing before entering communal water. Food preparation involves strict attention to ingredient separation — raw and cooked items never touch the same surface.

Even modern office buildings feature genkan entryways where street shoes are exchanged for indoor slippers, maintaining spatial hierarchy through footwear.

Harmony, or wa, functions similarly. Shinto sees mountains, rivers, and humans as containing kami, making any disruption of the natural relationship a violation of cosmic structure. Harmony becomes a practical necessity. This explains why Japanese meetings prioritize consensus over efficiency, why public confrontation is shocking, and why society functions with minimal trash bins. Creating waste that burdens others ruptures wa. Connection to nature operates by the same principle: seasonal ingredients dominate cuisine because eating what the land currently offers aligns human rhythm with natural cycles, maintaining the relationship between the kami in nature and the kami in people.

Millions of Japanese visit shrines on New Year's Day, but few identify as strictly religious. The ritual itself remains simple: toss a coin, bow twice, clap twice, bow again. This gesture signifies respect to kami and participation in a continuous cultural tradition passed down through generations. Corporate Japan absorbed this seamlessly. Companies routinely hold jichinsai ceremonies, where Shinto priests bless construction sites to appease land kami. New taxis undergo purification rituals. Department stores feature rooftop shrines. Even a CEO who might not believe in spirits would not skip these ceremonies — the perceived risk simply is not worth it.

Western visitors often misread this dynamic, wondering how Japan can be non-religious yet saturated with shrines. Shinto operates as cultural infrastructure. It is ambient and often invisible until needed. Its survival means it has become indistinguishable from normal life.

Buddhism's Impact – From Zen to Daily Practices

Zen Buddhism arrived in Japan during the twelfth century, carried by monks returning from China. Unlike earlier Buddhist schools that promised salvation through scripture or devotion, Zen dismissed textual authority entirely. Enlightenment came through direct experience — sitting meditation, physical labor, or sudden insight triggered by a master's question. This philosophy demanded practice, not contemplation.

The aesthetic revolution followed quickly. Zen monks designed rock gardens where raked gravel suggested water, with fifteen stones arranged so you could never see all of them simultaneously. These meditation tools trained the mind to accept incompleteness. The tea ceremony codified this into ritual: every gesture controlled, every utensil positioned precisely, yet the entire performance celebrated humility through rough pottery and asymmetrical arrangements.

Modern Japan inherited this aesthetic without realizing it. The sparse apartment with a futon stored during the day reflects Zen's rejection of excess. Bento boxes compartmentalize ingredients with spatial precision descended from tea ceremony protocols. Corporate employees at companies like Toyota and Sony often engage in Zen-derived mindfulness training, leveraging concentration techniques that Zen systematized centuries ago. Simplicity became cultural infrastructure, shaping everything from product design to daily routines.

Buddhist rituals reveal the depth of this integration with unusual clarity. When death arrives in a Japanese household, families instinctively contact a Buddhist temple, often regardless of the deceased's actual religious practice. The priest arrives to chant sutras while incense spirals upward. Cremation follows, leading to the bone-picking ceremony: relatives use special chopsticks to transfer bone fragments into an urn. This ritual is so distinctive that passing food chopstick-to-chopstick at meals remains deeply taboo, forever shadowed by its association with death.

The butsudan — the household Buddhist altar — occupies a quiet corner in countless Japanese homes, from rural farmhouses to cramped urban apartments. Families light incense there each morning, offer rice and tea, and speak to departed relatives as though they remain present. During Obon, the summer festival when ancestral spirits return home, these altars become focal points of reunion. Lanterns guide the dead back from the spirit world, and favorite foods appear as offerings. Buddhism provided the ritual vocabulary, but the practice addresses something older: the Japanese conviction that the dead remain woven into the living world, watching over descendants and requiring care.

Buddhist mindfulness saturates activities most foreigners assume are purely practical. Sweeping, polishing, washing rice — these are opportunities for zazen in motion, meditative focus extended into mundane rhythms. Watch a shopkeeper arrange fruit: each piece positioned deliberately, rotated to present its best angle, wiped clean. This is mindfulness practice disguised as commerce.

From this same Buddhist foundation comes mottainai — a word with no clean English equivalent. It expresses regret over waste, but not as an environmental concern. Discarding food carelessly or throwing away a functional object violates the Buddhist reverence for interconnection. Everything carries the labor, resources, and intention that brought it into existence; dismissing it dishonors those investments. An elderly woman carefully unwrapping a gift, folding the paper, and setting it aside to use again is not being frugal. She is practicing a form of respect — for the craftsman who made the paper, the person who chose it, and the object it once protected. Mottainai is why Japanese packaging is often more beautiful than its contents, and why discarding it without a second thought feels, to many Japanese, like a small act of violence.

The Beauty of the Imperfect – Wabi-Sabi and Mono no Aware

In a world that often chases permanence and polish, Japanese aesthetics offer a quiet reverence for the incomplete, the weathered, and the fleeting. Two concepts in particular shape this way of seeing: wabi-sabi and mono no aware.

Wabi-sabi is often translated as "beauty in imperfection," but it carries far more weight than the phrase suggests. It is the warmth of a handmade ceramic cup, slightly uneven at the rim. It is the silence in a weathered teahouse, the pause in a sentence, the space in a room that is left intentionally empty. Wabi-sabi values presence over flawlessness. It honors what is real, what has aged, and what carries the quiet dignity of use and time. A tea bowl deliberately thrown off-center on the wheel, its glaze pooling unevenly at the base, is considered more beautiful than a symmetrical one. The asymmetry signals a human hand, not a machine. Imperfection becomes the proof of authenticity.

Mono no aware, meanwhile, is the awareness of impermanence — the gentle ache that comes with knowing nothing lasts. This philosophy explains why cherry blossoms are so deeply loved in Japan. Their transience is the point. You enjoy them more precisely because they will fall within days. That tenderness, that quiet sadness that deepens appreciation, transforms transience from tragedy into a profound meditation on mortality.

Traditional ink painting follows identical logic. Artists spend years grinding ink and learning brush control, then execute entire compositions in minutes. The blank space — ma — carries as much weight as the brushstrokes themselves. Western viewers often ask what is missing from these sparse landscapes. Nothing is missing. The emptiness is the point, a visual expression of Buddhist śūnyatā, the fundamental emptiness underlying apparent form.

Modern Japanese media inherited this structure wholesale. Studio Ghibli films pause for silent sequences — characters watching rain, or walking without dialogue. These deliberate meditations trust the audience to inhabit stillness. Video games like Dark Souls encode Buddhist suffering directly, using endless death-rebirth loops to teach players to accept failure as instructive rather than punitive. Even manga page layouts manipulate time through panel size and spacing, allowing readers to control the narrative rhythm through their own attention — exactly how Zen training teaches awareness of breath.

To recognize Buddhist influence in Japan, watch for silence, negative space, and the acceptance of transience. These are spiritual architectures made visible.

Confucianism – The Invisible Hand in Social Harmony

Confucianism arrived in Japan through the same sixth-century conduit that delivered Buddhism: Korean emissaries bearing Chinese texts. While Buddhism offered salvation and aesthetic philosophy, Confucianism provided something the emerging Japanese state desperately needed — a manual for political order.

Prince Shōtoku's Seventeen-Article Constitution of 604 CE drew heavily on Confucian principles, establishing hierarchy as virtue and obedience as moral duty. Early adoption remained selective and elite, confined largely to court scholars who read Chinese classics without fundamentally reshaping society. For centuries, Confucianism existed as imported knowledge rather than lived structure.

The Tokugawa shogunate changed the trajectory entirely. When Ieyasu seized power in 1603, he needed an ideology to justify rigid social stratification and prevent the chaos that had plagued previous centuries. Neo-Confucianism became state orthodoxy. The shogunate established Confucian academies, required samurai to study the classics, and enshrined the five relationships as natural law: ruler and subject, father and son, husband and wife, elder and younger, friend and friend. Only one relationship was theoretically equal. Every other pairing encoded permanent hierarchy, with loyalty flowing upward and benevolence supposedly flowing down.

Those Tokugawa-era structures survived modernization intact. Walk into any Japanese corporation today and you will encounter a hierarchy that would make Confucian scholars nod in recognition. The sempai-kōhai system — senior-junior relationships — governs workplace interactions with ritualized precision. New employees bow lower, speak more politely, and pour drinks for seniors who joined the company even one year earlier. Junior employees frequently wait for cues from senior staff before contributing to discussions. Senior staff members, regardless of technical knowledge, typically lead conversations and decision-making. This top-down flow of communication is deeply ingrained cultural practice, invisible yet absolute.

The home reveals similar continuity. Filial piety remains visceral rather than philosophical. Adult children coordinate schedules around aging parents, often relocating to provide care rather than choosing institutional options. Nursing homes carry lingering stigma despite Japan's rapidly graying population, as traditional beliefs associate institutional care with an abandonment of Confucian duty.

If there is one thread that runs quietly through Japanese society, it is the value placed on wa — harmony. In Japan, the group often comes before the individual. This means personal desires are balanced against a deep awareness of context. A decision requires asking how an action will affect others. Tone matters. Timing matters. What is left unsaid often speaks louder than what is declared.

In conversation, this manifests as pauses, deferential language, and the habit of softening disagreement until silence carries the message more clearly than words ever could. Group behavior follows the same logic — lining up without fuss, leaving shared spaces exactly as you found them, removing shoes at the door without being asked. Each small act prioritizes smooth interaction over individual assertion. Wa functions as a cultural immune system, catching friction before it spreads.

Japan is not without conflict or complexity. But even then, wa shapes how tension is expressed, or often, how it is diffused. The goal is never to win the room. The goal is to keep the room intact. How does a society maintain cohesion in cities of thirty million people? By ensuring that every individual understands exactly where they fit within the whole.

Chapter Four

Speaking Without Words

Language and Communication

More Than Words – The Subtle Layers of Japanese

THE FIRST THING MOST people notice about spoken Japanese is the cadence. It sounds remarkably tidy, with a rhythmic structure that feels inherently polite. But the true complexity of the language lies entirely beneath the surface vocabulary. Speaking Japanese effectively requires understanding relationships before choosing words.

Japanese frequently leaves the obvious unsaid. A speaker rarely needs to say "I" or "you" because the context of the conversation makes the actors perfectly clear to anyone paying attention. Sentences trail off. Subjects vanish mid-thought. The language operates on the assumption of mutual awareness, rewarding restraint over assertion. Saying less consistently communicates more.

The system of honorifics, known as keigo, adjusts the grammar and vocabulary depending entirely on the speaker's relationship to the listener. Keigo maps social distance. It functions as a constant verbal acknowledgment of where two people stand relative to one another in terms of age, status, and familiarity. This constant calibration ensures that every interaction acknowledges the social structure.

Casual conversations carry this same demand for calibration. A simple "yes" (hai) frequently means "I understand what you are saying," rather than "I agree with you." A pause inserted before a reply often carries the actual weight of the response. Spelling out every detail of an opinion or a plan is considered clumsy, even awkward.

Mastering Japanese requires learning how to read the air, feeling the space between the spoken lines, and allowing communication to unfold with deliberate care.

The Language of Silence – High-Context Conversations

Silence in Japan carries meaning. It serves as a structural component of the conversation, often holding the most honest part of the exchange.

Linguists classify Japanese as a high-context language. The words themselves carry only a fraction of the communicative burden. The majority of the meaning resides in the context: the identity of the speakers, the physical location, the history of the relationship, and precisely what is left unsaid. A listener must notice the atmosphere, reading between the gestures and the pauses to grasp the full intent.

A speaker might trail off in the middle of a sentence, or answer a direct question with a soft laugh and nothing more. This signals trust. The speaker trusts that the listener is paying close enough attention to understand the meaning without forcing an explicit, potentially uncomfortable declaration.

The Japanese phrase for this skill is kuuki o yomu, which translates literally as "reading the air." People grow up learning this social reflex. It dictates when to speak and when to step back, recognizing when a joke has landed or when an opinion would unnecessarily agitate the group.

Missteps happen, and even native speakers occasionally misjudge the air. But the underlying intent remains constant: to preserve ease, to prevent friction, and to keep the social group functioning smoothly. Conversation functions as a shared space, and silence remains one of its most carefully deployed tools.

Bows, Pauses, and Glances – Non-Verbal Nuance

Picture a junior employee spotting his section manager on a crowded train platform. No words pass between them. The junior bows at roughly forty-five degrees and holds the position for two full seconds.

The manager returns a shallower bow of perhaps fifteen degrees and looks away first. The entire exchange lasts four seconds and communicates seniority, respect, and mutual acknowledgment with a precision that no spoken greeting could replicate. A significant portion of daily communication in Japan operates exactly like this — entirely without words.

The bow shifts constantly depending on depth, timing, and purpose. A quick nod between friends serves a entirely different function than the deep, sustained bend of a formal corporate apology. The bow offered during a greeting differs subtly from the bow expressing gratitude. To an outsider, they look identical. To someone raised within the culture, the angle and duration carry precise emotional weight, folding humility, respect, and acknowledgment into a single motion.

Eye contact operates under a different set of rules than in Western cultures, where a steady gaze often signals confidence or sincerity. In Japan, prolonged eye contact can feel aggressive or invasive. The culture prizes attentiveness, focusing on the balance of the gaze rather than its intensity.

Pauses dictate the rhythm of serious discussions. A moment of silence before answering a question signals reflection, demonstrating that the listener heard the question and is giving it proper consideration. Rushing to respond immediately often feels careless or dismissive.

The unspoken consistently carries more clarity than the spoken word. The challenge for any visitor lies in learning to listen with the entire body.

Lost in Translation – Humor, Ambiguity, and Meaning

Humor in Japan relies heavily on shared situational context rather than verbal sparring. It depends on timing, shared experience, and absurdity delivered with a perfectly straight face. Wordplay and puns (dajare) remain popular, particularly in television broadcasts. Humor that relies on sarcasm, irony, or direct confrontation rarely succeeds.

This failure occurs because confrontational humor pulls too hard at the fabric of social harmony, risking genuine offense.

Ambiguity commands deep respect. Japanese communication leans deliberately into the gray areas, creating space for nuance that blunt directness would collapse. A vague response often serves as the most polite way to deliver a refusal, preserving the relationship by leaving the other person's dignity intact.

A speaker might begin a sentence with chotto... — meaning "a little... " — and follow it with silence. Depending entirely on the context, this could mean "I would rather not," "That will not work," or "Absolutely not, but I would like to remain friends." The words leave the door slightly ajar, even when the underlying answer is a firm negative.

This subtle approach disorients outsiders accustomed to reading meaning head-on. A foreign executive who pushes past chotto to demand a direct yes or no has not extracted clarity — he has forced his Japanese counterpart into an uncomfortable corner and damaged the working relationship in the process. The answer was already there, delivered in the pause and the trailing syllable. He simply did not know how to listen for it.

What does it mean to live in a society where the most important things are never said out loud? It means developing an entirely different relationship with language — one where the spaces between words carry as much information as the words themselves, and where the ability to read silence is considered a mark of genuine intelligence.

The Language of Respect

Communication, Etiquette, and Social Manners

The Architecture of Indirection

A JAPANESE COLLEAGUE ONCE agreed enthusiastically to a proposal she had no intention of implementing. Her response — zenzen daijōbu, meaning "no problem at all" — appeared straightforward. The phrase carried a specific intonation, a slight pause before delivery, and a context understood by everyone in the room except the foreign consultant seated across the table. She had politely declined. The refusal was complete, precise, and entirely invisible to the one person it was directed at.

This reliance on implication over directness governs Japanese communication at every level. Meaning is transmitted through what remains unsaid — tone shifts, timing, physical positioning, and cultural reference points that require no explanation among insiders. The opposite approach, common in Western business cultures, makes everything explicit: "I disagree" or "That will not work." Japanese equivalents rarely surface; such bluntness violates foundational social contracts around wa (group harmony) and the preservation of face.

The linguistic architecture itself enforces indirection. The keigo honorific system requires constant calibration based on relative status, context, and relationship history. A single verb transforms through dozens of forms depending on who speaks to whom, about whom, and why. Mimasu (to see) becomes goran ni narimasu when a superior does the seeing, or haiken shimasu when the speaker humbly views something belonging to someone higher-ranked. This grammatical complexity does not merely reflect hierarchy — it constructs a social reality in which every sentence is simultaneously a statement and a declaration of one's position within the group.

The cognitive load is measurable. Companies develop templated phrases and internal guidelines so junior staff can deploy them without paralysis. Eliminating honorifics entirely would not simplify communication — it would render it socially incomprehensible.

Silence as Information

Silence in Japan carries active meaning. A manager who pauses for three full seconds before responding to a subordinate's suggestion is not gathering thoughts — that pause signals skepticism. Its duration and quality transmit more information than any spoken critique could, and everyone in the room reads it correctly except, often, the person who made the suggestion.

Linguists classify Japanese as a high-context language. The words themselves carry only a fraction of the communicative burden. The majority of the meaning resides in context: the identity of the speakers, the physical location, the history of the relationship, and precisely what is left unsaid. A listener must notice the atmosphere, reading between the gestures and the pauses to grasp the full intent.

The Japanese phrase for this skill is kuuki o yomu — reading the air. People grow up developing this social reflex. It dictates when to speak and when to step back, when a joke has landed and when an opinion would unnecessarily agitate the group. A speaker might trail off mid-sentence, or answer a direct question with a soft laugh and nothing more. This signals trust — the speaker trusts that the listener is paying close enough attention to understand without forcing an explicit, potentially uncomfortable declaration.

What does it mean to operate in a society where the most important things are never said out loud? It means developing an entirely different relationship with language — one where the spaces between words carry as much information as the words themselves, and where the ability to read silence is considered a mark of genuine intelligence.

The Body Speaks First

On his first day at a Tokyo trading firm, a new employee watches his department head take a phone call at his desk. The conversation lasts two minutes. Throughout it, the department head bows repeatedly — fifteen degrees, thirty degrees, back to fifteen — adjusting the angle with each exchange as though the person on the other end of the line can see him perfectly. They cannot. The body has simply learned what the mind no longer needs to consciously direct.

Bowing in Japan operates as a precise measurement system. A fifteen-degree bow (eshaku) handles casual greetings or brief acknowledgments between peers. Thirty degrees (keirei) appears in business introductions or when thanking colleagues. Forty-five degrees (saikeirei) is reserved for profound apologies, executive meetings, or deep gratitude. These angles are not suggestions — they are legible signals that everyone present can read. Deviations signal incompetence or disrespect, and experienced professionals decode status relationships instantly by observing who initiates, who bows deeper, and whose head rises first.

Children learn bowing mechanics in elementary school through daily practice. This physical memory becomes automatic, which explains why Japanese people bow during phone conversations despite having no visual audience — the body remembers what the mind no longer questions.

Eye contact operates under different rules. In many Western cultures, a steady gaze signals confidence or sincerity. In Japan, prolonged eye contact reads as confrontational or invasive. Averting one's gaze demonstrates deference, not dishonesty. The culture prizes attentiveness, focusing on the balance of the gaze rather than its intensity. A visitor who holds eye contact too long while making a request is not projecting confidence — they are creating discomfort and misreading the room entirely.

The Gift as Social Contract

Gift-giving in Japan functions as a binding social contract, not spontaneous generosity. The practice operates through giri — social obligation that creates reciprocal debt requiring equivalent return. When a colleague brings omiyage (regional souvenirs) after a vacation, recipients mentally catalog the gesture, ensuring they return with comparable items from their own travels. This reciprocal exchange maintains social equilibrium. The act centers on the preservation of harmony through acknowledged mutual obligation — the gift is simply its vehicle.

The selection process reflects this weight. Executives often spend considerable time choosing wrapped sweets from specific department stores, a process driven by careful calculation rather than indecision. The gift's wrapping, the store's reputation, its seasonality, and its precise price point all transmit measurable signals about relationship value and hierarchical awareness. Department store wrapping — crisp, precise, bearing the store's logo — validates the gift's quality before it is even opened. Generic wrapping diminishes value regardless of what lies inside, suggesting the giver did not invest proper care in the relationship.

Timing carries equal weight. Ochūgen (mid-year gifts) and oseibo (year-end gifts) arrive within narrow seasonal windows. Missing them signals a lapse in relational attention — not a delayed gift, but a gap in care. The presentation ritual stays constant regardless of context: offer with both hands, minimize the gesture verbally: "Tsumaranai mono desu ga" — "it is nothing special." Self-deprecation accompanies the gift regardless of its price tag, because the point is never to impress. The point is to notice someone.

What does it say about a culture that its most binding social contracts are never written down, never spoken aloud, and never explained to outsiders? It says that the contracts are enforced not by law but by something far more durable — the accumulated weight of ten thousand small gestures, each one a quiet confirmation that the relationship still holds.

Table Manners and the Precision of Respect

Chopstick etiquette reveals Japan's precision in translating respect into physical action. Resting chopsticks across a bowl appears innocuous — yet it violates spatial boundaries the same way leaning elbows on a train seat invades shared territory. Chopsticks belong on the hashioki (chopstick rest) or parallel to the table edge. Inserting them vertically into a bowl of rice — tatebashi — replicates funeral offerings to the dead. The error does not carry symbolic rudeness. It activates death ritual at the dinner table.

Before eating, there is a pause: itadakimasu. The phrase functions as a thank-you — to the cook, to the ingredients, to the chain of people and labor that brought the meal to the table. When the meal ends, gochisōsama deshita closes the moment with the same quiet acknowledgment. Both phrases are spoken even when eating alone, because the gratitude is not performative — it is habitual, embedded in the rhythm of the day.

Pouring soy sauce directly onto rice disrupts the carefully calibrated flavor balance the chef constructed. Sushi arrives pre-seasoned; additional sauce suggests the preparation failed. At formal meals, diners dip fish-side down into small individual dishes, preserving the rice while honoring the chef's intent. These rules function smoothly when everyone at the table shares cultural literacy. They fracture in mixed contexts. International clients unfamiliar with hashioki placement create no offense when Japanese hosts recognize genuine ignorance — but the system assumes shared fluency. Without it, gestures intended as respect become unreadable performance.

Tradition in Motion

Those historical patterns now absorb influences that would have been unimaginable a generation ago. Internal corporate messaging apps and Slack dominate Japanese workplaces, yet they simply digitize keigo rather than abolishing it. Younger employees still deploy formal verb endings in chat messages to supervisors, even as they drop them entirely with peers in adjacent channels. The platform changed; the calibration survived.

Western directness infiltrates through media, education, and multinational corporate culture. Business schools teach assertiveness; English-language instruction emphasizes declarative statements. Yet watch bilingual professionals switch between languages and the behavior switches simultaneously — more eye contact in English, bowing returns in Japanese. They are operating two systems in parallel, selecting which to activate based on context rather than abandoning either.

Rakuten, the Japanese e-commerce giant, adopted English as its official corporate language specifically to bypass the keigo constraints that historically prevent junior staff from contributing in meetings. English functions as a linguistically egalitarian medium that permits hierarchical flexibility structurally impossible in Japanese. Yet separate Japanese-language decision tracks persist in the same companies, where traditional communication and hierarchy reassert themselves the moment the meeting ends.

The friction surfaces when contexts blur. A video call mixing Tokyo headquarters with a Silicon Valley satellite office forces real-time negotiation over whose norms govern. Younger employees can execute both systems flawlessly but increasingly question why the elaborate version persists internally. The architecture adapts — not by collapsing, but by becoming conscious. No longer invisible reflex, but deliberate choice.

Chapter Six

Between Tatami and Train Stations

Decoding Daily Life

The Architecture of Home

TATAMI MATS PREDATE SKYSCRAPERS by seven centuries. First woven for Heian-era aristocrats around 900 CE, these rice-straw rectangles became Japan's spatial measuring system — rooms quantified not in square meters but in jō, standardized tatami units that dictated furniture placement, sleeping arrangements, and social hierarchy simultaneously. The mat's rigid dimensions — roughly ninety by one hundred and eighty centimeters — imposed mathematical discipline on architecture. Carpenters built structures around multiples of this module, creating proportional harmony without Western drafting tools. A six-mat room carried legible meaning to any inhabitant: the space was instantly comprehensible, its proportions a shared language.

Modern apartments still advertise size in tatami counts, though many no longer contain actual mats. The ghost of the system persists — an invisible grid structuring how Japanese people conceive domestic space, even when vinyl flooring has replaced woven straw.

Step inside a Japanese home — shoes off at the genkan, the entryway that functions as a deliberate pause between public and private life — and the philosophy becomes physical. A row of slippers set out. The floor level rising slightly. The shift is marked, not announced. Interiors are compact, especially in cities, but used with intention. Tatami mats, fusuma sliding panels, and low furniture make the home adaptable: a room might host tea in the morning and become a bedroom at night. Nothing is fixed. Space changes with the needs of the moment.

Minimalism here is philosophical inheritance, not decorative taste. Zen Buddhism's rejection of attachment meets Shinto's reverence for purity as a tangible, daily state. The result is space that breathes through ma, the deliberate void given equal weight to physical objects. Remove clutter and each remaining element intensifies. A single scroll mounted in the tokonoma alcove commands attention because nothing competes for the eye. Every object must earn its place through utility, beauty, or preferably both at once. Western minimalism copies the aesthetic. Japanese minimalism embodies the reasoning: impermanence teaches us to carry less.

Bathrooms reflect the same logic. The toilet occupies its own room — clean, discreet, often equipped with heated seats and bidet functions that visitors from abroad find simultaneously baffling and revelatory. The ofuro, or bath, is separate. You wash before entering, then sink into deep, hot water. The bath is quiet time, shared by family members in turn — not out of necessity, but tradition. It is restoration.

The Symphony of Transit

Japan's train system operates with precision so extreme it becomes invisible until you notice what is missing: chaos. Over three million passengers navigate Shinjuku Station daily without collisions — not through signage or enforcement, but through something more fundamental: a shared understanding of spatial choreography that begins in childhood and never ends. What does it mean to build a city where three million strangers coordinate daily without a single instruction? The answer is not infrastructure. It is inheritance.

The foundation is the painted line. Yellow tactile blocks guide the vision-impaired. Floor decals mark where doors will open. White stripes indicate queuing zones. Passengers form orderly columns at precise intervals, waiting for trains arriving within fifteen-second windows. This is collective muscle memory, not compliance.

When trains arrive thirty seconds late, conductors apologize. A two-minute delay warrants a written explanation posted at the platform. The 2005 Amagasaki derailment — the train running ninety seconds behind schedule when it crashed, killing one hundred and seven people — revealed how deeply temporal precision permeates operations. Recovery crews issued apologies for restoration delays measured in hours, not days. The standard had been set so high that deviation, even in the aftermath of catastrophe, required formal acknowledgment.

This infrastructure extends beyond machinery into human behavior. Passengers rotate bags forward to minimize space. Phone conversations cease upon boarding. The system functions because individual restraint enables collective efficiency — a principle so ingrained it feels less like rule-following than breathing.

Tokyo's street addresses confound Western logic not because they are poorly designed, but because they follow different principles.

Rather than sequential numbering along named roads, blocks receive numbers based on construction chronology. A house built in 1975 sits between structures from 2003 and 1960, their addresses reflecting not geographic sequence but temporal arrival. Delivery drivers develop encyclopedic spatial knowledge, their expertise built through years of repetition. First-time visitors clutch hand-drawn maps from shopkeepers who understand that finding a specific ramen counter requires landmarks, not logic — turn at the vending machine, past the shrine, third door after the bicycle shop.

Stand to the left of escalators in Tokyo, to the right in Osaka. This single regional variation, enforced by nothing more than collective habit, defines urban identity with a precision that no official rule could replicate.

The Rhythm of the Ordinary

A salaryman leaving his apartment at 7:14 a.m. does not simply exit. He straightens his shoes at the genkan, double-checks his bag, ensures the entryway remains uncluttered. The housewife wipes her doorstep. The shopkeeper moistens his noren before hanging it. The office worker arrives twenty minutes early to prepare tea. Each action compounds into the seamless choreography outsiders mistake for instinct. It is rehearsed constantly — from childhood onward — until precision becomes reflexive.

The Japanese concept behind this is kata — form, or pattern. Loosely translated, it means the right way to do things, passed down and polished over time. It is the bow at the beginning of a tea ceremony, but also the way someone bags your groceries at the konbini — smooth, intentional, done with care. Once you recognize kata, you see it everywhere: shoes lined up by the door rather than tossed. A clerk who hands you change with both hands. A plastic sleeve placed over your umbrella so the shop floor stays dry. These are small signs of consideration, offered without expectation of acknowledgment.

The konbini — that humble, neon-lit convenience store — may be the clearest symbol of how daily life here blends practicality with grace. It is where you buy lunch, pay bills, print concert tickets, send parcels, grab a fresh shirt, or get directions from a kind cashier at one in the morning. Fresh food arrives multiple times daily based on real-time sales data. Chains like 7-Eleven Japan rotate over one hundred new products monthly, constantly refining offerings through relentless small adjustments. The logic is kaizen — continuous improvement — applied not to a factory floor but to a refrigerated shelf of rice balls.

Toyota's production line in 1951 was failing. Workers waited for parts. Machines sat idle between batches. Defects surfaced too late to fix cheaply. Taiichi Ohno did not order a dramatic overhaul — he tinkered methodically. Repositioning a tool rack saved four seconds per assembly. Adjusting parts delivery eliminated waiting. Installing pull cords let any worker halt production at the first sign of error. Each worker proposed weekly modifications. Most saved seconds, not hours. Compounded across shifts, years, and thousands of employees, those seconds restructured global manufacturing. The same logic governs the konbini shelf. Progress, here, is patient and accumulating — refinement compounded across decades, not breakthroughs announced in press releases.

Objects That Carry Memory

A mother wakes before six to pack her child's lunch. She adds a favorite food, arranges the rice and vegetables into a small shape — a rabbit, a flower, nothing elaborate. The bento will be eaten in ten minutes at a school desk. She knows this. She does it anyway. A good bento is an expression of thoughtfulness that does not require an audience. Even the store-bought versions are neatly compartmentalized, seasonally appropriate, and tastefully packaged. A small box, but it tells a story: I made this for you. Or, failing that: someone made this with care.

Common phrases exchanged at home participate in the same honouring of the everyday. The word okaeri — said to welcome someone home — means simply "you have returned." The response, tadaima, means "I am home now." Both are spoken every day, often quickly, sometimes barely above a murmur. They are never empty. They remind the speaker and the listener that leaving and returning, even for something as routine as work or school, is never taken for granted.

Seasonal objects carry the same weight. Hand towels with cherry blossoms in spring, cooling wind chimes in summer, red maple designs in autumn. These are quiet acknowledgments of the changing world outside — a reminder to look up, to feel the season, to mark the passing of time in the fabric of daily life. The objects are not grand. The gesture is.

Behind the Pristine Door

The genkan tells the truth about Japan's relationship with public and private space. That lowered entryway — shoes removed, slippers waiting, the floor rising slightly to mark the threshold — is where the country's two faces meet. On one side: the street, swept clean, orderly, presented to the world with quiet pride. On the other: the apartment, which may be a different matter entirely.

This is not a contradiction the Japanese find troubling. It is a structural feature.

Urban apartments, particularly in Tokyo and Osaka, are compact by any international standard. A typical 1K apartment — one room with a kitchen alcove — runs between twenty and thirty square meters. A family of four in a 3LDK (three rooms, living space, dining area, kitchen) manages in roughly seventy. The space is not generous. What makes it liveable is a highly developed culture of functional storage, pragmatic accumulation, and the quiet understanding that the private home is a working space, not a showroom.

Walk into the average Japanese apartment and you will find plastic storage units from Nitori stacked in corners, folded laundry waiting on a drying rack because outdoor drying is restricted by building rules, a kotatsu table dominating the living room from October through March, and a kitchen counter holding a rice cooker, a toaster oven, and a portable IH burner because the built-in stove has only one gas ring.

The bathroom is a marvel of engineering compression: shower, bath, and laundry machine occupying a space smaller than many Western walk-in wardrobes. The toilet, in its own separate room, is often the most technologically sophisticated object in the building.

None of this is hidden with embarrassment. It is simply private. The distinction between public presentation and private reality is not hypocrisy in Japan — it is tatemae and honne operating as designed. The pristine street, the immaculate convenience store, the spotless train carriage: these are shared spaces, and shared spaces receive shared care. The apartment is personal territory, arranged for function rather than impression, and no one outside the household is meant to see it anyway.

This explains something that confuses many foreigners: the Japanese reluctance to invite people home. In Western social cultures, hosting at home signals trust and intimacy. In Japan, the home is simply not a social venue in the same way. Relationships are maintained in restaurants, izakayas, and coffee shops — spaces designed for hospitality. The home is where the armor comes off, where the shoes are replaced by worn slippers, where the television runs in the background and the laundry sits unfolded. Inviting someone into that space is a significant act of intimacy, not a casual gesture.

The minimalism celebrated in design magazines and travel writing is real, but it belongs to a specific register of Japanese life: the tea room, the ryokan, the carefully curated tokonoma alcove. These are ritual spaces, governed by aesthetic philosophy. The rest of the home is governed by the same pragmatic intelligence that organises the konbini shelf — everything in its place, nothing wasted, the system optimized for daily use rather than visual effect. The philosophy and the practicality coexist without conflict, each operating in its own domain, neither cancelling the other out.

Neighborhood as Infrastructure

Walk a residential street on a Saturday morning — before the city fully wakes — and you will encounter something invisible to guidebooks. Elderly residents sweep pavements they do not own, not from compulsion but inherited protocol. A woman waters plants outside her building's entrance. Another wipes down the neighborhood bulletin board. These are not isolated acts of civic pride. They are chōnaikai — neighborhood associations — made visible through embodied routine.

Most Japanese people belong to one without choosing.

These micro-governments predate the Meiji state, formalising Edo-period mutual surveillance networks into community infrastructure. Monthly fees fund streetlights, local festivals, and disaster supplies. Rotation schedules assign rubbish collection oversight, shrine cleaning, and fire-watch duties. Participation is not legally required, but refusal marks you as socially unreliable in ways that compound: fewer informal favors, colder greetings, exclusion from information networks about school changes or construction schedules. The social cost of opting out often exceeds the time investment of staying in.

Attend a neighborhood association meeting and observe who shows up: predominantly retirees sustaining systems younger workers inherited but rarely service. Note the meticulous record-keeping, the budget transparency, the consensus-building that can consume ninety minutes debating festival banner colours. This is jichikai — self-governance — operating exactly as designed, though increasingly strained as demographic decline leaves fewer hands to sweep shared streets.

Technology has not dissolved these bonds; it has merely updated the delivery mechanism. For decades, the kairanban — a physical clipboard of neighborhood announcements — circulated from house to house, requiring neighbors to physically hand it to one another and stamp their family seal to confirm receipt. Today, many urban chō-naikai have transitioned this system to dedicated community portal apps or automated email chains. Earthquake alerts, lost-pet notices, and festival preparation schedules transmit instantly to hundreds. Younger residents who never attend physical meetings check these digital kairanban during commutes, contributing financially to the association while bypassing the ninety-minute banner debates. The tension remains unresolved: can digital coordination sustain bonds forged through embodied routine? Can algorithms replace the knowledge gained from sweeping the same pavement for thirty years?

Technology in Its Place

Inside Kyoto's Fushimi Inari shrine, elderly miko sweep stone paths while visitors tap contactless offerings on NFC donation boxes mounted beside rope-pull bells. The juxtaposition registers as unremarkable to everyone present.

Japan never treated tradition and technology as opposing forces requiring resolution. Both serve the same underlying purpose: maintaining functional order through continuous refinement. When railway operators introduced automated ticket gates in the 1990s, they retained white-gloved attendants who bow deeply to passengers upon entry and exit. The technology handles throughput; the attendants preserve omotenashi hospitality. Sushi chains install conveyor belts and tablet ordering while chefs still compress rice by hand. Buddhist temples livestream sutras but burn incense in bronze bowls cast centuries ago. Department store elevators run on computer systems, yet operators announce each floor in practiced, melodic Japanese.

The integration has limits that only become visible under stress. When Rakuten mandated English as its official corporate language in 2010, the stated goal was efficiency — eliminating the keigo constraints that prevent junior staff from contributing freely in meetings. English, being grammatically egalitarian, permits a junior analyst to address a division head without navigating five levels of verb conjugation. The experiment worked, partially: cross-departmental communication accelerated, and international hires reported fewer barriers. What persisted was a parallel track — separate Japanese-language decision-making channels where traditional hierarchy reasserted itself the moment the meeting ended. The medium changed. The underlying architecture did not.

During the pandemic, major financial institutions like Nomura discovered that transposing deeply ingrained corporate protocols onto virtual platforms created unexpected strain. Senior managers expected younger employees to perform the same deference through screens that they would in person. The result was exhaustion, disengagement, and declining productivity. The technology worked perfectly. What failed was the assumption that it could sustain unmodified sempai-kōhai relationships across physical distance, as if a Zoom call could carry the same weight as a bow.

The concern is the erosion of ba — the shared physical space where trust forms through repeated, low-stakes interaction. Japan's answer, so far, prioritizes adaptation: implementing device-free meetings as recalibration; open-space architecture that creates daily touchpoints between neighbors who might otherwise never speak. The tools change. The architecture underneath them does not.

Chapter Seven

Meals with Meaning

Reading Japan Through Food

The Architecture of Seasonality

KYOTO'S OLDEST KAISEKI KITCHENS do not open for lunch. Seating be-gins at six sharp, tables accommodate no more than eight, and the meal unfolds over three deliberate hours. The ingredients were harvested that morning, prepared through techniques refined across centuries, and assembled with botanical precision. Each course arrives as edible proof of shun: the two-week window when bamboo shoots taste of spring rain, when autumn matsutake mushrooms carry the forest floor in their flesh.

Kaiseki emerged in sixteenth-century Kyoto as tea ceremony cuisine, designed by Sen no Rikyū to complement bitter matcha without overwhelming its subtle flavours. The name itself — kaiseki — translates as "breast stone," referencing the warm rocks Zen monks tucked into their robes to suppress hunger during meditation. What began as ascetic necessity evolved into Japan's most sophisticated culinary expression, where every element operates under constraint: seasonal imperative, regional specificity, aesthetic restraint.

The same logic governs the neighborhood izakaya that never advertises its menu. What is available depends on what arrived at Tsukiji before dawn — October's Pacific saury, January's Hokkaido crab, May's first katsuo bonito. The wooden placard listing today's offerings is operational reality, not quaint decoration. Seasonal availability dictates what you can order.

Home cooking operates identically. Japanese grocers do not stock tomatoes year-round because demand exists — they stock what the season provides. Winter means daikon radish in miso soup, kabocha squash simmered until tender, nabe hot pots assembled from root vegetables that store through cold months. Summer brings sōmen noodles served ice-cold, cucumber sunomono salad, eggplant grilled until the skin blisters. The typical Japanese home kitchen contains no spice rack promising global cuisine on demand — it contains dashi stock,

soy sauce, mirin, and whatever this
week's harvest offers.

Street food follows suit. Festival stalls sell yakiimo roasted sweet potatoes only when autumn varieties arrive, never in July. Kakigōri shaved ice disappears after September. This is cuisine structured by agricultural reality, where flavour peaks within narrow temporal windows and eating means aligning with what the land provides now.

Tokyo's modern kaiseki establishments layer international techniques onto seasonal foundations. Chef Yoshihiro Narisawa famously serves "Satoyama Scenery" — a dish replicating forest floor ecosystems using only ingredients foraged that morning. French sous-vide precision applied to Kyoto vegetables harvested at dawn. Liquid nitrogen freezing wild mountain herbs picked six hours earlier. The technology changes; the shun calendar does not.

Miss this month's shirako — cod milt, a winter delicacy — and you wait eleven months. That scarcity, enforced not by pricing but by planetary rotation, makes each encounter irreplaceable. Seasonality persists because it restores stakes to eating, transforming meals from refuelling into moments that will not repeat until Earth completes another orbit.

Building an entire cuisine around the idea that the best ingredient will disappear next month infuses every meal with quiet urgency and deep attention. The bamboo shoot on your plate exists in a two-week window. Eat it now, or miss it entirely.

The Foundations — Rice, Miso, Dashi

Every morning in Japan begins the same way. Gohan — cooked rice — arrives in a bowl before anything else. The word itself means both "rice" and "meal," the two concepts so inseparable in the language that the Japanese never needed to distinguish between them. That linguistic fact is three thousand years old.

Rice farming shaped Japan with a precision most civilisations never achieved. By the Yayoi period around 300 BCE, wet-paddy cultivation required engineering prowess — levelling fields, constructing irrigation channels, coordinating planting cycles — that forced scattered communities into permanent cooperation. One family could not manage flooding schedules or transplant thousands of seedlings alone. This was social architecture disguised as agriculture.

The rice calendar became Japan's organizing principle. Shinto festivals aligned with planting and harvest cycles. Tax systems measured wealth in koku — rice volume — and samurai stipends arrived as grain rations rather than currency. When Tokugawa officials calculated domain productivity, they counted rice; when farmers paid tribute, they delivered it. The substance itself became governance, a single crop holding together the architecture of an entire civilisation.

Every Japanese person still encounters this legacy daily. Restaurant menus list rice as the anchor, not a side dish. Convenience stores stock twenty onigiri varieties, each region claiming distinct cultivars: Niigata's Koshihikari, Akita's Akitakomachi. The grain remains Japan's gravitational centre, roughly three millennia after its introduction.

Miso occupies the same foundational role, though its history diverges sharply. Fermentation arrived from China around the seventh century, carried by Buddhist monks who refined the technique into something distinctly Japanese. Soybeans, salt, and koji mould — left to transform over months or years — created a living paste that preserved protein through brutal winters while delivering umami depth no other ingredient matched.

Every regional variant carries geological memory. Sendai's red miso ferments longer, darker, saltier — a response to

Tōhoku's punishing cold. Kyoto's sweet white miso requires minimal aging, reflecting both milder climates and the refined palates of the old imperial court. Nagoya's hatcho miso uses only soybeans, no rice, producing an almost chocolate-dark intensity born from specific water chemistry and temperature patterns. These were survival strategies encoded in paste, not aesthetic preferences.

Hundreds of distinct regional varieties still exist, each meticulously adapted to local microclimates, each harboring living cultures — lactobacillus, yeast — that shift subtly between prefectures. Yet most Japanese households now buy mass-produced versions. Regional specificity collapses into convenience, one batch at a time.

Dashi functions as Japanese cuisine's invisible architecture. Without this clear broth — kombu kelp simmered with katsuobushi bonito flakes — miso soup, noodle broths, simmered vegetables, and countless other dishes lose their structural foundation. Western stocks require hours of extraction, bones and aromatics slowly yielding flavour. Dashi takes seven minutes.

The technique emerged from necessity: island geography limited meat access while surrounding oceans provided kelp forests and migratory fish. Somewhere during the Edo period, cooks discovered that dried bonito shavings and kombu produced umami — the fifth taste, though no one named it until 1908, when chemist Kikunae Ikeda isolated glutamate. What they knew empirically, science confirmed: these two ingredients contain the highest natural concentrations of glutamates and nucleotides, compounds that trigger savory depth receptors.

Traditional preparation demands precision. Water heated to 80°C, not boiling — excess heat makes kombu slimy, bonito bitter. Steep briefly, strain immediately. The result tastes like distilled ocean.

Most home cooks now use instant granules. Convenient, shelf-stable, adequate — but something fundamental disappears when seven-minute discipline becomes thirty-second dissolution. The short-cut works. It severs the connection between technique and taste that defines Japanese culinary philosophy.

Tea, Sushi, and Sake

Tea ceremony — chadō — reflects centuries of aesthetic refinement, precise choreography unfolding on four-and-a-half tatami mats. Sen no Rikyū formalized its principles in the sixteenth century, distilling Zen and Shinto purity into codified movements: folding the silk cloth (fukusa), rotating the bowl, ladling water. Every gesture follows sequence, yet mastery makes rehearsed motion appear spontaneous.

Before the tea arrives, there are wagashi — seasonal confections crafted to reflect the world outside the tearoom window. A maple leaf pressed from red bean paste in October. A plum blossom shaped from soft rice flour in February. They are never overly sweet — just enough to prepare the palate for bitter matcha. Each one is served on a lacquered dish, turned to face the guest, offered without commentary. The sweetness is the commentary.

Wabi-sabi — the philosophy animating tea ceremony — defies simple translation, evident in the objects themselves. Tea masters prize bowls with irregular glazing, asymmetrical lips, and visible thumb marks — each one a record of the potter's hand rather than a factory mould. This aesthetic emerged from fifteenth-century monks who rejected Chinese porcelain's flawless surfaces, choosing instead Korean peasant ware — rough, cracked, alive with the maker's intention.

The tearoom itself embodies these principles. Low doorways force guests to bow, shedding rank at the threshold. Natural light filters through rice paper, softening shadows across aged wood grain. Nothing announces itself. Beauty operates through restraint, through what remains unsaid.

Sushi began as narezushi, a Southeast Asian fermentation technique over a millennium old. Rice preserved fish for months through lactic acid, then was discarded once the fish was ready. The Edo period reversed this formula: vinegar-seasoned rice eliminated the need for fermentation entirely, shifting the focus to fresh fish and the precision of presentation.

Jiro Ono spent seventy years perfecting nigiri at his three-Michelin-star Sukiyabashi Jiro. Apprentices massage octopus for forty minutes. Rice is aged. Vinegar is blended from three types. Each fish receives temperature-specific treatment — tuna rested at room temperature, kohada gizzard shad marinated for seventy-two hours. His humble commercial rice cooker proves that true alchemy lies in attention, not exotic equipment.

This obsessive refinement reflects shokunin kishitsu — the craftsman's spirit that demands decade-long apprenticeships before a student touches fish independently. Conveyor-belt kaiten-zushi now dominates, offering adequate nigiri for around ¥100 per plate. The gap between Jiro's counter and the rotating plates reveals which cultural values survive commodification — and which do not.

Sake consumption in Japan follows three rules that reveal whether you understand its cultural function. Pour for others, never yourself — the empty cup signals trust that someone will notice and reciprocate, transforming drinking into continuous mutual attention. Hold your cup when receiving, lifting it slightly with both hands to acknowledge the gesture. Accept the first pour even if you do not drink — refusal breaks the social circuit.

Temperature matters functionally. Less refined sake often tastes better warm because heat masks imperfections and enhances umami notes. Premium daiginjo — rice polished to forty percent or less — should be served chilled to preserve delicate aromatics that evaporate above 10°C. The vessel changes the experience: ochoko ceramic cups retain warmth, glass reveals clarity, wooden masu boxes add cypress fragrance.

At formal dinners, the senior person pours first, activating hierarchy through liquid. In izakayas, colleagues pour in descending order of rank. Watch who refills whom — it maps the room's real structure more accurately than business cards ever could.

Order nihonshu, not "sake" — that word means all alcohol in Japan. Specify junmai for pure rice sake, or let the shop choose by describing the food you will eat.

Fusion and the Modern Table

Japanese fusion cuisine operates through strategic adaptation. Yoshoku dishes like hayashi rice trace their lineage directly to French demi-glace but arrived during the Meiji period, when Western techniques were methodically absorbed into Japanese kitchens. The dish survives today as reinvention — smaller portions, pickled garnishes, a fundamental shift in how richness is balanced. Walk into a yoshoku restaurant and the menu becomes a historical document: European techniques alongside Japanese aesthetics, cream ratios adjusted, miso additions that never existed in the original.

Then there is mentaiko pasta, where spicy cod roe meets Italian spaghetti. The fusion holds because it operates on texture and umami rather than novelty — the cod roe coats the noodles the way a cream sauce would, but with a salinity and depth that no dairy product replicates. Matcha tiramisu does not replace coffee; it augments the structure, creating something that honors both traditions without apologizing for either.

Modern Japanese kitchens employ technology with the same precision once reserved for blade-making. Zojirushi rice cookers monitor grain moisture through fuzzy logic algorithms, adjusting heat and timing to compensate for humidity variations. At Narisawa, chefs use liquid nitrogen to flash-freeze seasonal ingredients at peak ripeness, preserving qualities that icebox storage would destroy. The technology extends what hand-selection and timing once accomplished alone.

Japanese chefs introducing plant-based menus encounter an unexpected challenge: customers mistakenly believe that expertise in Buddhist shōjin ryōri translates seamlessly to modern veganism. Temple cuisine refined umami extraction from kombu and shiitake over centuries, yet contemporary vegan diners expect Western substitutes — cashew cream, nutritional yeast, aquafaba — ingredients entirely foreign to traditional Japanese pantries.

The most accomplished establishments resolve this by committing to a clear direction. Some honor shōjin principles completely, educating diners why no cheese substitute exists because the original dish never required one. Others embrace fusion openly, wielding Japanese technique as methodology rather than dogma. Tokyo's Ain Soph exemplifies the latter: their vegan ramen harnesses miso complexity and kombu depth while acknowledging the cashew-based broth follows no classical lineage.

Japanese restaurants dominate global cities, but most dishes abroad bear only passing resemblance to what exists in Japan. The California roll — invented in Los Angeles or Vancouver to comfort Western diners uncomfortable with raw fish — never appears in Tokyo sushi-ya. This is adaptation, not corruption. Ramen shops in London cannot source the kelp varieties or pork bones available in Fukuoka. Chefs improvise with local ingredients while preserving technique. The best distinguish between immutable principles and flexible components: a Paris ramen-ya might substitute French pork for chashu, but cannot compromise on broth clarity or noodle texture without abandoning the form entirely.

Someone discovering California rolls at twenty might seek out edomae sushi at thirty, their palate educated through gradual exposure rather than shock immersion. Japan's culinary influence abroad functions less as preservation than as negotiation — tradition adapting to local reality, dish by dish, city by city.

Living inside a culture where the calendar itself functions as a form of obligation carries distinct psychological weight: by insisting that the principles — seasonality, restraint, attention — remain non-negotiable, while everything else remains open to revision.

Chapter Eight

A Year in Bloom

Festivals and Seasonal Traditions

The Cycle of Seasons

EVERY JAPANESE SHRINE FEATURES a massive twisted rope at its entrance. These shimenawa, made of rice-straw, delineate the sacred from the profane — a distinction preceding Buddhism, Confucianism, and even written history.

Festivals evolved as calendrical negotiations of this boundary. Early rituals arose with Yayoi period rice cultivation (three hundred BCE to three hundred CE), when survival hinged on precise seasonal timing. Farmers sought kami blessings for spring plantings, typhoon prevention in summer, and autumn harvests. The word itself derives from matsuru — to enshrine or worship — but originally meant propitiating the deities inhabiting mountains, rivers, and storms that controlled crop yields.

Gratitude and appeasement were operational necessities, the only available insurance against starvation. Shinto's nature reverence formed the skeleton. Buddhism added ancestor veneration and philosophical depth after five hundred and thirty-eight CE, while Confucian ethics formalized social roles and hierarchies. Each layer accumulated rather than replaced what came before.

Modern matsuri preserve this accumulated logic intact. Kyoto's Gion Matsuri still purifies the city against plague — a function unchanged since eight hundred and sixty-nine CE, though few participants consciously remember why they are pulling the massive floats through the July heat. The rituals endure because they articulate something deeper than belief. The Gion Matsuri procession does not merely commemorate the eight hundred and sixty-nine CE plague response — it re-enacts it, purifying the same streets, in the same month, using the same ritual logic.

What does it cost, psychologically, to live inside a culture where the calendar itself is a form of obligation? The cherry blossoms open in April regardless of what the previous year delivered. The cicadas hum in August. The snow buries Hokkaido in January. The passing of time is felt in the smell of rain on warm pavement, and in the shift from plum blossoms to fireflies. This rhythmic certainty forms the emotional architecture of Japanese life — and the weight of it is inseparable from its beauty.

A Calendar of Rituals

Japanese seasonal traditions unfold with quiet specificity, anchoring people to the year in ways that Western holidays, fixed to historical dates or religious events, rarely achieve. The New Year does not begin with a countdown and a toast. It begins with housecleaning — a full scrubbing of the home called osoji — followed by a return to the family, bowls of ozoni soup eaten on the first morning, and then hatsumode: the first shrine visit of the year. At Meiji Jingu in Tokyo, two million people queue in the January cold to approach the main hall, clap twice, bow, and exchange last year's omamori charm for a new one. The old charm is returned rather than kept because the kami's protection is understood to be finite — it depletes over twelve months and must be renewed. That single detail reframes the entire ritual. This is maintenance, not ceremony.

Spring brings Hina Matsuri, the doll festival observed on the third of March. Families with daughters display tiered platforms of delicate figures dressed in Heian court robes — the Emperor and Empress on the top tier, court ladies and musicians arranged below. The dolls must be packed away promptly after the festival ends. Leave them out past March third and, according to a superstition that persists across modern households, a daughter's marriage will be delayed. The belief has no logical foundation and everyone knows it. The dolls are packed away anyway.

Spring's arrival is tracked with almost meteorological precision. Forecasts map the "cherry blossom front" as it moves north across the archipelago, and all eyes turn to the trees. The blossoms open and offer something rare in Japanese society: permission. Permission to pause, to gather, and to look up.

Hanami, or flower viewing, remains the country's most beloved seasonal ritual. Families, coworkers, and students spread out blue tarps beneath sakura trees, sharing bento lunches and cans of beer under a canopy of pink and white. The atmosphere is festive but rarely chaotic. Even when the portable karaoke machines appear later in the evening, a quiet reverence underpins the gathering.

The poignancy of hanami stems from what it honors: impermanence. The blossoms arrive quickly and vanish just as fast, scattered by wind or rain within two weeks, leaving behind bare branches and the soft ache of something beautiful having passed. The Japanese call this mono no aware — the awareness of transience, the gentle sorrow that makes a moment more vivid precisely because it cannot last.

Hanami centers on being present for a moment that refuses to endure. Sitting with colleagues or strangers, looking up, knowing this will be over in a few days — that shared acknowledgment of fleeting time provides a collective exhale for a society that otherwise values relentless forward momentum.

Autumn brings Tsukimi, the moon-viewing festival. People gather to watch the full harvest moon rise, eating tsukimi dango — round white rice dumplings stacked in towers of three — and taking in the light without ceremony. No fireworks, no speeches, no program. The festival asks only that people stop and look at the sky, which in a country of sixty-hour working weeks is a more radical instruction than it sounds.

Summer Heat and Ancestral Return

Summer in Japan is heavy, humid, and loud with cicadas, but its central festival, Obon, operates on a quieter frequency. Every August, the country pauses. Trains pack with people heading back to their hometowns, city streets empty, and windows open to the warm night air.

Obon marks the return of the spirits. For a few days, the boundary between the living and the dead softens. Families return to ancestral graves out of rhythm, memory, and inherited courtesy. They pull weeds, rinse stone markers, and light incense — acts of company rather than grief. The visit is unhurried, practical, and entirely without drama, which is precisely what makes it moving. Inside homes, altars are cleaned and favorite snacks left out. Some families hang small lanterns near the entrance, a physical gesture signalling that the light has been left on for the visitors.

That protective impulse crystallized into movements that endure unchanged across centuries. Bon Odori — the dance performed during the festival — originated in twelfth-century Buddhist practice, when the monk Kūya popularized dancing while chanting nembutsu to welcome ancestral spirits returning from the afterlife. Villagers formed circles around drum towers, their synchronized steps guiding the dead homeward. Today, in parks and temple courtyards, people gather in yukata summer robes, maintaining these slow circles. The choreography varies dramatically by region: Tokushima's Awa Odori employs energetic, improvised movements suggesting intoxicated joy, while Gifu's Gujo Odori maintains precise formations learned over generations.

Every version serves the same function: physical repetition that opens the boundary between living and dead. When the music begins, you copy the person ahead — clockwise shuffling, clapping on specific beats, hand gestures representing waves or harvest motions. The point is embodied participation in cyclical return. After three circuits, muscle memory overrides conscious thought, triggering the same neurological shift that transformed rice planting into ritual a millennium ago.

When the festival ends, small paper lanterns are sent down rivers, out into the dark. They drift rather than race, disappearing one by one, a quiet way of remembering that those who have gone still matter, and that the space held for them still exists.

Regional Resilience and Civic Architecture

Japan's festivals resist national uniformity because the problems they were built to solve were never national. Each region's matsuri evolved to address the specific dangers and gifts of its own landscape, and the solutions they arrived at are radically different from one another.

In Aomori Prefecture, where snow drifts reach second-story windows and summer lasts barely three months, the Nebuta Matsuri emerged from tangible need. Luminous warrior floats parade through August darkness, a material manifestation of neputa — the drowsiness threatening rice farmers during crucial harvest weeks. Exhausted laborers sought an embodied expulsion of fatigue itself. The floats, towering constructions of wire, washi paper, and electric bulbs, depict fierce warriors whose painted faces glow with defiant vitality. Each float becomes a weapon against exhaustion, a blazing rejection of sleep when sleep meant failed harvests.

Hokkaido's Yuki Matsuri, born in nineteen fifty, arrived at a different solution entirely. Rather than fighting winter, it made winter the spectacle. Ice sculptures tower three stories high, celebrating the same snow that buries roads and isolates communities for months. Snow becomes sacred material.

Kyoto's Gion Matsuri unfolds across the entire month of July, embodying a fundamentally different principle than Aomori's luminous spectacle. Here, the festival functions as neighborhood sovereignty made visible — a living map of Kyoto's invisible social architecture. The yamaboko floats, massive two-story wooden structures weighing up to twelve tons, belong not to the city but to individual chō, the merchant neighborhoods that commissioned their construction centuries ago. Each district maintains its own float, storing disassembled components in dedicated warehouses, employing specialist carpenters who reassemble them annually without a single nail. The Naginata Boko float alone stands twenty-five meters tall, requiring coordinated effort from dozens of neighborhood volunteers.

This decentralized ownership distinguishes Gion Matsuri from state-sponsored pageantry. Neighborhoods compete through craftsmanship rather than hierarchy — textile quality, bronze fittings, imported tapestries transformed into moving exhibitions. The festival thus reveals power structures invisible on ordinary days: which neighborhoods command resources, skilled labor, and continuity sufficient to sustain traditions requiring multigenerational commitment.

Okinawa's Eisa festivals operate on entirely different logic. Subtropical August heat dictates timing, and drumming intensity mirrors island rhythms entirely foreign to mainland sensibilities. These evolved through Ryukyu Kingdom independence, with origins linked to Buddhist Obon dances performed for ancestors for hundreds of years before annexation in eighteen seventy-nine. Each neighborhood forms a team of dancers wielding large barrel drums, moving in circular patterns synchronized to sanshin lute melodies. The accessibility serves a specific historical function: Eisa originated as a homecoming ritual for diaspora communities, requiring frameworks that accommodate strangers returning after decades abroad.

Each region's matsuri solves distinct environmental and historical problems. They create orchestrated plurality — a shared form containing radically different content.

The Infrastructure of Participation

A visitor who arrives at Gion Matsuri without knowing which chō owns which float is not merely uninformed — they are invisible to the event's actual social logic. The floats are not decorations. They are territorial markers, each one a declaration of neighborhood identity, financial capacity, and generational continuity. To watch the procession without that knowledge is to see the surface of something whose depth runs centuries downward.

Regional festivals reveal themselves fully only to those who commit. Choose Gion Matsuri, Nebuta, or Eisa and secure lodging months in advance, blocking calendar days around the event. Research the festival's internal structure before arrival. For Gion Matsuri, identify which chō maintains which float and examine their textile collections. For Nebuta, trace corporate sponsorships behind specific warrior designs. For Eisa, contact community centers weeks early — many welcome observers at rehearsals, offering insight into the preparation that sustains tradition.

During the event, arrive ninety minutes before official start times. Watch organizers communicate through gesture alone. Notice how neighborhoods deploy members across simultaneous roles — some pulling floats, others coordinating crowds, still others managing ritual sequences. Follow one element — a single float, dancer, or coordination team — through the entire route, observing how tradition adapts in real time to modern crowds and urban constraints.

The infrastructure supporting spontaneity is worth studying on its own terms. Printed dance diagrams posted near loudspeakers. Volunteer coordinators wearing identifying sashes, positioned to gently redirect rather than scold. Refreshment stalls accepting credit cards alongside cash, digitising exchange without eliminating omiyage gift logic. This scaffolding is how tradition survives — not through rigid preservation, but through the deliberate lowering of barriers around an essential core.

Adaptation and Survival

The friction surfaces when preservation confronts demographic reality. Aging villages struggle to muster forty men to shoulder the mikoshi portable shrines. Before any shrine can move, priests perform shubatsu — purification using sacred sakaki branches dipped in salted water, striking the air in prescribed patterns. The norito prayers recited have remained unchanged since the tenth-century Engishiki codified them. Whether at Tokyo's Yasukuni Shrine or rural Shimane Prefecture, identical syllables intoned in rhythms predating written Japanese fill the air.

Yet, adaptation occurs. Some villages now hire young workers from cities, paying strangers and severing traditional lineage. Others permit women in processions previously reserved for men, disrupting gendered spiritual logic unchanged since Tokugawa rule.

Digital platforms now saturate festivals that survived centuries without screens. QR codes at shrine entrances unlock multilingual histories. Augmented reality apps overlay historical procession routes onto modern streets during Kyoto's Jidai Matsuri, showing where samurai formations once marched through what are now parking lots. During Takayama Matsuri, participants livestream float preparations to diaspora communities worldwide, transforming private rituals into public documentation.

This adaptation is strategic preservation. Aging artisan communities use video tutorials to transmit float construction techniques that once passed through decades of apprenticeship. Nebuta float builders in Aomori now crowdfund materials through social media campaigns, bypassing traditional corporate sponsorships that demanded creative control. Festival committees track participation demographics through digital registration systems, identifying which age groups are disappearing from ceremonies.

The tension remains visible. At Gion Matsuri, neighborhood associations debate whether Instagram-friendly lighting installations honor or corrupt yamaboko float aesthetics. Technology becomes most valuable when invisible — when digital ticketing systems prevent overcrowding that would destroy ritual pacing, or when translation apps allow foreign participants to understand purification protocols rather than merely photograph them.

Environmental consciousness has entered festival culture as a form of reverence. Tokyo's Sumida River Fireworks Festival now emphasises waste reduction and sustainable logistics, with designated sorting stations staffed by volunteers who treat the clean-up as an extension of the ceremony itself. The logic is consistent with the festival's origins: a community that once gathered to propitiate the river now gathers to protect it.

The intrusion of global cuisines has transformed Japan's festival food scene in unexpected ways. At Osaka's Tenjin Matsuri, vendors now sell Korean fried chicken alongside traditional yakitori, while craft beer from American microbreweries competes with sake stalls. Festival organisers recognize that younger Japanese attendees, raised on diverse flavours through travel and social media, expect variety that mirrors their everyday eating habits. Traditional foods persist through clever reinvention. Takoyaki vendors experiment with cheese fillings and truffle oil. Taiyaki, the fish-shaped cake traditionally filled with red bean paste, now appears stuffed with chocolate, custard, or matcha ice cream. These innovations exist alongside classical offerings, creating choice rather than erasure.

The younger generation transforms festivals by participating rather than copying them perfectly. University students in Shimane Prefecture who cannot execute traditional kagura dances flawlessly simply show up anyway, learning through repetition rather than waiting for mastery. Rural shrines, facing depopulation, now run weekend workshops because imperfect transmission beats no transmission. The mikoshi carrier who fumbles this year becomes next year's coordinator.

Hokkaido's Yosakoi Soran festival grew from ten teams in nineteen ninety-two to nearly three hundred today because organisers valued participation over perfection. Rough choreography and mismatched costumes are welcomed. The barrier to entry dropped, and the festival expanded. Most traditional roles demand presence more than expertise: carrying portable shrines builds muscle memory within hours, lantern painting requires enthusiasm rather than credentials, festival cooking teaches itself through repetition.

Young Japanese often discover that festivals welcome meaningful contribution long before mastery is achieved. Traditions survive through imperfect continuity, each generation contributing what they can rather than abandoning what they cannot yet master. The festivals persist, but an unresolved question haunts them: which elements constitute sacred essence, and which are merely historical accidents now eligible for sacrifice?

Chapter Nine

Stillness in Motion

Traditional Arts and Aesthetics

Arranging Silence

I N JAPAN, SILENCE IS a material. Something you shape, arrange, and listen to. That idea runs like a current through the country's traditional arts, where beauty arrives with restraint rather than noise or colour — a vase holding one wild branch angled toward the light, a brushstroke that lands slightly off-center, a masked actor holding a gesture for a breath longer than expected.

A thirteenth-century monk named Murata Jukō once proclaimed that the finest tea bowl was one that appeared ready to collapse. He valued its asymmetry and rough glaze because those qualities represented a theological revolution. This framework inverted conventional beauty: perfection became suspect, impermanence became precious, and the incomplete held more truth than the finished.

The terminology itself reveals this inheritance. Wabi originally meant the misery of living alone in nature, disconnected from society. Sabi described the patina of age, the rust and wear that marks time's passage. Zen practice transformed these negative states into spiritual ideals — solitude became tranquillity, decay became wisdom. Together, wabi-sabi emerged as the beauty of imperfection.

Zen temples tested these principles through daily practice. Monks raked gravel gardens where patterns dissolved overnight. They conducted tea ceremonies using cracked bowls. They practiced calligraphy that celebrated the brushstroke's unrepeatable gesture. Each ritual reinforced Buddhism's core teaching of impermanence — that grasping for permanence causes suffering, while accepting transience brings liberation.

The aesthetic infiltrated domestic life through everyday objects that embodied imperfection as practice rather than theory. Pottery from Bizen kilns emerged unglazed, marked only by wood-ash deposits and flame patterns. Each piece remained unique because each occupied a different position in the kiln. Sake cups often developed subtle thumbprint depressions that felt awkward until use revealed their ergonomic logic. Rice bowls bore hairline cracks that tea masters considered improvements, demonstrating that the object had lived.

Kintsugi made this philosophy explicit. Artisans repaired broken ceramics with lacquer mixed with powdered gold, making the fracture lines prominent rather than concealing them. The repair became the story. Modern homes still choose ikebana arrangements emphasising empty space over abundance, placing single flowers in asymmetrical containers.

Wabi-sabi migrated into workshops and studios where contemporary creators wield asymmetry and imperfection as active design principles. Architect Tadao Ando pours concrete that celebrates its own irregularities — formwork patterns, air bubble traces, subtle colour shifts from curing conditions. Each panel documents its specific creation moment. At the Church of Light in Ibaraki, visitors confront raw concrete that triggers rejection in Western minimalism yet reads as refinement to Japanese eyes trained to perceive wabi in material honesty.

Fashion designer Rei Kawakubo builds garments with exposed seams, deliberate asymmetries, and raw-edged fabrics. Her clothing announces its construction rather than concealing it beneath polished surfaces. Her nineteen eighty-two Paris debut shocked critics who dismissed the work as "Hiroshima chic," missing entirely how those torn hems and frayed edges carried forward the same philosophy sixteenth-century tea masters encoded in cracked bowls.

Contemporary ceramicists still fire in wood-burning kilns specifically to capture unpredictable ash patterns, rejecting electric kilns that offer perfect control. Ryokan owners commission carpenters to leave visible wood grain and natural edges in renovation projects, paying premiums for materials industrial suppliers discard as defective. The philosophy endures because it addresses something industrial perfection cannot: the reassurance that beauty accommodates damage, that age enriches, and that cracks prove survival.

Building an entire aesthetic tradition on the premise that damage requires celebration, rather than solution, fundamentally alters how objects are valued. That question sits at the centre of everything that follows in this chapter.

Space, Light, and Paper

Walk into a traditional Japanese home, and the first thing you notice is the restraint. No towering ceilings. No ornate chandeliers. No over-stuffed furniture calling for attention. Instead, there is light, shadow, air, and a purposeful quiet. Japanese architecture frames space rather than filling it.

This design philosophy is rooted in ma — the space between things. Ma applies to physical space and emotional space equally. It is the pause in music, the silence in conversation, the bare alcove in a room that draws your eye precisely because it is empty. Rooms are shaped to breathe. Sliding doors made of rice paper diffuse sunlight into a soft glow. Tatami mats hush your footsteps. The architecture invites your presence rather than demanding your gaze.

Materials are humble and deliberate. Wood, bamboo, earth, paper. Natural elements age gracefully and bring the outside in. Rooms often contain a tokonoma — a recessed niche holding a seasonal flower or a scroll — and it changes with time, reminding the inhabitants to honor impermanence rather than resist it.

In traditional minka rural dwellings, roofs are steep and floors are raised, adapted to the elements. In urban machiya townhouses, rooms are long and narrow, filtering light through a courtyard. Whether countryside or city, the principle holds: architecture should serve life, not the other way around.

Contemporary Japanese design often holds onto these values even when using modern materials and angles. Clean lines, modular spaces, and a reverence for craftsmanship persist. The architect Kengo Kuma has described his approach as "erasing architecture" — designing structures that recede so the materials and the landscape can speak. In Japan, a building that disappears into its surroundings earns the highest possible compliment.

The Art of Stillness

Spend an afternoon in a traditional calligraphy studio and the first thing that strikes you is the silence before the brush moves. The ink stick has been ground for ten minutes. The paper is laid flat. The calligrapher sits without moving. Then the brush descends, and the stroke is over in a second — unrepeatable, unrevocable, complete.

Japanese calligraphy — shodō, literally "the way of writing" — functions as both functional literacy and spiritual practice. A master calligrapher channels breath, posture, and mental clarity through a bamboo brush to ink paper in movements that cannot be revised, erased, or hesitated over. Washi paper absorbs ink instantly and permanently. Animal-hair brushes hold moisture unpredictably. By the time the first stroke touches paper, the calligrapher has already committed to irreversibility.

This commitment separates shodō from Western calligraphy, where preliminary sketches and correction fluid accommodate human error. Japanese practitioners train for years to accept mistakes as evidence of presence. The brush records everything: hesitation appears as pooled ink, anxiety as jagged edges, distraction as misaligned balance.

A character written while thinking about dinner looks demonstrably different from one created in focused stillness. The paper becomes a diagnostic tool revealing the calligrapher's mental state with unforgiving precision.

Outsiders perceive beautiful imperfection in ink that bleeds beyond ideal boundaries or spacing that shifts irregularly. Practitioners recognize these elements as nijimi and kasure, technical terms for controlled unpredictability. These elements prove that a human hand guided the brush. The eighth-century monk Kūkai described each stroke as containing the entire universe in miniature: beginning in emptiness, manifesting as form, returning to void.

Modern calligraphy studios teach through rinsho — copying masterworks stroke by stroke until muscle memory internalizes rhythm, pressure, and timing. Students might spend six months practicing a single character. They learn that speed indicates focus; many classical works were executed rapidly because hesitation produces visible tension. The goal is embodiment, transferring philosophical principles from teacher to student through repeated physical gesture.

Ikebana operates on the same logic, though its medium is living material. The practice is often translated as "flower arrangement," but that framing misses the point entirely. A practitioner arranges space — a line of stem and shadow, a bend that echoes the wind outside. One blossom placed high, one low, one tilted sideways, because they speak to one another rather than merely coexisting in a vase.

The practice emerged in fifteenth-century Kyoto as spiritual discipline. Zen monks positioned evergreen branches beside altar scrolls to honor Buddha, creating asymmetrical compositions that rejected Chinese symmetry for spatial tension. The earliest documented school, Ikenobo, codified principles still governing practice today: heaven, earth, and humanity expressed through three primary stems whose angles and lengths convey cosmic relationships. Sogetsu, founded in the twentieth century by Teshigahara Sofu, embraced bold experimentation with wire, plastic, and driftwood while preserving core principles of asymmetry and negative space. Ohara developed moribana, arrangements piled in shallow containers, to accommodate Western flowers entering Japan after eighteen sixty-eight — proof that adaptation need not mean abandonment.

The materials themselves embody the philosophy. Branches selected for ikebana often bear damaged bark, lichen growth, or irregular curves that would disqualify them from Western arrangements. Practitioners manipulate stems through bending, stripping leaves, or deliberate breakage to reveal what the plant might become. Sogetsu's Teshigahara described the practice as making flowers stand — giving them presence through emptiness. Negative space between stems carries equal weight to physical material, mirroring the concept of ma. What remains absent matters as much as what appears.

The Harmony of Movement

Noh theater is the only major theatrical tradition in the world where the primary technique is not acting but the deliberate suppression of expression. The goal is not to convey emotion but to create a container in which the audience supplies it. That inversion — the performer withdrawing so the audience can enter — defines everything about how Noh works.

The form emerged in fourteenth-century Japan when actor Kan'ami merged folk performance with Zen philosophy. His son Zeami refined this approach into precise theory, codifying techniques that remain unchanged after six centuries. The stage enforces constraint: bare hinoki cypress with four pillars, a painted pine backdrop, no scenery, no curtain. Performers wear carved wooden masks that appear expressionless yet convey shifting emotion through minute head tilts. A shite protagonist might take eight minutes to cross fifteen feet, each step deliberate, each pause calculated. What looks like inaction is meticulous control.

This aesthetic principle is called yūgen — profound grace, the beauty of what remains unsaid. Zeami described it as "a white bird with a flower in its beak," an image that suggests rather than defines. The audience witnesses a meditation made visible, where meaning accumulates in silence and empty space carries weight.

Kabuki emerged in the early sixteen hundreds as Noh's scandalous counterpoint. Izumo no Okuni, a shrine maiden turned performer, staged provocative dances along Kyoto's Kamo River. Her troupe wore Portuguese pantaloons, carried swords, and performed bawdy skits that drew crowds and official fury. By sixteen twenty-nine, authorities banned women from the stage entirely, citing moral corruption.

The ban transformed Kabuki. All-male troupes developed onnagata — actors who devoted their lives to embodying femininity through gesture, voice, and movement. These specialists created an idealized femininity more exquisite than any woman could perform onstage, achieved through pure technique. Some onnagata never broke character, living as women between performances.

Where Noh whispered, Kabuki roared. Elaborate revolving stages appeared by the seventeen fifties. Mie poses froze actors mid-gesture as percussionists struck wooden blocks, crystallising climactic moments into tableaux. Aragoto style showcased warriors in exaggerated makeup performing superhuman feats that thrilled commoners.

Yet beneath its flamboyance, Kabuki delivered serious social commentary. Sewamono plays portrayed merchant-class tragedies: lovers choosing death over separation, commoners crushed by rigid hierarchy. The seventeen-oh-three play Sonezaki Shinju depicted actual lovers who died together, triggering such widespread copycat suicides that authorities banned new domestic tragedies for decades. Kabuki reflected Edo-period tensions while offering visual spectacle that made social constraint temporarily bearable.

Wearing the Seasons

To wear a kimono is to step into a language without verbs or nouns, full of meaning all the same. Every fold, every layer, every subtle pattern quietly speaks of season, occasion, age, formality, and the wearer's mood. The garment is composed, not simply put on.

The kimono is deceptively simple in shape — a straight-cut robe, symmetrical and structured. Within that simplicity lives a deep sense of nuance. The fabric might feature falling plum blossoms for early spring, or cranes soaring above pine for a New Year's gathering. The rules govern awareness: noticing where you are in time, who you are with, and what kind of space you are entering.

For women, obi belts are the boldest statement — a wide sash tied at the back, each knot style carrying different social weight. For men, the palette tends to be more muted, the message quieter but still precise. Formality dictates the cut, the length, and the way the collar sits at the neck. Wearing a furisode — the long-sleeved formal kimono of an unmarried young woman — to a casual summer festival is not merely overdressed. It misreads the entire social register of the event, announcing the wrong relationship to the occasion and to everyone present. The kimono does not forgive inattention.

Wearing one is also an exercise in humility. It slows you down. The weight of the fabric and the structure of the layers ask you to move with intention. A mindful dignity emerges — not stiff or severe, but present.

Three pathways reveal how the kimono transformed from everyday garment to cultural statement. First, observe its current use: elderly women in subdued patterns on New Year's Day, twenty-year-olds in rented furisode at coming-of-age ceremonies, professionals who touch one only at weddings. This generational split shows what happened — the nineteen sixties shift to Western clothing was economic necessity, as kimono's handwashing, seasonal storage, and complex dressing became incompatible with postwar work life.

Construction details remain untouchable. Kimono pieces are cut in straight lines, sewn without darts, creating flat panels that can be completely disassembled, washed, and reconstructed. This practical innovation originated centuries ago when silk carried generational value. Modern designers preserve this structural geometry even when introducing denim fabric, motorcycle prints, or asymmetric hemlines.

Younger practitioners reimagine tradition without abandoning it. Hiromi Asai maintains traditional yuzen dyeing techniques while creating high-fashion designs suitable for contemporary runways. Kyoto Denim constructs kimono from selvage denim using historical patterns, producing garments that function as both fashion statement and cultural inheritance. Each generation decides which elements serve contemporary life and which can transform, refusing to treat craftsmanship as a museum artifact.

Mastery Through Repetition

The Japanese word for mastery does not translate cleanly into English. Shokunin — often rendered as "craftsman" or "artisan" — carries a weight the English words do not. It implies a life organized entirely around a single skill, a commitment so total that the boundary between the person and the practice dissolves. A shokunin does not have a craft. A shokunin is the craft. This way of learning is captured in the idea of shuhari — a concept used in everything from martial arts to flower arranging. It breaks down into three stages: shu (to obey), ha (to break), and ri (to transcend). First, you copy. Once the foundation is solid, you adapt. Finally, the technique dissolves, and the expression becomes your own. There are no shortcuts. You must live inside the form before you can move beyond it.

A potter spends years making the same shape. A sushi chef polishes rice for months before touching a knife. The humility in that is not false modesty — it is an acknowledgment that some things cannot be rushed, and that the act of repetition, when done with care, becomes devotion.

Watch a tea master fold a cloth. The same way, every time. Or a Noh actor rehearsing a single gesture, refining the angle of a wrist or the depth of a breath. This repetition is meditative. Meaning lives in the motion. Practitioners believe that through staying with the form long enough, the spirit will eventually speak.

Japanese artisans have discovered something Western innovation culture often misses: technology amplifies mastery. A ceramic artist in Bizen designs tea bowl forms using 3D modelling software, then fires them in traditional anagama kilns for ten days straight, sleeping beside the kiln to monitor temperature shifts. Digital precision meets wood-fired unpredictability. The software codifies centuries of proportion and balance, but the final judgment — whether a piece embodies wabi-sabi's honest imperfection — remains irreducibly human.

This pattern repeats across craft traditions. Textile workshops in Kurume use computer-aided design to map intricate kasuri ikat patterns, then execute them through hand-dyeing techniques unchanged since the Edo period. Sword polishers analyse blade metallurgy through electron microscopy, then apply findings using water stones and muscle memory passed down through five generations. The question is which elements serve timeless function and which merely replicate historical limitation.

Even once mastery is achieved, it is not flashy. A calligrapher's brushstroke might look effortless, but behind it lie decades of quiet mornings, wrists learning the weight of ink, eyes trained to see balance in negative space. The essence of refinement here is not striving to stand out, but striving to belong more fully to your craft. Whether that craft survives the next generation — whether the artisan who masters both algorithm and fire represents Japan's creative future or its nostalgic last stand — is a question nobody has answered yet.

Learning, Earning, Belonging

Inside Japanese Work Culture

The Classroom as Society

S CHOOL IN JAPAN FUNCTIONS as the first introduction to the collective rhythm of national life. From the moment students slip into their uniforms, they receive a physical reminder of their position within a structure larger than themselves. Individual expression remains possible, but it is channelled through the group.

The day begins with a bow. Students greet their teacher in unison and end class the same way. The gesture provides daily practice in spatial and social respect. Most public schools employ no janitors. Students clean their classrooms and hallways themselves, sweeping floors, wiping down desks, and emptying trash while a collective cleaning song echoes from the speakers. The task is framed as responsibility, teaching children to maintain the spaces they share.

Uniforms flatten economic status. A crisp navy blazer or sailor-style top ensures that a student's identity is defined by behaviour and contribution rather than brand affiliation. Group activities, club participation, and school festivals reinforce the expectation that belonging requires effort. Cooperation, modesty, and endurance are treated as measurable skills.

The hierarchy that will govern their adult lives begins here through the dynamic between senpai (senior) and kohai (junior). A senpai is someone with more experience — a guide to watch and learn from. The kohai offers deference, support, and effort in return. The relationship requires a specific social choreography: the senpai leads by example, the kohai follows with trust.

You see this dynamic in language and gesture. A kohai uses polite speech when addressing a senpai, while the senpai speaks more casually in return — a shift that signals familiarity rather than condescension. At a club gathering, a junior member pours the senior's drink first and helps with cleanup. These actions maintain group balance. Ideally, the relationship creates continuity: a senpai offers guidance and quiet advocacy, knowing the kohai will eventually provide the same support to the next generation. In a culture where harmony is prized, this structure provides a social shorthand reminding everyone they are not navigating the system alone.

The Sorting Machine

Beneath the orderly surface of neat uniforms and silent train commutes lies a pressure that starts early and rarely lets up. You see it in the crowded juku cram schools operating late into the evening, filled with elementary students preparing for exams that will determine their future.

Shiken jigoku — examination hell — originated during the Meiji era when scarce university seats created brutal zero-sum competition. That scarcity endures in the prestige economy. Entrance exams measure single-day performance under extraordinary pressure rather than cumulative knowledge or aptitude. Tests occur once annually. No retakes exist. No appeals process. Students who stumble face an entire year's delay, watching peers advance while they remain behind.

Exam failure in Japan reshapes life trajectories in ways outsiders rarely grasp. The journey from elementary school through university functions as a merciless sorting mechanism, determining corporate recruitment, lifetime earnings, and marriage opportunities decades before those futures arrive. Success requires stamina and the unspoken belief that trying hard enough should always yield results.

Innovation enters this system through calculated evolution rather than disruption. The Ministry of Education recently permitted high schools to reduce rote memorisation in favour of critical thinking exercises, though implementation varies dramatically by prefecture. Universities now offer English-language degree programs as strategic responses to demographic reality. Temple University Japan and Waseda's international initiatives attract Southeast Asian students, filling classrooms that declining birth rates have emptied. Delivery methods adapt to survival imperatives while academic rigour remains uncompromising.

The Broken Bargain

The exam mindset does not end at graduation. It transforms into the defining ethic of the Japanese workplace, symbolized by the salaryman — a figure in a dark suit leaving the office well past sunset, embodying dedication, routine, and corporate loyalty.

Post-war Japan's work culture crystallized around a specific bargain: companies offered lifetime employment, and workers delivered total commitment. Firms rebuilding from rubble could not afford turnover, so they guaranteed security in exchange for absolute loyalty. A fresh university graduate joined a company and stayed for life. Promotions were based on seniority. The ringi consensus system meant decisions required multiple approvals across departments, stretching projects across months. Nominication — drinking sessions with colleagues — functioned as mandatory networking where actual business occurred. Refusing invitations signalled disloyalty. Work time and personal time were concentric circles, one contained within the other.

Then came the asset price bubble collapse in the early nineteen nineties.

The economic foundation cracked, but the cultural superstructure remained standing. Lifetime employment guarantees weakened, then vanished for many workers. Yet the expectations persisted — arriving before your supervisor, staying until the office lights dimmed, demonstrating commitment through visible presence rather than measurable output. The old bargain broke, but nobody renegotiated the terms. Workers still performed the rituals of total dedication, now without the security that once justified the sacrifice.

What happens to a workforce when the loyalty demanded by the system outlives the protection provided by it?

The human cost of this model has a name: karōshi, meaning death by overwork. It is a structural reality that Japan has been forced to confront openly. The country records approximately two thousand karōshi deaths annually — workers who die at their desks from stroke, cardiac arrest, or sheer exhaustion. The government recognizes these as legitimate workplace casualties, compensating families when monthly overtime exceeds eighty hours. The actual number is almost certainly higher.

Depression and anxiety rarely surface in corporate wellness reports. A twenty nineteen Ministry of Health, Labour and Welfare survey revealed that nearly sixty percent of workers experiencing mental health issues never sought treatment, citing workplace stigma as the primary barrier. Asking for help signals weakness; taking psychiatric leave permanently damages promotion prospects. Employees facing relentless corporate demands internalize severe anxiety in silence. Many resign quietly, citing vague "personal reasons" that obscure the true scale of workplace mental health crises. These invisible exits leave no official record.

Hikikomori — prolonged social withdrawal lasting months or years — now affects an estimated one point four six million Japanese citizens. Many retreat after educational or professional setbacks that seem to foreclose any viable future. This phenomenon represents a rational response to systems that define success narrowly and punish deviation harshly.

Women and the Workforce

Confucian orthodoxy arrived in Japan alongside writing systems and state bureaucracy, embedding gender stratification into the social architecture. The Tokugawa shogunate formalized these distinctions through legal codes separating uchi (inside) domestic spheres from soto (outside) public realms. Women managed household economies and wielded considerable informal authority, but legal personhood remained exclusively with fathers and husbands.

Meiji industrialisation complicated these divisions. Thousands of women entered textile factories, their wages funding brothers' educations and family land purchases. This labour was framed as temporary service before marriage, never a permanent career. The eighteen ninety-eight Civil Code enshrined male household headship, mandating wives obtain spousal permission for contracts, property transactions, or legal proceedings.

Post-nineteen forty-five reforms granted legal equality on paper, and the Labor Standards Act prohibited workplace discrimination. Reality diverged sharply from statute. By the nineteen sixties, the salaryman-housewife model became aspirational: men provided lifetime employment, women managed intensive child-rearing. This arrangement was a modern invention serving rapid economic growth, not a traditional one.

Government statistics illuminate the current structural realities. Women's labour force participation has climbed above fifty-four percent for those aged fifteen to sixty-four, yet they occupy only twelve point nine percent of managerial positions. At board level, women hold just thirteen point four percent of seats in listed companies, among the lowest rates in developed economies.

The system filters women out at predictable intervals. Marriage and childbirth function as departure points because structural accommodation remains rhetorical. Companies maintain formal maternity leave policies as mandated, yet matanto harasu — maternity harassment — operates as an informal penalty. Women face reassignment to peripheral duties, exclusion from advancement tracks, and ambient pressure signalling that motherhood indicates diminished commitment. Approximately thirty percent of women exit employment after their first child.

Recent initiatives address these patterns directly. The government's womenomics platform mandates diversity reporting, subsidises childcare expansion, and incentivises flexible scheduling. Some multinationals have implemented blind résumé screening and enforced parental leave for fathers, normalising career interruptions beyond gender. Progress unfolds unevenly, revealing which organisations treat equality as compliance versus operational transformation. The mechanisms preventing women's advancement now face scrutiny they previously evaded.

The Generational Fault Line

Walk into Toyota's headquarters and you encounter fifty years of working life compressed into one space. Baby Boomers who joined during Japan's economic miracle work alongside Generation Z employees fluent in technologies their seniors struggle to comprehend. The friction is real, if invisible from outside.

Senior engineers carry knowledge that exists nowhere else: how particular alloy batches respond under extreme stress, which supplier inconsistencies require vigilance, and troubleshooting approaches never committed to paper. Younger colleagues command AI-assisted design platforms, sophisticated data analytics, and cross-cultural fluency essential for global markets. Neither generation possesses sufficient capability alone.

Companies successfully managing multigenerational teams demonstrate measurably higher innovation rates and stronger financial results. Yet informal mentorship withers. Older workers bristle when juniors question established methods, while younger staff view seniority-based authority as arbitrary gatekeeping divorced from actual competence.

Toyota created structured ba — intentional spaces where knowledge flows deliberately rather than accidentally. Veteran craftsmen conduct workshops where physical intuition matters more than digital simulation. Junior employees run reverse-mentoring sessions on automation capabilities and emerging market intelligence.

Hierarchy endures: thirty-year-old insights still require managerial approval before reaching decision-makers, regardless of merit. The gap narrows through institutional design, not cultural shift. Younger generations are beginning to question the cost of the traditional model — the missed time with family, the burnout, the lack of work-life balance.

Structural reforms targeting mental health and overwork have begun to take root, though their implementation varies widely across industries and regions. The twenty nineteen work-style reform legislation capped overtime at forty-five hours monthly and three hundred sixty hours annually, backed by meaningful penalties for violations. Major corporations like ITOCHU Corporation now mandate at least five days of annual paid leave. ITOCHU Corporation restructured its working day from the opposite end: instead of capping late hours, it incentivized early arrival. Employees who began work before eight in the morning received premium wages and complimentary breakfasts; overtime past ten at night was banned entirely. The reform attacked the visibility problem at its root — in Japanese offices, staying late signals dedication regardless of output. By rewarding early arrival instead, ITOCHU broke the equation between long hours and loyalty without requiring anyone to formally acknowledge the old system had been extracting more than it returned. Mental health apps designed for Japanese workplace contexts — prioritising anonymity and accessibility over conventional counselling — saw sharp adoption after twenty twenty. Technology firms lead this shift; traditional manufacturers follow more cautiously, if at all.

The Demographic Reckoning

Japan's working-age population has contracted by over thirteen million since nineteen ninety-five. By twenty forty, projections show a further decline of sixteen million — roughly one worker in five disappearing from the labour pool. The numbers dictate the future before policy catches up.

Walk through any construction site in rural Akita or Shimane, and you notice grey hair under hard hats. Crews where half the workers are past sixty have become commonplace. Department stores actively recruit septuagenarians for customer service positions that once went to fresh university graduates. The traditional retirement age of sixty has quietly shifted to seventy, then seventy-five, as companies scramble to retain workers who carry decades of institutional knowledge. Keeping employees well past their expected retirement has become a survival strategy.

Companies are redesigning factory floors with lighter equipment, implementing flexible hours, and creating mentorship roles that allow older workers to train younger replacements who may never arrive in sufficient numbers. The economic implications extend beyond individual workplaces. A shrinking tax base must support expanding social services. Regional economies collapse as young people flee to cities, leaving behind aging populations and shuttered businesses.

Japan added nearly three hundred ninety thousand foreign workers between twenty nineteen and twenty twenty-three under the Specified Skilled Worker visa program. A Filipino engineer arriving in Osaka might receive months of training in Japanese language and workplace protocol, only to find reality far more complex. Senior technicians speak exclusively in regional dialects. Unspoken seating hierarchies govern lunch breaks. Crucial after-work social sessions remain inaccessible without fluency in cultural subtext. Language training focuses on transactional competence — reading safety manuals, filling forms — but does not prepare workers for the silent codes that determine belonging.

Integration remains structurally superficial. The tatemae (public facade) welcomes foreign labour; the honne (true feelings) preserves cultural boundaries. Foreign workers fill critical gaps in construction, nursing, and manufacturing, occupying a liminal space: essential yet peripheral, needed yet never quite integrated.

How does a society maintain its cultural identity when the workforce required to sustain it must be imported from the outside? Workplaces accommodate foreign labour because the alternative — production lines stopping, hospitals closing wings, construction projects abandoned — imposes costs no organisation tolerates indefinitely. The friction continues, but the direction has already been determined by forces larger than consensus.

Chapter Eleven

Between Generations

Family, Love, and Gender Roles

The Architecture of the Household

THE MODERN JAPANESE HOUSEHOLD balances the old and the new with a quiet pragmatism. A living room might feature a leather sofa resting on tatami mats, while the alcove once meant for seasonal scrolls now holds a flatscreen television. The cultural heartbeat of the home endures in small rituals — taking shoes off at the door, saying itadakimasu before a meal, placing a seasonal flower by the window.

Yet the structure beneath these rituals has fractured. Extended families used to be the norm, but today, multi-generational households are increasingly rare. In nineteen seventy-five, three-generation households comprized sixteen point nine percent of the total. By twenty nineteen, that number had collapsed to five point one percent.

This shift dismantled a legal and social architecture that governed Japanese life for decades. In eighteen ninety-eight, the Meiji government formalized the ie system — a legal framework binding property, inheritance, and identity to the patrilineal household rather than the individual. The household head held absolute authority over marriage approvals, asset distribution, and residence. Women married into a family, their names transferred from one koseki (family registry) to another, erasing legal ties to their birth families.

The ie system was deliberate social engineering designed to consolidate wealth, prevent land fragmentation, and create stable tax units during Japan's rapid modernisation. Only the eldest son inherited. Younger sons left to form branch families or marry into households lacking male heirs. Daughters provided no continuity; they became members of their husbands' households upon marriage, expected to serve their mothers-in-law before nurturing their own children. Filial piety demanded unquestioning obedience upward while promising authority downward — a generational contract where subordination guaranteed eventual control.

The postwar constitution abolished the ie system entirely in nineteen forty-seven, granting women equal inheritance rights and marriage autonomy. Legal transformation happened overnight. Cultural transformation did not. The abolished ie continues shaping expectations around caregiving, surname changes, and elder care obligations decades after its formal dissolution. It functions as a ghost architecture still structuring millions of lives.

Forces of Fracture

Urbanisation, credentialism, and technology systematically dismantled what the ie system had encoded for generations.

Urbanisation physically separated families. As employment shifted from agriculture to manufacturing and services, young workers migrated to Tokyo, Osaka, and Nagoya, leaving aging parents in depopulating rural towns. The multi-generational household fractured into nuclear units scattered across prefectures. Distance complicated obligation.

Education became the new inheritance mechanism. Where land once passed to eldest sons, parents now invested everything in juken — entrance exam success for all children regardless of birth order or gender. Mothers became kyōiku mama (education mothers), orchestrating tutoring schedules and school choices with the intensity previously reserved for household management. This created the first generation of women whose primary identity derived from their children's academic achievement rather than domestic labor alone. The examination system redefined what mothers owed their children and what children owed their lineage.

Technology introduced asynchronous connection. Email, LINE messages, and video calls allowed children to maintain relationships with parents without physical proximity. A son in Tokyo could fulfil filial obligations through weekly video check-ins rather than daily meals prepared by his wife for his aging mother. These shifts made generational expectations negotiable for the first time in centuries.

Modern Japanese families navigate this tension through selective preservation. A Tokyo family might observe obon meticulously — cleaning ancestral graves and preparing ritual foods — while simultaneously accepting their daughter's decision to delay marriage until thirty-five for career advancement. The same grandmother who insists on formal keigo during New Year visits welcomes her grandson's non-Japanese girlfriend at the dinner table. The expectation that wives serve tea to in-laws persists in rural Kyushu but has largely vanished in urban Kanagawa. This is not hypocrisy; it is calibration.

The Invented Tradition of Gender

Gender roles in Japan were engineered through specific policies during periods of state consolidation. The Meiji government systematically encoded female domesticity into law. Education bifurcated: boys received academic training for professional work, while girls studied sewing, etiquette, and household management. Textbooks taught that women achieved fulfilment through service to husbands and sons. This borrowed selectively from Confucian hierarchy while discarding Edo-period precedents where merchant wives managed finances and samurai women occasionally controlled estates. The ryōsai kenbo ideal — "good wife, wise mother" — defined female purpose entirely through domestic service and child-rearing.

The postwar occupation reformed family law but left workplace structures untouched. Companies built around the salaryman model, with men as permanent employees and women as temporary clerical workers who resigned upon marriage or childbirth. Tax policies penalized dual-income households, corporate benefits flowed through male household heads, and daycare remained scarce by design. By nineteen seventy-five, the "professional housewife" had become the statistical norm — an arrangement barely two generations old presented as timeless tradition.

Those foundations are now cracking under demographic pressure. Female CEOs remain vanishingly rare; as of fiscal twenty twenty-three, only thirteen women led firms among the one thousand six hundred forty-three companies listed on the Tokyo Stock Exchange's Prime Market. The stagnation reveals structural barriers that outlasted legal reform. Companies technically permit women to compete for management positions, but promotion systems reward continuous tenure — precisely what motherhood disrupts.

Japanese corporations still expect employees to work unlimited overtime and attend mandatory after-hours drinking sessions. These unstated requirements function as biological filters. Watch couples on the Yamanote line during evening commutes: notice who handles the shopping bags, who occupies the seats, or who manages the childcare logistics while balancing a briefcase. These patterns reveal underlying structures more reliably than official statistics. Documenting workplace communication meticulously reveals the same bias — meetings scheduled after standard hours, informal mentorship offered selectively, and opinions misattributed in formal minutes. This is what resistance looks like in practice.

A professional woman in Japan often follows a familiar trajectory: rigorous education, steady corporate advancement, and a management position secured by her mid-thirties. Yet after taking maternity leave, she frequently encounters matahara — maternity harassment. The signs are unmistakable. Invitations to client meetings stop arriving, key projects shift to colleagues deemed "more available," and within months, a lateral transfer appears. It is functionally a demotion wrapped in bureaucratic language.

A twenty seventeen workplace survey found that approximately twenty-six percent of pregnant women experienced this harassment, including pressure to resign or accept demotions after announcing pregnancy. The penalties persist even when women return quickly: colleagues question their commitment, managers assign less critical projects, and salary increases stall. Women strategise in response, deliberately postponing motherhood until management roles are secured and irreversible, or negotiating flexible arrangements quietly to avoid visibility that might invite career penalties. This pattern fuels Japan's infamous M-curve, where female labor participation plummets during childbearing years and recovers only later, if at all.

The Quiet Language of Love

In Japan, love rarely arrives with fireworks. It tiptoes in through a shared umbrella, a quiet train ride, or a carefully prepared bento lunch. Romance is careful. Public displays of affection remain rare; couples might hold hands, but kisses on the street draw stares. Saying "I love you" is not taken lightly. Affection is shown through care rather than words — making time, offering a favor, remembering a favorite tea.

Marriage has long been viewed as a social contract joining families as much as individuals. For older generations, arranged introductions (omiai) were common — respectable, structured, and endorsed by elders. Today, the path to partnership takes more organic routes through online dating, college crushes, and workplace flirtations.

Yet the average age of first marriage tells a story of economic precarity rather than changing romantic preferences. By twenty twenty-three, men were marrying at thirty-one point one years and women at twenty-nine point seven.

These figures have climbed steadily since nineteen ninety. Singlehood has become a pragmatic choice. By twenty fifteen, twenty-three point four percent of men and fourteen point one percent of women had never married by age fifty. These numbers reflect deliberate decisions made in response to structural constraints — housing costs in Tokyo, stagnant wages, and the impossibility of balancing child-rearing expectations with professional ambitions.

Technology reshapes how connections form. The phenomenon of konkatsu — marriage hunting — treats partnership as a project requiring strategy, effort, and sometimes professional assistance. What appears cold becomes necessary when traditional matchmaking networks have dissolved and organic meeting opportunities have narrowed. Marriage rates fell below five hundred thousand in twenty twenty-three, the lowest since the nineteen thirties. A twenty twenty-one survey revealed that seventeen point three percent of men and fourteen point six percent of women aged eighteen to thirty-four had no intention of ever marrying.

The Ikumen Generation

Walk through a Tokyo park midday, and you see a slow revolution: fathers holding toddlers and pushing strollers. The word ikumen — a blend of ikuji (child-rearing) and men — has become a cultural nudge encouraging men to be active, present fathers.

The government has set ambitious targets for male paternity leave uptake, aiming for fifty percent by twenty twenty-five and eighty-five percent by twenty thirty. In fiscal twenty twenty-three, eighty-four point one percent of mothers took parental leave, but only thirty point one percent of fathers did, exposing a persistent cultural gap despite universal eligibility. This pragmatic adaptation mirrors Japan's historical pattern: survival imperatives drive institutional change that ideology alone never achieved.

Implementation remains uneven. Taking paternity leave still signals insufficient dedication in many corporate environments. The same workplace praising diversity in recruitment materials often penalizes men who actually use accommodation policies. Younger couples negotiate division of labor their parents never considered — shared surnames through legal workarounds, collaborative child-rearing schedules, deliberate choices to remain childless without shame. These decisions accumulate quietly, reshaping expectations one household at a time.

Japan's public discourse around gender inequality now appears in bestselling books like Chizuko Ueno's influential Misogyny and in legislative debates. Younger women speak openly about career obstacles their mothers endured silently. The pressure comes from labor scarcity, not just activism; demographics force what protest alone could not. Recruit Holdings and Shiseido now publish gender equity metrics publicly, knowing that university graduates increasingly screen employers for advancement data before accepting offers. The twenty sixteen Act on Promotion of Women's Participation mandates that companies with over three hundred employees set numerical targets for female leadership. Compliance remains uneven, yet the framework exists.

Aging and the Shared Chapter

Adult daycare centers host karaoke afternoons, while temples offer memory circles for those with dementia. Grandparents FaceTime grandchildren they used to hold daily. Home-care robots exist alongside centuries-old customs. Japan stands at a cultural crossroad: how to honor old age in a society speeding forward.

Traditionally, aging was embedded in community. Elders were the keepers of wisdom and the moral anchors. Filial piety was a daily rhythm. The respect remains in the language — honorifics that change with age — and in customs like keirokai (Respect for the Aged Day) celebrations.

But the structure holding that rhythm is shifting. The old system of care, where the eldest son's wife was expected to care for in-laws, has frayed. More elderly people live alone, and more adult children live far from home. Economic necessity accelerates adaptation. With almost a third of the population now over sixty-five, elderly parents increasingly depend on daughters-in-law who work full-time. Families solve this through improvized combinations — hiring Filipino caregivers, rotating responsibilities among siblings, utilising adult day-care facilities.

What has not changed is the emotional current running through it all: the quiet promise that aging is not a burden, but a shared chapter. A bow, a warm bowl of soup delivered to a neighbor, a seat offered on a crowded train. In these everyday acts, Japan continues to write its story of care with tenderness and time. This represents evolution. Each conversation, each decision to delay marriage or split household labor differently, compounds into something resembling cultural drift as the society navigates entirely new forms of connection.

Chapter Twelve

Modern Japan Decoded

Pop Culture, Technology, and Digital Life

The Medium That Made Itself

IN NINETEEN SIXTY-THREE, OSAMU Tezuka released Astro Boy into weekly television syndication. Within months, forty percent of Japanese households tuned in to watch a robotic child navigate ethical dilemmas through stark black-and-white animation. The series was not technically sophisticated. Tezuka's studio produced episodes for a fraction of Disney's per-frame budget, compensating through limited animation techniques that maximized narrative impact while minimizing drawing labor.

This economic constraint became an aesthetic foundation. What emerged was a distinctly Japanese form prioritizing psychological interiority over fluid motion. Tezuka used static frames and dramatic closeups to convey emotional states that movement alone could not capture. He had studied wartime propaganda films and absorbed cinematic techniques — jump cuts, perspective shifts, speed lines — that transformed budget limitations into visual language. Manga provided the structural blueprint, its panel-based storytelling already conditioning Japanese readers to fill gaps between images and infer motion from stillness.

Anime and manga encode Japanese culture rather than escaping it. What appears to outsiders as escapist fantasy frequently operates as symbolic processing of pressures too immediate to address directly. Studio Ghibli's Spirited Away follows ten-year-old Chihiro into a bathhouse serving spirits, where her parents transform into pigs after gorging on food. The narrative depicts work culture with ethnographic precision. Chihiro scrubs floors, learns hierarchical protocol, memorizes clients' preferences, and earns her name back through unpaid labor that proves devotion. The bathhouse operates exactly like a traditional ryokan, complete with senpai-kohai dynamics and ritualized service standards.

Neon Genesis Evangelion presents teenage pilots controlling giant bio-machines against existential threats, but director Hideaki Anno embedded Japan's generational trauma directly into the structure. The absent parents, the surveillance, the expectation that children will sacrifice themselves for collective survival — these are direct diagnoses of national psychology through mecha battles. The mirror clarifies through displacement.

The Global Export

Japanese pop culture's global reach stemmed from structural advantages few nations possessed. By the nineteen eighties, Japan had industrialized animation production into assembly-line efficiency. Toei Animation employed specialized departments for key frames, in-betweening, coloring, and photography, reducing costs while maintaining an output volume that American studios could not match.

When Pokémon launched globally in nineteen ninety-eight, it arrived as a coordinated media ecology. Games, anime, trading cards, and merchandise synchronized across markets simultaneously. This replicated strategies zaibatsu conglomerates had perfected across manufacturing sectors decades earlier.

The content traveled because it addressed universal adolescent experiences through culturally specific frameworks. Dragon Ball Z's training montages and hierarchical power systems, Sailor Moon's friendship-obligation tensions, Death Note's rule-bound moral complexity — all embedded Japanese social logic so thoroughly that international audiences absorbed Confucian values without recognizing them as such.

Japanese pop culture now generates thirty point eight billion dollars annually, a figure more than double Rwanda's entire GDP. When Demon Slayer: Mugen Train became the highest-grossing film in Japanese history during a pandemic, it demonstrated recession-proof cultural production thriving precisely when tourism, manufacturing, and retail collapsed. Entertainment exports constitute core infrastructure amid manufacturing migration and demographic contraction. Pop culture operates as soft diplomatic power in ways automotive exports never could. Attack on Titan screenings in Seoul draw crowds despite historical tensions. Indonesian youth learn Japanese through manga before English. Nigerian cosplayers adopt Japanese aesthetics without ever visiting Tokyo. This cultural reach creates influence that transcends traditional geopolitics.

Invisible Infrastructure

Tokyo's convenience stores reveal technology integration that most visitors walk past without noticing. Every 7-Eleven coordinates temperature, inventory, and staffing through machine-learning systems that predict demand two hours ahead, rerouting delivery trucks in real time. The same store interface accepts multiple cashless methods — QR codes, IC cards, digital wallets — without requiring manual intervention from either customer or clerk.

Home technology follows an identical philosophy: invisible infrastructure that anticipates need. Integrated home energy management systems learn household consumption patterns, optimising electricity use and anticipating peak demand before it arrives. Air conditioning units adjust not just to temperature but to occupancy patterns learned over months. Rice cookers compensate for humidity variations that would otherwise ruin texture. These systems do not announce themselves; they simply work.

This represents kaizen — continuous incremental improvement — applied to everyday friction points. Japanese engineers identify annoyances Westerners accept as inevitable, then eliminate them through patient refinement.

Transportation infrastructure crystallizes this approach. Tokyo's trains do not just run on time. Platform doors align within centimeters of carriage doors, smartphone apps show which car deposits a passenger nearest their destination exit, and IC cards have evolved into wallet-enabled wearables that passengers tap without breaking stride. The technology disappears into seamlessness.

Yet ruthlessly optimising friction creates unexpected casualties. Sumida Ward's twenty nineteen study on elderly technology adoption revealed that the elderly were becoming socially isolated by digital convenience. ATMs replaced bank tellers who offered daily conversation. Automated checkout eliminated cashiers who remembered their preferences. Each efficiency gain systematically removed the low-stakes social contact that had structured their days.

The response demonstrated Japan's capacity for deliberate recalibration. Major retailers like Aeon introduced "silver shopping lanes" — slow checkout areas designed for conversation, not speed. Japan Post Bank began promoting in-person assistance, particularly around pension distribution dates, treating human contact as infrastructure worth maintaining. These were strategic decisions to engineer friction back into systems.

The Social Architecture of Digital Life

Social media penetrated Japan through a cultural filter. LINE, the dominant platform with ninety-six million users, functions as digital neighborhood infrastructure — delivering earthquake alerts, coordinating municipal announcements, and hosting work hierarchies via formal group chats. Users maintain keigo honorifics in text messages, transforming ephemeral communication into preserved social architecture.

Twitter became Japan's second-largest market because its character limit aligned with cultural preferences. Compressed expression rewards wit, and anonymity enables candour impossible in hierarchical face-to-face settings. The platform hosts freelance creators promoting work, political organizing disguised as fandom discussion, and complaint cultures that would violate wa (harmony) if voiced openly. A salaryman critiquing corporate overtime culture can tweet freely at midnight, his identity shielded, his frustration validated by thousands of silent likes from colleagues who will never acknowledge the sentiment in daylight.

Instagram curates aesthetics over authenticity. Users post seasonal moments — cherry blossoms, autumn leaves, meticulously plated meals — reinforcing traditional appreciation for fleeting beauty through digital curation. The platform becomes a contemporary expression of mono no aware, that poignant awareness of impermanence, now archived in pixels and hashtags.

Japan architected virtual worlds as social infrastructure. Final Fantasy XIV hosts over thirty million registered accounts, and players organise into "Free Companies" that mirror Japanese corporate structures: formal hierarchies, scheduled meetings, collaborative projects spanning continents. When Naoki Yoshida rebuilt the game from its catastrophic twenty ten collapse, he engineered systems demanding interdependence. Dungeons require coordinated teamwork. Crafting economies reward specialisation. Housing districts force neighbor interaction. Elderly players combat isolation here. Hikikomori individuals practice social skills through avatars. Foreign workers master conversational Japanese in spaces where mistakes carry no professional weight.

VRChat pushes this further into embodied experience. Japanese creators design virtual shrines, bathhouses, and clubs where global participants learn etiquette through gesture — bowing at thresholds, removing virtual shoes, maintaining conversational distance. Cultural transmission happens through imitation. Westerners see escapism; Japanese society sees deliberate social scaffolding for a generation whose physical infrastructure increasingly fails to foster human connection.

Wearing the Culture

Japan's fashion system operates as visible contradiction made coherent. Walk through Harajuku and observe a seventy-year-old woman in perfect kimono stepping past teenagers in deconstructed streetwear. Both expressions are equally valid. Fashion became the arena where Japan resolved its deepest tension: how to honor inherited forms while creating something utterly new.

Traditional elements persist with ruthless precision. Kimono construction still follows straight-cut geometry unchanged since the Heian period, sized through body measurements that reject Western fit-and-flare silhouettes. Indigo dyeing techniques perfected in Tokugawa workshops now appear on Comme des Garçons runway pieces. The wabi-sabi aesthetic manifests in deliberately frayed hems and asymmetrical cuts that command premium prices precisely because they violate industrial perfection.

When Yohji Yamamoto draped models in oversized black silhouettes during his nineteen eighty-one Paris shows, Western critics called it anti-fashion. He was translating ma — negative space as a structural element — from temple gardens into fabric.

Japanese gadgetry embodies cultural logic made tangible. The Zo-jirushi rice cooker uses fuzzy logic algorithms to perfect rice cooking, encoding centuries of traditional culinary instinct into microchip technology. Sony's nineteen seventy-nine Walkman succeeded by creating private mental space in dense urban settings, offering commuters psychological boundaries in a culture that values group harmony yet craves personal sanctuary. Smart toilets translate Shinto purity rituals into advanced technology — cleanliness as a spiritual state, not mere hygiene. Panasonic's nanoe air purifiers embody concern for atmospheric harmony within domestic space, echoing traditional sensibilities about environmental balance.

Innovation With Heritage

Japanese tradition survives by finding new forms without losing its core. The tea ceremony persists because it offers deliberate slowness, ritualized attention, and a space where technology intrudes only by permission. Walk into a contemporary tea house in Tokyo, and you will find tatami mats paired with climate control, bamboo whisks alongside precision-engineered ceramic bowls. The ceremony itself remains unchanged in structure — guests still bow, sip in silence, and admire the scroll hanging in the alcove. The participants may arrive via smartphone calendar invite, and the tea master might maintain an Instagram account documenting seasonal wagashi sweets. This is cultural resilience in action.

Festivals demonstrate the same principle. Gion Matsuri in Kyoto has run for over a millennium, yet its massive floats now incorporate LED lighting and sound systems. The sacred portable shrines (mikoshi) carried through neighborhoods still receive Shinto blessings, but organisers coordinate routes using GPS and crowd-management software. Tradition demands that innovation serve continuity rather than replace it.

What makes Japan's cultural architecture durable is strategic selectivity about which innovations matter. Robotics engineers at Honda do not see conflict when they program ASIMO to bow at precise angles based on Confucian hierarchy. The technology exists to extend social protocols, not abolish them.

This pattern repeats across industries. When Kengo Kuma designs buildings, he integrates cutting-edge environmental systems with façades employing traditional Japanese woodcraft. The intricate wooden lattice work at the Nezu Museum breathes modern efficiency through an aesthetic vocabulary centuries old. Even Japan's gaming industry follows this logic. The Legend of Zelda borrows narrative structures from folklore, Dark Souls embeds Zen patience into punishing gameplay loops, and Animal Crossing digitises the seasonal attentiveness that once governed agricultural rituals. Players worldwide absorb Japanese philosophical frameworks without recognizing them as such.

Japan demonstrates that the most resilient cultures integrate selectively, preserving the underlying logic and applying it to whatever tools the present offers. What happens to a society when its most successful exports are the very coping mechanisms it built to survive its own internal pressures?

Chapter Thirteen

Embracing Japanese Paradoxes

How Contradictions Make Sense

The Shrine Beneath the Billboard

S HINJUKU STATION'S EAST EXIT displays a paradox in three layers. Beneath a neon-bright Uniqlo billboard, the Hanazono Shrine — an Inari shrine dating from the Edo period — receives offerings from salarywomen clutching Starbucks cups. Their bows are brief but executed with full precision, interrupting commutes measured in seconds. The shrine's wooden architecture has not changed in two hundred years. The smartphone each woman uses to photograph her visit did not exist a decade ago.

Neither element feels out of place.

Japan's cultural continuity operates through active integration, treating tradition and innovation as complementary technologies.. What appears contradictory to outside observers functions as a deliberate strategy to participants who never learned these elements should conflict.

The distinction matters because most analyses frame Japanese modernisation as a tension requiring resolution — ancient temples versus bullet trains, kimono versus streetwear, calligraphy versus emoji. This framework misreads the actual mechanism. Japanese culture does not balance contradictions. It deploys them simultaneously, activating whichever system serves the immediate context without requiring philosophical reconciliation.

Consider a construction site where workers in cutting-edge safety equipment pause for Shinto purification ceremonies before operating GPS-guided excavators. The jichinsai rite is not a performance for tradition's sake. It addresses spiritual obligations that engineering degrees do not cover: acknowledging the kami inhabiting the land, requesting permission for disturbance, and ensuring collective harmony before beginning work that demands absolute coordination. The ceremony takes twenty minutes. The project timeline accounts for it the exact same way it accounts for concrete curing time.

This operational logic appears throughout Japanese systems. Department stores like Mitsukoshi install digital payment infrastructure while maintaining rooftop shrines where employees pray for business prosperity during New Year. The Tōkaidō Shinkansen — an icon of technological precision since nineteen sixty-four — runs alongside sections of the original walking route marked with eighteenth-century stone markers.

Technology updates the tools. The underlying framework persists. Understanding this integration requires abandoning the assumption that modernisation demands replacement. In Japan, the old does not resist the new. It teaches the new how to function properly.

Contextual Activation

Contradiction coexistence describes Japan's functional method for operating multiple incompatible systems simultaneously without requiring synthesis. The term itself would not appear in Japanese discourse — the phenomenon operates as default logic.

Japanese individuals commonly navigate distinct social spheres that Western frameworks might treat as mutually exclusive. An office worker might deploy full keigo formality in a client meeting, with bows calculated to exact angles, navigating Confucian hierarchies through every verb conjugation.

Hours later, the same person attends a Harajuku streetwear pop-up, wearing experimental fashion that deliberately contrasts with morning protocol. No cognitive dissonance emerges. The contradiction is not resolved; it is compartmentalized. The key mechanism is contextual activation rather than unified identity.

A salaryman might participate in traditional matsuri festivals wearing historical costumes, shouldering portable shrines through neighborhood streets while chanting centuries-old rhythms. Monday morning, he returns to a glass-tower office filled with cutting-edge robotics prototypes. These are not separate people or performative code-switching. They are contextual modes, each fully authentic within its domain. The festival self and the corporate self coexist without requiring philosophical reconciliation because Japanese culture does not demand they align.

Technology integrates into sacred spaces without diminishing their spiritual authority. Temples accept digital payment systems for omikuji fortune slips. Monks maintain social media accounts documenting meditation practices. Shinto shrines install QR codes for contactless donations. The sacred and the digital occupy the same physical space, serving different functions simultaneously. Neither compromizes the other.

This operational paradox extends beyond individual behavior into institutional design. Department stores dedicate entire floors to traditional crafts — handmade ceramics, artisan textiles, centuries-old confectionery techniques — while upper levels showcase the latest consumer electronics and fashion imports. The building itself embodies contradiction: preservation and innovation under one roof, each thriving precisely because the other exists.

The Architecture of Resilience

Western observers frequently mistake this coexistence for dysfunction — structures that "should" have collapsed but somehow persist through inertia or cultural stubbornness. That diagnosis fundamentally misunderstands the strategic architecture at work.

Maintaining contradictory structures simultaneously creates resilience impossible within unified frameworks. When Japan faced post-war reconstruction, it did not choose between traditional values and Western modernisation; it activated both. Companies adopted American management techniques while preserving Confucian hierarchies. Cities rebuilt with concrete and steel while maintaining shrine networks and seasonal festivals. The contradiction was not a compromize. It was deliberate redundancy.

This matters because singular systems contain singular failure points.

A culture organized around pure efficiency optimizes brilliantly until external shocks — economic collapse, demographic crisis, technological disruption — expose fatal brittleness. Japan's overlapping systems provide what engineers call graceful degradation. When lifetime employment fractured economically, the underlying Confucian obligation structure remained intact, allowing companies to preserve loyalty expectations even as contractual guarantees dissolved. The system adapted without collapsing because it never relied on a single operational logic.

For travellers and cultural observers, this explains persistent confusion. Guidebooks present Japan as either timeless tradition or futuristic innovation, forcing a false binary. Visitors arrive expecting consistency and encounter deliberate contradiction instead: vending machines outside wooden temples, businessmen in suits performing tea ceremonies, teenagers coding apps while studying classical calligraphy. The disorientation stems from expecting a unified cultural identity when Japanese culture operates through activated contexts.

Understanding this transforms observation from confusion to recognition. That elderly woman performing traditional dance at the community centre while wearing a fitness tracker is not caught between worlds — she inhabits both fully, activating whichever framework serves immediate needs. The temple accepting credit cards has not compromized its sacred function. It has preserved accessibility by updating infrastructure while maintaining ritual structure.

When the Systems Held — The 2011 Tōhoku Earthquake

The most legible demonstration of this principle in living memory occurred on March 11, 2011, when a 9.0-magnitude earthquake struck off the Pacific coast of Tōhoku, triggering a tsunami that reached forty meters in height and killed nearly twenty thousand people. The scale of the disaster overwhelmed every digital and institutional system it touched. Power grids failed across entire prefectures. Mobile networks collapsed under simultaneous demand. Government emergency broadcasts reached only those with battery-powered radios. The infrastructure of modern Japan — the trains, the internet, the ATM networks, the supply chains — simply stopped.

What did not stop were the neighborhood associations.

In coastal towns where the tsunami arrived within minutes of the earthquake, chōnaikai members already knew their evacuation routes because they had walked them during annual drills. They knew which elderly residents could not move without assistance because they had maintained the neighborhood welfare registers that local governments had long since digitized and then effectively abandoned. They knew where the community emergency supplies were stored because they had restocked them the previous autumn. When the official systems went dark, the analogue infrastructure of mutual obligation activated with a speed and precision that no emergency management algorithm could have replicated, because it had never been switched off in the first place.

In the weeks that followed, the same networks organized food distribution, coordinated temporary shelter, and managed the extraordinarily complex social dynamics of displaced communities — who had lost everything but had not lost their relationships with one another. International observers noted with something approaching disbelief the absence of looting, the orderly queues at relief distribution points, the collective restraint of populations under conditions of genuine scarcity. This was not stoicism performing for cameras. It was gaman — the cultivated endurance of hardship without public complaint — meeting the practical infrastructure of chōnaikai obligation, two systems that had been maintained in parallel for generations precisely because no one could guarantee the digital alternatives would hold.

The redundancy was not accidental. Japan sits on the Pacific Ring of Fire, experiences over one thousand earthquakes annually, and has been building disaster resilience into its social architecture for centuries. The chōnaikai system, the community emergency drills, the neighborhood welfare registers — these are not charming anachronisms. They are load-bearing structures, maintained at considerable cost in time and social obligation, because the country has learned through repeated catastrophe that singular systems fail at the worst possible moments. The earthquake of 2011 did not reveal a Japan that had preserved tradition out of sentiment. It revealed a Japan that had preserved redundancy out of hard-won wisdom.

Beyond Resolution

Japan's contradiction coexistence offers a model increasingly relevant as other cultures face similar pressures: how to modernize without erasing heritage, how to preserve identity while adapting to survival imperatives, how to hold incompatible truths simultaneously without demanding they resolve into false coherence.

Identifying paradoxes in any culture starts by recognizing patterns that have been naturalized into invisibility. Most people notice contradiction only when encountering other systems. Japanese visitors to America express genuine confusion at the simultaneous celebration of individualism and intense workplace conformity, just as Americans puzzle over Japan's coexistence of cutting-edge technology and fax-machine bureaucracy. The contradictions most difficult to see are those inhabited daily.

Every culture operates through unacknowledged contradictions. Environmentalists drive alone to purchase organic groceries wrapped in plastic. Privacy advocates scroll social media for two hours nightly. Professionals valuing work-life balance check email during dinner. Japan's cultural resilience emerges partly from allowing these contradictions to exist without demanding artificial resolution.

Inherited structures are often mistaken for natural law. Americans treat the forty-hour workweek as inevitable, despite its codification by the Fair Labor Standards Act in nineteen thirty-eight. Many Europeans assume August vacations reflect a timeless rhythm rather than origins in nineteenth-century industrial scheduling. A firm handshake, formal email signatures, and Sunday as a default rest day are not mere customs but encoded hierarchy, group membership, and temporal organisation.

The harder practice involves strategic activation rather than philosophical consistency. Japan's contextual deployment — formal keigo at work, casual speech with friends, ancient ritual at shrines — offers an alternative to Western pressure toward unified authentic selfhood. Maintaining an "outdated" practice specifically because it contradicts modern efficiency tests whether holding incompatible truths simultaneously offers advantages that optimized consistency cannot.

Contradictions generate friction, but they also provide redundancy. A years. There are things we need to learn, but there are also things that need to be unlearned — behaviors and attitudes, deeply held beliefs and selfish desires that need to be unearthed and brought under the direct influence of the Holy Spirit. Where do we begin? Let me encourage you to do what you can.

Do What You Can

"Do what you can," I've heard people say, "not what you can't." For example, everyone knows that the Bible, the Word of God, needs to be a regular part of your life. But maybe you're not a reader, it's not your primary learning style. As a result, every time you sit down to read the Bible, your mind wanders. You have a hard time keeping your eyes open. You might even fall asleep. You know you need to read the Bible, but you simply can't focus. You want to read through the Bible in a year, you've tried multiple reading plans but never completed them and you've been beating yourself up, "What's wrong with me?" you wonder. "Why is it so hard for me to read the Bible?" Well, it could be a demonic attack — demons have a vested interest in you *not* reading the Bible — or maybe you're simply an auditory learner. Maybe you're in a season in your life, for whatever reason, where reading is a chore. What do you do? I would encourage you to engage the Bible the way you can, not the way you can't.

Recently, I downloaded the *Listener's Audio Bible* with vocal performance by Max McLean, the director of the Fellowship of Performing Arts in New York City, and it's phenomenal! There's an arresting musical background. He has an amazing voice. And the drama? Wow! I listened to him read Genesis 1, and I was hooked. It's so engaging. Besides, the Bible was meant to be heard, not just read. In cultures that were illiterate, the words of Scripture were passed down from one generation to another verbally through what's known as the oral tradition. If you struggle to read the Bible, stop reading and start listening to the Bible or read it aloud. Do what you can, not what you can't. It doesn't mean you won't ever be able to sit and read the Bible. It might just be the season you're in right now. Instead of trying, trying harder and feeling like a failure, ask God to show you another way.

Several years ago, I had lunch with a young man who was attending my church and felt a call on his life to ministry. He was in his late twenties, newly married, and in great shape. He was tall and thin, unusually fit for a guy pushing thirty. I asked him about it because I was sure he was a personal trainer or an athlete of some kind. He smiled and said, "Let me show you something." He then pulled out his phone and showed me a picture of an enormous guy, several hundred pounds overweight, sitting on a couch. I said, "Who is it? A family member, a friend, a motivational picture you pulled off the internet?" "No," he said, "It's me, four years ago." I was shocked. I would never have recognized him. "What happened?" I asked. "What did you do?" He went on to tell me that, for a variety of reasons, he was eating himself to death in his early twenties when he found Jesus. And finding Jesus, he found the strength to do what the human will alone simply cannot do. And this is how it began. While he was watching TV, he asked Jesus to help him get up during the commercials and walk around the couch. He'd be sitting there with his bag of chips, watching TV, and when a commercial came on, he'd stand up and start walking. That's all he did. He did it for weeks and his body changed. He lost some weight, not a lot, but it was noticeable. He was getting stronger, which enabled him to take longer and longer walks. Eventually he found himself at a gym walking on a treadmill, then he started taking classes and eventually he became a personal trainer. All the little things add up to something. Are you doing what you can, not what you can't?

Transformation takes time, but more than the simple passage of time, you have to participate. You have to practice. You will not enjoy a life with

God automatically, magically. You will not learn to live freely and lightly, you will not discover the secret of the easy yoke and the light burden, the secret to contentment, unless you rearrange your life around spiritual practices and do what you can. Something is better than nothing. Even the smallest thing, or what might seem small to you, could make all the difference. It could, eventually, enable you to swim in deeper waters.

Start Small

I don't know where I got this idea, but it's been incredibly helpful to me. Whole life transformation is overwhelming. We need to make it simpler, make a start. What is God highlighting for you? What about you needs to change? Is it fear, lust, greed, selfishness, or anger? Do you struggle with perfectionism, pride, the good opinion of others? What has power over you? What severely reduces your freedom or ability to respond to the promptings and invitations of God? What do you need to work on the most? Galatians 5:22 says, "The fruit of the Spirit is love, joy, peace, forbearance, kindness, goodness, faithfulness, gentleness and self-control." It's a good place to start. Pick one thing. Do you need to grow in love for others? Do you want to be more patient? Do you need more self-control? Pick one thing and hold it before the Lord. Now, what could you do, what practice could you engage in that would put you in a place where God can begin to change that one thing?

I talk to God a lot. I'm good at talking, not so good at listening. So I'm practicing silence these days as a soul-training exercise. Silence, for me, is fasting from talking so I can listen to God. It's difficult and I'm not very good at it, but I'm practicing. I'm training myself to listen quietly for God's voice, ten minutes a day. Running around after my intersecting thoughts is like chasing cats more days than not, but it's okay. I'm in training. I'll get better at listening if I continue to apply myself and practice.

What are *you* working on? The beauty of spiritual disciplines is they can be customized. I love the story about, author and teacher, Dallas Willard. He was finishing a lecture at university when a student took exception with his point of view and disrespectfully and persistently pressed his argument. They had a brief exchange. Willard was calm and respectful. The student was agitated and disrespectful. While he spoke, Dallas listened patiently until the student had finished, then smiled, looked at his watch and said, "Well, thank you. That's all the time we have for today." Immediately following the class, some of the other students came up to him and said, "Why didn't you put him in his place? Why would you let him talk to you that way?" And Willard replied, "I'm practicing the discipline of not having to have the last word."[18] It was something he was asking God to work on in his life. What are you working on?

I like to watch the Kansas City Chiefs play football. I'm a fan, but I wasn't always a fan. I grew up in Western Pennsylvania, Steeler country, black and gold until I'm dead and cold, as we like to say. But, after twenty-plus years of watching the Chiefs, reading about the Chiefs, hearing people talk about the Chiefs, I suddenly cared. I was no longer ambivalent to the outcome. That's when I noticed something needed to change. When I watched them play, my temperature would rise, my heart would race, and my blood pressure would spike. I'd talk to the TV as if they could hear me, fussing over poor tackling, bad play calling and stupid mistakes.

Recently, when the Chiefs played the Buffalo Bills, I turned on the TV as Dianne was sitting in the room at her sewing table. She was not even aware the Chiefs were playing. "What are you watching?" she asked. "The Chiefs are on," I replied. "It's a playoff game." "Do I need to leave the room?" she asked quietly. "No," I said, raising an eyebrow, "Why would you need to leave the room?" "Well, you know how you get watching football," she said. "It makes you angry." "Angry?" I replied, wide-eyed. "Yes," she said, giving me that look. "So," she continued with a smile, "what are you going to do that would enable me to be with you while you watch the game?" I laughed, then instantly bowed my head and said aloud, "Dear Jesus, I'd like to invite you to watch the Chiefs with me. I'm inviting you into this experience to give me the power to enjoy the game, regardless of the outcome." Dianne laughed. Jesus laughed. I enjoyed the game. And I only yelled at the TV once or twice in the second half when she was upstairs and Jesus was at *your* house helping *you* hold on to *your* peace!

Choose One Thing

As John Ortberg wrote, "The disciplined person is not someone who does a lot of disciplines. The disciplined person, the disciple, is someone who is able to do what needs to be done when it needs to be done. The whole purpose of disciplines is to enable you to do the right thing at the right time in the right spirit, so if something doesn't help you do that, then don't do it."[19] We're all at different stages in life. We have different learning styles and unique life experiences. We're all at various stages of spiritual growth and development. Some are introverts, others are annoying — I'm kidding! Some are more contemplative, others learn by doing. Not every spiritual discipline or practice will be helpful for everyone. They're tools! Put them in your toolbox. How many tools do you have in your toolbox at home that you've only used once or twice? How many tools do you have that you make space for in your toolbox on the off chance that you might need them someday? I have tools I've never used. I don't even know what they're for, what they're called or where they came from, but I'm not getting rid of them because the moment I do something will break at my house that requires the use of that tool and nothing else.

Look. As I talk about taking the time to cultivate the habits and practices that will enable us to swim in deeper waters — see the *Spiritual Disciplines Handbook* by Adele Calhoun for a wonderfully comprehensive list — I want you to know you don't have to use them all. Some are more foundational, for general use — like a screwdriver, a pair of pliers or a crescent wrench — and some are more situational, like a pipe wrench, a coping saw, or a stud finder. The idea is to gather as many tools as you can, learn how to use them and apply them as necessary. If you're just getting started, identify one thing you want to work on in your life, led by the Holy Spirit, and choose one tool. One tool, one soul-training exercise, one spiritual discipline, used faithfully for an extended period, is far more effective in the long run and far more valuable than spending your time collecting tools or the endless search for the perfect tool.

That's where I was. I was always looking for the perfect tool. I collected as many tools as I could — Bibles of all shapes and sizes, countless devotional books, various kinds of journals. They were good tools, helpful tools or they probably would have been if I'd faithfully applied them. Do you know what I'm talking about? For years, the enemy tried to get me to believe that if I couldn't spend an hour in prayer every day, if I couldn't read through the Bible in a year, if I couldn't keep a regular journal, write my prayers, memorize huge sections of Scripture, read devotional literature and Christian biographies, if I couldn't do all these things then I might as well give up. I had an all-or-nothing approach, an idealized mental picture of how a good Christian should behave and I told myself, "If you can't do all these things, then why bother?"

"All-or-nothing" is rarely helpful. It doesn't make sense in any other area of life. Why, then, do we insist on applying it to our relationship with God? For example, I simply don't have the time to be a bodybuilder. I know those of you who know me might find that hard to believe, but there it is. For years, I had an all-or-nothing approach to exercise. If I couldn't do an hour of cardio and an hour of weight lifting every single day, then why bother exercise at all? I'd start "the program," rearranging my life around what I thought I should do and I'd inevitably fail. Then I'd wait until I felt like trying again and start over. Are you familiar with this pattern? It's embarrassing, but it took me a while to give myself permission to do *some-*

thing when I couldn't do *everything*. Have you given yourself permission to do something when you can't do everything?

It reminds me of the ninth grade aquatics class I had to take in high school. Every Monday, Wednesday and Friday we would interrupt a perfectly normal day by donning a swimsuit and spending an hour with our peers in a highly chlorinated pool. It wasn't fun. We weren't frolicking or horsing around. They taught us to swim freestyle, and that's what they expected us to do. For weeks, we'd line up in the Olympic-sized pool and swim lap after lap, with our heads underwater, popping up to breathe every other stroke. I just couldn't get the hang of it. My ever-present allergies made it hard for me to exhale out of my nose underwater. I was gulping, sputtering, my eyes were burning. It was miserable. I was always the last to finish. After a week or so, I thought, *"This is not for me."* I couldn't wait to get out of the pool...*until* week four when the instructor introduced the backstroke. Suddenly, I was in my element. I could finally breathe! I went from worst to first! I loved it so much I started doing everything backwards — walking backwards, running backwards. I'm one of the few people in America who's actually faster backwards than forwards...okay, I'm making that up. I even figured out that my name, backwards, is Renraw Rotciv Kram. The backstroke was a revelation! I could swim! I was finally at home in the water. I could venture out into the deep without fear. I just needed the right stroke, the right technique, the proper tool. Choose one tool, one spiritual practice. What is God inviting you to do in this season of your life?

A Sampling

I've used a variety of spiritual disciplines, practices and soul-training exercises. Some I've known about and practiced on-and-off-and-off-and-on for years — Bible reading, memorization, worship, intercessory prayer. Others were introduced to me for the first time through the

Ignatian Exercises. Some I've discovered through reading. Others have been recommended by family and spiritual friends. Here are a couple of my favorites.

1. *Breath prayers*. When this idea was first explained to me, I realized I'd been doing it, in one way or another, most of my adult life. I'd feel stressed and in an effort to relieve that stress I'd unconsciously take a deep breath, hold it for a moment, then let it out, saying, "Lord, have mercy" or "Lord, give me strength." It was a reflex, something I did out of necessity when I felt overwhelmed. Now I do it intentionally as a daily practice. It helps me slow down, focus my heart on Jesus and attend to His presence in my life. I'm sure you've heard about the health benefits of deep breathing. Apple even includes a *Mindfulness* app on the Apple Watch to encourage the practice. But mindfulness — "a mental state achieved by focusing one's awareness on the present moment, while calmly acknowledging and accepting one's feelings, thoughts, and bodily sensations,"[20] whatever that means — is empty, limited and ultimately unsatisfying apart from Jesus. Only Jesus can calm your heart, alleviate your fears, and heal your troubled mind. Only Jesus can help you get to the root of the problem. Deep breathing is helpful. You need to breathe. You should breathe. I highly recommend it. Prayer is something else. Jesus prayed. Prayer is conversation with God. Breath prayers combine the natural, familiar, God-given rhythm of breathing in and out with a short, memorable, biblical phrase. It's a way of using your body to focus your heart and mind on Jesus, inviting Him into every aspect of your life.

Thankfully, the Bible is full of short, memorable prayers and phrases that can easily be prayed this way. Emulating the prophet

Samuel from the Old Testament, you might pray, "Speak, Lord," as you inhale and "your servant is listening," as you exhale.[21] Or like Jesus, you might pray, "Not my will," as you inhale and "but yours be done," as you exhale.[22] It's a prayer of surrender. My favorite is a simple prayer I learned from my wife, Dianne. It was meant to be done with hand motions, but it works as a breath prayer just as well, even better in combination. As I inhale, I lift my hands to heaven and pray, "God, my Father," then, stretching my arms out like Jesus on the cross, I exhale and say, "Jesus, my Redeemer." Then, putting my hands over my heart, I inhale and pray, "Holy Spirit within me," then, bowing low at the waist, I exhale and say, "I surrender my life to you." "God, my Father / Jesus, my Redeemer / Holy Spirit within me / I surrender my life to you." I've taught it to my congregation. It's a wonderful way to begin or end a day, to quiet or realign your heart with God or prepare your heart for worship. I find myself breathing that prayer multiple times throughout the day as a regular rhythm. Why? I'm practicing the surrendered life, putting myself in His hands. I'd encourage you to try it.

2. *Journaling.* I love listening to the audio version of *Living in Christ's Presence* by Dallas Willard. The book was created from the transcripts of a conference Dallas did with John Ortberg a few months before he died. The audio version is not an audiobook, as such, but an actual recording from the conference and it is rich with truth, incredibly moving and well worth your time. I wish I had been there. There were several memorable moments, but one of the things God highlighted for me was something John Ortberg said about journaling. He said, "Because we tend to gauge spiritual maturity by devotional practices, we get guilty about them. My wife loves hearing that Jesus never journaled. The Bible is full of people who loved God, who lived under the Spirit, who

fought sin, who grew in virtue, but they never went down to the stationery store and bought a little blank leather book and started filling it out. Now, if journaling helps you, if it helps you focus your mind as it does mine, sometimes, by all means, do it. If it doesn't help you, don't do it."[23] This goes back to "do what you can, not what you can't."

I have had a lukewarm relationship with the soul-training exercise of journaling most of my adult life. I love the idea of journaling — keeping a record of God's activity in my life and my response to that activity over a sustained period — but I've struggled with the practice. I've started more than my share of journals over the years, handwritten and digital, only to abandon them, defeated, when I inevitably missed a day, a week or more. Add to that the niggling feeling that someone might, one day, happen upon my journal and read it (horrors!) and my ongoing struggle with having to write well — using proper grammar, syntax and the like — so as not to offend God and you can see my dilemma. It wasn't until I invited Jesus into my journaling, gave myself a break on the days I wrote less or wrote nothing at all, and started incorporating a little creativity — drawing, coloring, writing poetry and prayers — that I was able to unlock the riches of this beautiful spiritual practice.

Each journal entry makes a mark "on your spiritual wall, recording and denoting growth."[24] If you grew up, like I did, standing tall against a door jamb on your birthday while your mom or dad measured and marked your height, you know how encouraging that can be. The door jamb leading to the den, in the house I grew up in, provided a reference point that I was, in fact, a growing boy. We all are encouraged by seeing our progress. A journal acts like a spiritual door jamb. It reveals where you've been and how far you've come.

The Need for Grace

A couple of final thoughts on training. First, we all need grace. We need to give ourselves grace as we practice. I talked about my practice of silence earlier. Silence is a wonderful spiritual discipline. Nevertheless, when I felt God's invitation to sit quietly before Him — "Be still, and know that I am God" (Psalm 46:10) — it was a struggle at first. I'd set a timer on my phone, close my eyes and invite His presence and, immediately, my mind would remind me of what I had to get done, replay my last conversation or urgent email or simply go on an adventure to some far off land. It was a wrestling match, more an exercise in daydreaming or worrying than attending to the presence of God. "Silence is hard," I concluded. Not the silence part, mind you. Silence is easy. As an introvert, I have no trouble sitting in silence. It's the listening part. Listening for God's voice among all the other voices. And there are so many other voices — the world, the flesh, the devil — whispering, shouting, talking over each other, elbowing their way forward, like overstimulated children vying for my attention. "Look at me," they'd shout insistently the moment I set about listening to God. It was frustrating.

I talked with a friend about my struggles and he asked me, "Where do you meet Jesus when you're practicing silence?" "Where do I meet Him?" I asked curiously. "Yes," he replied. "I sometimes find it helps to join Him at a coffeeshop in my mind or take a walk with Him." Intrigued, I started using my imagination to walk with Jesus through a meadow on a bright, sunny day. Though I'm not much of an outdoorsman, it helped to picture myself walking beside Him in a companionable silence, me just enjoying His presence and waiting for Him to take the conversation where He wanted it to go. I had some sweet times with Jesus in that meadow. Then, one day, all the old, familiar voices showed up, spoiling the meadow in my mind, crowding into my time with God. That's when my friend suggested I take those random thoughts, walk them to the edge of the meadow, and leave them there. "If they're really important," he said, "they'll come back to you when you're ready to address them." *"Could it really be that easy?"* I thought.

Well, it wasn't easy. It was still really hard. I was always excusing myself from the conversation and walking intrusive thoughts to the tree line like they had to go to the bathroom. "Keep a paper and pen handy and write those thoughts down," I can almost hear you saying as you read this. "It works for me." I'm glad it works for you but for me, jotting down all my random thoughts in a ten-minute time of silence before the Lord was more like the Lord watching me make a to-do list then the two of us having a conversation. The time flew by, my alarm would go off and I'd end my time of silent reflection wondering why God had invited me into such an exasperating practice. But the more I tuned my heart to hear Him, the more I practiced listening, the easier it got. I'm still wrestling with intrusive thoughts from time to time, but now I'm doing it with the strength that God provides. The goal was never to be good at the practice. The goal was always, and is now, to attend to the loving presence of God, to learn to keep company with Jesus. This was huge for me. In the shallow end of the pool, I didn't think I needed to sit with God in silence. My relationship with Him was more about being good and getting things done. Since the Bible gave me an adequate list of what to do and not do, to be good and get things done, I didn't think I needed to listen to God in real time. But a healthy relationship, really any healthy relationship, is not just about doing — what He's done for you and what you do for Him — it's about being, talking and listening, yes, but also just being together. Silence is a way for me to push against my tendency to do, do, do for God and just be with Him.

Should you practice the spiritual discipline of silence? I don't know. You're asking the wrong guy. But whether he leads you to do it or not, don't feel guilty about how well you do it. Give yourself grace because God does. God has grace for you.

It's Not About the Practice

We have to be careful not to make it about the practice. As author Jan Johnson wrote, "Concentrating on practices and tools of our faith (and how well we're doing them) can be a sign of self-centeredness rather than God-centeredness: *Have I prayed today? Did I pray long enough, sincerely enough for it to 'count' with God?* We may congratulate ourselves for our consistent practices or regret our lack. We focus on our efforts so that we essentially trust in ourselves, as the Pharisees did (Luke 18:9). We become, in effect, 'stars' of our own spirituality, concentrating on our own performance. In fact, Jesus must be the star of our spirituality — the focus of our attention and the one who does the heavy lifting."[25] Is Jesus the focus of your attention or is it more about your performance, about practices performed properly or consistently? Do you see spiritual practices as a means to an end, a way of connecting with God, or an end in themselves?

I'd also encourage you not to compare your spiritual practices with the practices of others. These comparisons are rarely helpful, more often a desolation in our lives than a consolation, leaving us with a sense of inadequacy. Look. We're all on the same path, walking with Jesus, but we're not all in the same place. He may be working on one thing with you, using a particular set of tools, and another thing with me requiring a whole different set of tools. This is the thing that's so frustrating about reading Christian biographies. We read that George Mueller prayed three hours a day and we shake our heads in despair. "If that's the bar, I have no hope. I'll never learn to walk by faith." We read that John Wesley preached nineteen times every Sunday, circuit riding from one location to another, and we can't help but feel like a slacker. So, how, then, do we learn to walk by faith and not by sight, always comparing? How do we grow in grace for others and for ourselves? That's where spiritual practices come in. They're the means by which God changes our lives.

Now, disciplines are not the *only* means by which God changes us. He'll often use life circumstances, significant relationships and pain and suffering to bring about change. You might also have an arresting dream, a vision, a prophetic word or a notable encounter with the Holy Spirit, all as a catalyst for change. These memorable, joyful, sometimes painful moments serve as catalytic events in our life with God. We need catalytic events, watershed moments. But catalytic events always need to be accompanied by a continuous process. You can't simply live for the next catalytic event — the next prophetic word, vision, angelic appearance, or whatever. You need a continuous process, a way to regularly engage with God. Spiritual practices are that continuous process. They are a fundamental way God pours His grace and favor into our lives and makes us more like Jesus. Why? Because they put us in a place where God can get at us. Does God have access to you? Are you making yourself available to Him? Are you training or just trying?

This was the first thing that changed for me on the road to a deeper, more intimate love relationship with Jesus. I stopped merely trying and started training. But my paradigm shift, my way of relating to God, didn't end there. I also needed to get off the merry-go-round of my driven life so I could learn to be with Jesus.

Drawn, No Longer Driven

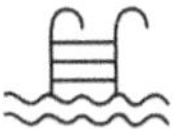

"And I [Jesus], when I am lifted up from the earth,
will draw all people to myself."
~John 12:32

"If you don't come apart for a while,
you will come apart after a while."[26]
~ Dallas Willard

Are you a driven person? "Driven" is the word we often use to describe someone who's motivated, ambitious, or compelled by the desire to accomplish a goal. It's a compliment. That's what I've always believed. And most of my life, I have been driven, running headlong down a path I thought would lead to success, recognition and so much more. And, in truth, it led to so much more, but it wasn't the more I wanted. I talked a bit about that in chapter one, about climbing the ladder I thought would lead to success only to discover it's leaning against the wrong wall. For me to grow in my love relationship with Jesus, I needed a paradigm shift — from trying to training and driven to drawn. Let me explain.

Most of the driven people I know either don't think they're driven or they wear it like a badge of honor, something to be proud of. I know I did. I even put in on a résumé and used it as a buzzword in a cover letter, "A driven, ambitious and self-motivated individual seeking a forward-thinking opportunity…" and on it goes. That was par for the course when I worked in the corporate world several years ago. I shake my head in wonder today when I read stuff like that in a cover letter for a position in ministry. "Drivenness is next to godliness," said no one ever, but you'd never know it watching driven pastor after driven pastor "burn out for Jesus." Despite the abundance of cautionary tales, I was convinced I'd be the exception to the rule. I used to describe myself as driven, self-motivated, high-functioning, and hard-working, with no small amount of pride.

Now, please understand, there's nothing wrong with hard work, nothing inherently wrong in pressing toward a goal. But drivenness, as I'm using the word in this chapter, is less about how you do what you do and more about *why* you do it. Why do you do what you do? Have you ever stopped to think about that? Have you ever taken the time to examine your motives? What are you hoping to gain from all that activity? What are you hoping to achieve? What legacy are you hoping to leave behind?

It might help to picture yourself actually achieving your goals. There you are, one day in the future, admiring the work of your hands, basking in the culmination of a dream, celebrating the fruits of your labor, your life's work, and as the celebration winds down, the music fades, and the crowd of revelers slips away, what are you left with? How do you feel? Content, fulfilled, satisfied or something else? Drivenness is a condition of the heart, more about the motive than the opportunity. Whatever drives you, whatever your motives, the results are often the same. Contentment is fleeting, at best, and elusive, at worst, and you're left to wonder who you are when you're not doing something, striving toward something or achieving something. Drivenness, as desirable as it might be in a life apart from God, is counterproductive to a life *with* God. He doesn't drive us, He draws us. We're meant to live in response to His invitations. My drivenness, for the first fifty years of my life, was fueled, in large part, by what the New Testament calls *selfish ambition*. It's one of those things that's easy to see in others but hard to see in yourself.

Pretty Girl

Several years ago, I was on my way home from church on a Sunday afternoon. It was just an ordinary Sunday, as I remember it. I got up early, hurried my family into the minivan, drove to church, taught two services, led ministry time, talked with a handful of people, and then rejoined my family after the last service to go to lunch. What follows is an account of what happened on that particular Sunday. I emphasize the point because it could have been any Sunday. This could have happened on any given Sunday, and I'll tell you why.

I was suffering under the illusion that it all depended upon me, that one fantastic sermon could launch the church into a season of unparalleled growth while a single stink bomb would cause people to leave in droves, holding their noses. As a result, I had unknowingly slipped into the habit of reliving the details of my sermon in the car every Sunday, obsessing over every triumph, witticism and clever turn of phrase, as rare as those might have been, along with every ill-advised rabbit trail, joke or vaguely inappropriate illustration, which were far more common. I was processing out loud, looking for affirmation, asking my wife, Dianne, to reassure me. "Did it make sense? Was it too long? What did you think about my second point? Did I communicate well? Did I hit the right note?" As I wrestled with myself aloud, the regrets always drowning out the joys, my obsession with perfection and success made me oblivious to the fact that my children were forced to endure this as well. Week after week, like clockwork, I would preach and lament, preach and lament and every week the kids would listen in as Dianne tried to talk me off the ledge.

Finally, on the Sunday in question, while I was standing in the rut I'd grooved out for myself over several years, singing the same old song, my teenage daughter, Brittany, piped up from the backseat. "You're a pretty girl, Dad," she said with a smirk on her face. "What?" I asked, perplexed, as everyone laughed. They got it immediately, but I was so deep inside myself, so lost in my macabre weekly ritual that it went right over my head. "You're a pretty girl," she said again, laughing. I shook my head and smiled as the truth came home to me. Brittany had had her fill of teenage girls obsessing over their looks. "Does this look good on me? Does this shade enhance my eyes? Do these shoes go with my outfit? Do you like my hair this way?" "You're a pretty girl," was her way of addressing my self-obsession. She might as well have said, "Look down, look down, you'll always be a slave. Look down, look down, you're standing in your grave."[27]

In a way, I *was* standing in my grave. I was a slave to selfish ambition, driven to succeed, to prove that I was just as talented, just as smart, just as worthy of adulation as the next guy. I wanted the approval of others so badly at that time in my life, affirmation, if not conclusive proof, like Bruce Willis' character at the end of the movie *The Kid*, that I was not, in fact, a loser! I was obsessed, full of nagging questions. "Am I worth anything if I'm not out there proving myself? Who am I when I'm not busy doing things that tell the world who I am? Why is it so hard to stop the frantic pace of my life even when I know it's hurting me and those I love? What do I do with this pain and sadness? What is true and real in my relationship with God and what is merely illusion — things I would like to believe are true but really aren't? Is God really enough to satisfy the loneliness, the emptiness, the longing of my soul?"[28] Brittany's comment was like holding up a mirror for me. It provided an opportunity for some painful self-reflection. "Kids say the darnedest things," and, in my experience, so do teenagers!

Dianne had been pointing it out to me for years. "Does one sermon really matter that much? Why are you so obsessed?"

Well, for one thing, I was raised to believe that the sermon on Sunday really does matter. It was the main event, the thing that kept them coming back. "Preach the Bible," I was told by a mentor who was assigned to me in those early days. "Preach the Bible and they will come." I'm pretty sure he got that last part from *Field of Dreams*. He kept repeating the refrain as if he'd hit on something profound though, bless his heart, he couldn't remember my name. In the year and a half I met with him he called me Mike or Matt or Milt even, but never Mark. You would think, if you were running through your mental Rolodex of four-letter boys' names that begin with the letter M, Mark would eventually come to mind, especially for a preacher, but it never happened and I grew weary of correcting him. It didn't matter. What mattered in the moment, and for thirty years thereafter, was that I agreed with him. I thought my future "success" in ministry was tied to my communication skills. If I could just write the perfect sermon — be suave, interesting and entertaining, as well as deep, learned and profound — every week for the rest of my life, my church would grow. "It's just that simple," I'd often say to myself. Talk about a burden!

Selfish Ambition

The seed, once planted, quickly took root as I looked out at all the famous pastors in America who were also great communicators and tried to emulate them. I launched a radio show at the tender age of twenty-two with dreams of becoming the next Chuck Swindoll. I started writing a book in my early thirties, not because I had anything to say but because famous pastors wrote books. If I were thirty years younger, I probably would have launched a YouTube channel, produced a series of TikTok videos and started a blog. Please understand, there's nothing necessarily wrong with any of those things if you're drawn to them, invited into them by God. It's not so much about what you do. The *why* matters more than the *what*. I did a lot out of selfish ambition, plain and simple. Come to find out, it's a fairly common motivation in our celebrity-oriented culture, even among pastors, but there are a number of other unhealthy motivations as well — envy, jealousy, lust, greed and pride. What motivates you to do what you do? What drives you, fuels you, compels you?

The last thing I ever wanted for myself, or anyone else, for that matter, was to be someone's whipping boy. Do you know that phrase, "whipping boy"? It conjures a fairly graphic image for me. I picture myself bound to an overloaded wagon, staggering under the weight of a heavy yoke while selfish ambition snarls at me maniacally from the driver's seat, cracking a whip, urging me on. That's how I often felt in the years leading up to my transformation, compelled along by an angry task master, browbeaten by a relentless bully. But that's not even the origin of the phrase "whipping boy." Intrigued, I had to look it up. A whipping boy, according to Dictionary. com, was a boy educated alongside a prince or child monarch who would bear the punishment for the prince's transgressions in his stead while he watched. Feels like one of those modern parenting techniques that sounds like wisdom until you try it. Who, in the world, ever thought that was a good idea? I can't think of a more surefire way to train a child in sadism. Truth or fiction, nobody knows, but I can tell you, this is not the life Jesus envisioned for us. He bore our sins on Himself. He took our punishment so we could live freely and lightly. He said His "yoke" was easy and His "burden" was light.

The Apostle Paul mentions selfish ambition on four separate occasions in the New Testament, setting it alongside slander, jealousy, gossip, arrogance and fits of rage as things that should be avoided. He specifically warned the church in Philippi that it was possible to preach Christ "out of selfish ambition, not sincerely."[29] He went so far as to say, "Do nothing out of selfish ambition or vain conceit. Rather, in humility value others above yourselves..."[30] I like to think Paul mentioned selfish ambition because he struggled with it himself. I don't know if that's true, but it makes me feel better. If Paul struggled with it, at least I'm in good company. And it's true, few were more ambitious than Paul [Saul]. He says as much in Philippians 3, running his long list of earthly accomplishments before putting them in perspective. He writes, "The very credentials these people are waving around as something special, I'm tearing up and throwing out with the trash — along with everything else I used to take credit for. And why? Because of Christ. Yes, all the things I once thought were so important are gone from my life. Compared to the high privilege of knowing Christ Jesus as my Master, firsthand, everything I once thought I had going for me is insignificant — dog dung. I've dumped it all in the trash so that I could embrace Christ and be embraced by Him (Philippians 3:7-9 MSG)."

I wasn't quite there yet, not in my twenties, thirties, forties or early fifties. I hadn't reached the "dog dung" stage. I was still largely motivated — driven is the word — by selfish ambition. Not all the time, mind you. It wasn't my only motivation. My motives were often pure, but that's not what drove me. What drove me, the wind in my sails, was my determination to achieve. I needed to prove that I was unique — uniquely gifted, uniquely called, uniquely set apart by God — like Paul, Moses, Martin Luther, John Wesley, and Dietrich Bonhoeffer. This underlying motivation colored nearly everything I did — every decision I made, every sermon I wrote, every person I hired — in one way or another. There's a poison in self-obsession. People in pain, living out of their false selves, often can't see anything or hear anyone but themselves. They're like a person who's hit their thumb with a hammer. Everything else and everyone else around them disappears and all they can think about is their own pain. I kept waiting for God to do something that would launch me to a position of prominence. And as the years went by, I couldn't understand how others succeeded where I failed, how others were celebrated and I was ignored, how others gained notoriety — as if that's the measure of anything — and I was left to toil away in obscurity. Selfish ambition had its claws in me and the consequences were obvious to anyone who loved me. I was struggling with identity, trying to soothe my self-doubt and "find myself" in roles, titles, and achievements. For years, I thought of myself as less than, a failure, as not enough. These were the tapes playing in my head. Jesus' invitation, in my early fifties, was far more than simply surrendering a sinful attitude like selfish ambition. He invited me into love, to discover my belovedness, to live out of my true identity as a dearly loved child of God.

The Invitational Jesus

Did you know Jesus is very invitational? He means to draw you, as you respond to Him, not drive you, compel you, or coerce you. When He chose His first disciples, His invitation couldn't have been more straightforward. To the fishermen, Peter and Andrew, He said, "Come, follow me," and they immediately left their nets and followed Him.[31] To Matthew, the tax collector, He simply said, "Follow me," and Matthew got up and followed Him.[32] They were responding to His invitation. He made no demands on them. He didn't try to persuade them. He simply invited them. God is often the initiator. You see this throughout the Bible. When Adam and Eve sinned in the Garden, God came looking for them, kindly asking questions He already knew the answer to. When Cain killed his brother Abel, again, God came to him. He inquired about Cain's emotional state. He asked probing questions. He offered hope and a caution. He invited Cain into a relational dialogue. God is regularly the initiator, always looking to draw us back to Himself, to the constancy of His love.

God gives all of us ample opportunities to come to Him, respond to Him. He regularly steps through our carefully designed defenses and comes to us, calls to us. You might hear a message from the Bible. You might have an arresting dream. You might have an amazing answer to prayer or your life is suddenly and inexplicably spared. The point is — God will often use life's circumstances to get your attention and you need to respond. I have often wondered about those who don't respond to the regular in-breaking of God, the gentle whisper of God, the invitation of God in their lives, those who have an encounter with God only to return to life as usual, poisoned by self-obsession or selfish ambition or something else. What will become of them? I'm grateful, in the words of Yogi Berra, that it's never over till it's over, that life is full of invitations, loving invitations from God.

The Merry-Go-Round

In this way, we're like a child riding a horse on a merry-go-round. As we go spinning round and round, up and down, our loving Father stands to one side, reaching out to us, offering us His hand, hoping to touch us in some way. This invitation repeats itself hundreds and hundreds of times over the course of our lives, revolution after revolution. And if we respond to His invitation and extend our hands to Him, He will draw us to Himself, show us how to get off the merry-go-round and live a different kind of life, the life Jesus said we could have. But if we procrastinate, if we ignore the Father's invitation, the merry-go-round quickly whisks us away until it ultimately comes back around again, giving us yet another opportunity. That's the good news. The good news is that God is very invitational. His hand is always extended. He wants a relationship with you. He offers what's known as an "open invitation." You can respond whenever you like and people often do. They respond whenever they like, treating God's invitation like a get-out-of-jail free card, promising to love Him and follow Him so long as He bails them out or fulfills their dreams or helps them escape the consequences of their choices. Have you ever met anyone like that? They "try" God when the chips are down, but only when the chips are down. They'll even own up to it. They'll say, "I tried God. I really did. I did everything I was supposed to do — I went to church, I served, I gave money and nothing changed. God didn't hold up His end of the bargain" and back on the merry-go-round they go. Do you ever wonder what it's going to take for them to stretch out their hand again? You wonder, when life brings them back around in six months or six years, what is it going to take to cause them to reach out to God, to accept God's invitation?

Why is the sin of procrastination so great? Because every day is not the same! We don't always have the same impetus to respond to God. Maybe you feel prompted by the Holy Spirit to write a note of apology to someone you've offended. You were insensitive; you told a thoughtless joke. Or the Holy Spirit might prompt you to do some act of service for your spouse or children. Whatever it is, you sense the prompting of the Spirit but if you delay, if you make excuses, if you say, "Now is not the time," those little knocks on the door of your heart get quieter and quieter until you're completely deaf to them.

The stories of Lot, King Nebuchadnezzar, Absalom and Judas are biblical examples of those who did not RSVP. They're also a testimony to the constant love of God. Remember, only God fully knows you and yet constantly loves you. We'll talk more about that in a later chapter. For now, I want you to consider the fact that Jesus is very invitational. His invitation is as constant and strong today as it was yesterday and will be tomorrow. The problem is us. We change. We may not be as sensitive or attentive or responsive tomorrow as we are today, let alone years from now. Still, some people say, "I can always do it later. I can accept Jesus' invitation later, after I've lived my life my way and done everything I wanted to do, then I'll surrender my life to Him." On the surface, it sounds like a plan. Jesus never changes. He'll always be standing there offering you His hand. The problem isn't Him, it's you. The longer you live apart from God, going your own way while trying to make it look like it's God's way, your heart grows harder, less responsive, like a bored child on a merry-go-round who smiles and waves enthusiastically the first time around but can't be bothered to even make eye contact with you on the tenth time around. How are you responding to Jesus' invitations?

Drawn, No Longer Driven

Perhaps His most famous invitation is the one I mentioned earlier. It's found in Matthew 11 and it's wonderful in any version, but I especially love how it reads in *The Message*. Talking to His followers who were living under the burden of man-made religion, Jesus said, "Are you tired? Worn out? Burned out on religion? Come to me. Get away with me and you'll recover your life. I'll show you how to take a real rest. Walk with me and work with me — watch how I do it. Learn the unforced rhythms of grace. I won't lay anything heavy or ill-fitting on you. Keep company with me and you'll learn to live freely and lightly (Matthew 11:28-30 MSG)."

The reality is, we are often weary and burdened. The words here could also be translated "toiling" and "loading." They refer to the effort it takes to bear up under the accumulated difficulties and pressures of life. Life is full of difficulties and pressures. I'm sure I don't need to convince you. For the follower of Jesus, the pressure grows even more intense when you turn your heart toward Him, when you set your heart to go against the grain of the world and truly follow Him. I have heard it said that Christianity is, by definition, a counter-culture. Being out of step with the world puts you in Satan's crosshairs and he loves to pile on, adding trouble to trouble. That's why we regularly need to step away from the noise of everyday life and learn to be with Jesus. We need rest, rest for our souls. As Wayne Muller wrote, "Because we do not rest, we lose our way…Poisoned by the hypnotic belief that good things come only through unceasing determination and tireless effort, we can never truly rest. And for want of rest our lives are in danger."[33] Is your life in danger? Have you been poisoned by the hypnotic belief that good things come only through unceasing determination? That was certainly true for me.

Parker Palmer put it this way. "The active life carries a curse. Many of us know what it is to live lives not of action but of frenzy, to go from day-to-day exhausted and unfulfilled by our attempts to work, create and care. Many of us know the violence of active life…Action poses some of our deepest spiritual crises as well as some of our most heartfelt joys."[34] Do you know the violence of active life? Are you painfully aware that endless activity might be a blessing, but it's not an unmixed blessing? I certainly felt that way before I accepted Jesus' invitation. I felt cursed, shackled to a life of endless activity, resigned to go from day-to-day exhausted and unfulfilled, working away the best years of my life, envious of those who had options.

My frustration with the active life would bubble to the surface at the oddest times. Sitting down with my family to watch a period-piece set in Victorian England — movies like *Emma, Pride and Prejudice* and the like — I enjoyed the storyline but couldn't help but marvel at how aimless, lazy and shiftless the "gentlemen" were, with little more to do all day than preen about, look down their noses at others and take a turn about the room. "They need to get a real job," I'd grumble periodically throughout the film while my son agreed and my daughters simply rolled their eyes. When you live a frenetic life, it's hard to see those who are merely active as anything less than somnambulant.

That brings me to something Julian of Norwich wrote in the early 1400s. She said, "This is the only reason why we are not fully at ease in heart and soul; that we look to find our true rest in these things [in other things, things] that are so little that they contain no rest."[35] Are you looking for rest in things that are so little that they contain no rest, so exhausted you're often hanging by a thread? Are you toiling away, loaded down, weary and burdened, what Ruth Haley Barton calls "dangerously tired?"[36] That's the reality for many of us. We feel stretched, hard pressed, under constant pressure — squeezed like a tube of toothpaste in the hands of a toddler, where everything on the inside is now outside and we feel exposed. Weariness creeps up on us like a malevolent, shape-shifting golem. We're often completely unaware of how weary and burdened we truly are. That's where I was, for years, dangerously tired, driven to tears, driven to distraction, driven to the edge. I still feel that way sometimes, when I haven't kept company with Jesus, I haven't come away with Him in a while. I feel overwhelmed, empty, vulnerable.

Martha, Martha

I was talking to a spiritual friend recently. At the end of the conversation, he asked me a question he often asks, "Mark," he said gently, "how's your soul?" There was a time when I wouldn't have known how to answer that question, but I'm learning to pay closer attention to what's going on inside me and put it into words. "I feel thin," I said honestly, "emotionally exhausted." We talked about that for a bit and he said, "Close your eyes for a moment. I want you to picture Jesus walking up behind you, putting His arm around you and whispering something in your ear. What do you think He would say to you, right now, in the situation you find yourself in?" I paused for a moment and replied with a sigh, "I don't know. Nothing really comes to mind. If I have to give you an answer, I guess He might say something like, 'Martha, Martha, you're worried and upset about many things!'"[37] My friend chuckled and said, "That's funny, but I don't think He'd have a rebuke for you. I think He wants to encourage you. Close your eyes and try again. Really listen this time. What is Jesus saying to you?" It proved to be an exercise in futility. In that moment, in the midst of the swirl around me, I simply wasn't able to receive what Jesus might have for me. Even with all I've learned about rest and responding to Jesus' invitations, I still sometimes find myself there, weary from the battle and burdened over many things, just like Martha. This is the reality for many of us. What might Jesus say to us in times like these? If Jesus walked up beside you, put His arm around you and whispered something in your ear, what might He say?

At a minimum, I think He'd say, "Come to me. Get away with me and you'll recover your life." I think He'd say, "Walk with me and work with me — watch how I do it. I'll show you how to take a real rest." The word translated "rest" in Matthew 11:28 literally means "to make to cease" or, as we might say today, "make it stop!" Another translation could be, "you will find relief for your souls."[38] Jesus is offering relief, respite, the slowing of the merry-go-round, the quieting of the voices, the end of hostilities, the absence of all your striving, what you might call breathing room for the soul! He's talking about that place at the center of every storm, where everything is still and calm. We need that. I need that. So what, exactly, is rest for the soul? What is Jesus talking about when He offers us rest for the soul?

Rest for the Soul

1. *Rest is a gift from God that dates back to creation.* Think about it for a moment. If God had wanted to, He could have created human beings without the need for sleep. Why, then, did He do it? Why make us in such a way that we needed to shut it down for several hours every day? I mean, you spend one-third of your life asleep, some of us, even more! If God is only going to give you seventy, eighty, or ninety years here on earth, why wouldn't He give you one hundred percent of the time? Why would one third of that time be "wasted" in sleep? Because God wants you to learn the importance of rest. Rest is so important God modeled it. When He finished with the first six days of creation, the Bible says, "On the seventh day He rested (Genesis 2:2)." Why did God rest? He wasn't tired. He was modeling the importance of rest for us. Rest is "a God-practiced, God-given rhythm woven into the fabric of

human life."[39] God gave it to us for our good, for the good of our souls. Rest is a gift from God and…

2. *Rest is a form of worship.* When we quiet the voices, slow the merry-go-round and regularly pull away from our active, sometimes frenetic lives, we finally find the space to simply be with God, to be who we truly are — His dearly loved children — and experience Him as He really is, our loving, attentive Father. In this way, rest is a form of worship, a place where we rediscover, embrace, and celebrate the ever-present Lover of our souls. As King David wrote, "The LORD Almighty is with us…He says, 'Be still [cease your striving,[40] step out of the traffic[41]], and know that I am God…' (Psalm 46:7,10)." We have to cease your striving, step out of the traffic of our everyday lives to know Him as He longs to be known. I know, it's easy to say, hard to do. So much of the stress we feel in life results from busyness. We're always rushing somewhere, always in a hurry. We might be tempted to see it as a symptom of our culture, but we really need to see it for what it actually is — a self-inflicted wound. How often do you feel like you're behind the 8-ball, like you'll never get caught up? I used that phrase for years to describe the burden of work I had yet to finish. "I'm behind the 8-ball," I'd say to my wife, exasperated. "You're always saying that," she would often reply. "What does that even mean?"

What does it mean? It's a term borrowed from the game of pool which means, "I'm in an uncomfortable or unfavorable position." My options are limited. I'm stymied, blocked, frustrated. For me, it meant that, right at that moment, I had a growing pile of unread emails full of requests, encouragements, demands, solicitations and accusations, with more being added to the pile every day. It meant that I had enough projects on the back burner to cause a four-alarm fire. I would never get to some of that stuff and I knew it. I would never have a week where I'd have the time to answer every email. There was no way I'd ever catch up. So what did I do? I was tempted, at times, to delete them all and pretend I'd never received them. I never did that, as far as you know, but I was tempted. What do you do? What should you do? You should look to God to meet your needs and despite all that is undone, step out of the traffic of your everyday life to allow Him to do for you what you can't get any other way. He will lovingly reset you, recharge you, recreate you and remind you of who you really are! You have to build rest into your schedule or you'll fall apart. That's why Jesus offers you this invitation. He says, "Come to me, come away with me and you'll recover your life."

I could stay up for the next three months, working around the clock, and I still wouldn't be caught up. But it's not just the amount of work I have to do. I've actually caught up several times over the years — returned every phone call, made every decision, answered every email — and I still felt pressed, exhausted, behind the eight ball. That's when I realized, if you're going to make room to be with God, it's not as simple as an adjustment to your schedule. Satan is warring against this. If you're going to consistently find rest for your soul, to live as Jesus said you could live, freely and lightly, you have to change your whole orientation. You have to start seeing rest as a gift from God, as a form of worship, as essential to your spiritual health and well-being. Otherwise, you'll end up like the Israelites in the Old Testament. As Isaiah wrote, "This is what the Sovereign LORD, the Holy One of Israel, says: 'In repentance and rest is your salvation, in quietness and trust is your strength, but you would have none of it (Isaiah 30:15).'" You need repentance *and* rest, quietness *and* trust. They would have none of it and they suffered terribly as a result. Let's build off this idea of trust for a moment. As I've read the Scriptures, I've come to believe that…

3. *Rest is a declaration of trust.* As Dallas Willard wrote, "Rest is an act of faith."[42] It's the same basic idea. Your willingness to push away from the noise, stepping out of the traffic and demands of your everyday life, to simply be with God in deeper water, is a declaration of trust. It's you saying to the world that God is more than able to keep you, sustain you and provide for you, regardless of your circumstances. Probably the best example of rest as a declaration of trust is found in Psalm 3. Psalm 3 was written by King David when his own son, Absalom, was trying to end his father's life and take the throne. Uncertain of the extent of Absalom's support and wanting to spare the city a potential bloodbath, David fled Jerusalem.[43] From that point forward, he's on the run. But despite his tenuous circumstances, David writes, "I call out to the LORD and He answers me…I lie down and sleep; I wake again, because the LORD sustains me. I will not fear though tens of thousands assail me on every side (Psalm 3:4-6)." Rest in the midst of trouble, in dire circumstances, in your anxieties is a declaration of trust in God.

4. *Rest is also an assertion that God cares.* It's an affirmation that we're valued and loved for who we are and not for what we do. Jesus Himself said, "The Sabbath was made for man, not man for the Sabbath (Mark 2:27)." The Sabbath was a gift from God. Do you know that word, *sabbath*? Exodus 34:21 says, "Six days you shall labor, but on the seventh day you shall rest [completely];[44] even during the plowing season and the harvest, you must rest." Even in your busiest season, He says, it's no excuse. You still have

to take a day off. God said it because He knew you would need it. You weren't designed to work non-stop, seven days a week, fifty-two weeks a year. Your relationships will come apart if you insist on doing that. Your mental health will come apart. Your relationship with God will come apart. See, when Jesus said, "The Sabbath was made for man, not man for the Sabbath," He was reminding his listeners of God's original design. Jewish tradition, in the first century, had so multiplied the requirements and restrictions for keeping the Sabbath that the burden had become intolerable. Jesus cut across these traditions and emphasized the God-given purpose of the Sabbath — a day intended for our benefit, for spiritual, mental and physical restoration.[45] God made the Sabbath for you because He loves you. It's not just about physical rest. It's not simply a "mental health day." It's meant to restore your soul. Jesus offers us rest for the soul.

"But, Mark," you might say, "I feel so guilty when I relax." Well, as I heard one pastor say, "Jesus didn't!" When you study Jesus' ministry, He often took time to relax. He'd pour Himself out in an intense period of ministry, preaching the good news of the Kingdom, healing the sick, driving out demons and then, He'd say, "Okay, we need to get away for a while. We need some downtime. We need to come apart before we come apart. Let's go to the mountains. Let's go to the desert. Let's go fishing. I'm going to take a nap in this boat." Jesus was in demand, but He didn't feel guilty about what He couldn't get done. You'll never meet everyone's expectations. Did you know that during the French Revolution, the French government cancelled the Sabbath and said every day is going to be a workday? After a couple of years, they had to reinstate it because the health of the nation had crumbled. You need this in your life. You need to rest. I heard about a guy who said to his pastor, "Pastor, I tried to get ahold of you all day on Monday." And the pastor said, "I'm sorry. That's my day off." And the man said, "The devil never takes a day off!" And the pastor said, "Yeah, and if I didn't take a day off, I'd be just like the devil." Some of you, that's why you're so surly! It's certainly why I was so surly. I wasn't getting enough rest. I wasn't getting enough time with the only one who can restore my soul.[46]

Practicing Sabbath

The Sabbath is a time to savor God. It's about turning aside, slowing down, and allowing yourself to be caught by God. It's a time to be refreshed and recreated, a time to separate yourself from the people who cling to you, from the demands you put on yourself, from the demands and expectations of others, from the routines you maintain and the roles you play. Sabbath is a time to develop a contemplative heart toward life and God, to invest in your own growth as a child of God. It's a time to enter into and fully embrace the twin disciplines of silence and solitude. It's a time for receptivity, not necessarily inactivity. It's a time to stop, be still (cease striving) and know God while allowing yourself to be known by God.[47] As Marjorie J. Thompson wrote, "Rest is a chance to gaze on God, to readjust our minds, realign our hearts, reassess our priorities, clarify our commitments and enlarge our perspectives."[48]

What are you supposed to do on your Sabbath? Three things.

1. <u>Rest your body</u>. Physically rest.
2. <u>Refocus your spirit on God</u>. Worship.
3. <u>Recharge your emotions</u>. Recreation.[49]

Different things recharge different people. You need to do something that restores you and re-energizes you. It could be a hobby. It could be a sport. It could be music. It could be a walk in the woods or time spent with friends who don't need you, who allow you to be your truest self. These are all good things that God has given us as gifts that can help you rest, refocus, and recharge. My wife is always asking me, "What recreates you? What do you enjoy doing that gives you life?" For her, the answer is obvious. Time spent in her garden recreates, recharges, and refocuses her, drawing her attention to the Creator and Sustainer of all things. For me, it's a bit more difficult. I've had various interests over the years, the most enduring of which is baseball, but I can't say that my interest in baseball recharges me, recreates me and refocuses my spirit on God. I love the daily rhythm of baseball. I love the pace of a game that forces you to focus on one thing at a time. I love that it's untimed, and it's never really over, but my rooting interest in the Royals works against my desire to refocus my spirit on God. It's one thing to have a hobby, something you enjoy, but that hobby is not necessarily a Sabbath. For me, Sabbath always includes solitude and silence. I need time alone, a regular place of refuge and rest. My office at home is more like a sanctuary. I often retreat there on a Sunday afternoon and tinker with words — not working, just being — with God. Are you resting your body, refocusing your spirit on God, and recharging your emotions?

Saying "Yes"

Here, once again, is the invitation Jesus offers you. He said, "Come to me, all you who are weary and burdened, and I will give you…" more work to do? No! It doesn't actually say that, but you'd never know it watching some followers of Jesus. You'd never know it watching me the first fifty-two years of my life. I was driven, not drawn, working for Jesus instead of with Jesus. That's why Jesus' words mean so much to me. He said, "Come to me, all you who are weary and burdened, and I will give you rest. Take my yoke upon you and learn from me, for I am gentle and humble in heart, and you will find rest for your souls. For my yoke is easy and my burden is light (Matthew 11:28-30)."

For many years, I never fully understood these verses. In the first place, as a kid, I didn't know what a yoke was. I thought it was part of an egg. I later discovered a yoke is a wooden crosspiece with two arches that's fastened over the necks of a pair of oxen so the oxen can pull together. The value of a yoke is that it halves the load, it distributes it evenly. Without a yoke, one ox might end up pulling more than they can bear, or the oxen might pull against each other, making it harder for them both. So, when Jesus says, "Take my yoke upon you," it may sound like He's got something more He wants you to do, something more you have to deal with, some heavy burden He wants you to shoulder. "Take your yoke upon me? Are you kidding? I've got a heavy enough burden already, Lord. I don't need to shoulder your burden as well. I don't need to take on any more." But that's not what He's saying at all. When He says, "Take my yoke upon you," He's not saying, "I'm going to give you my problems." As I'm sure you're aware, Jesus doesn't have any problems. He's saying, "I'll shoulder *your* problems, *your* load and lift you, if you'll let me!" Will you let Him?

A Drawn, Not Driven Story

When my wife, Dianne, was twelve years old, her missionary family returned to the United States for a year of furlough. Dianne was born and raised in Congo, then Zaire, and lived there and Côte d'Ivoire for the better part of her life until graduation. The year in question, 1976, was special for a number of reasons. The country was celebrating the bicentennial, a peanut farmer from Georgia was elected President and Dianne was given the responsibility of caring for three horses on a farm near her home — Roan, Lady and Shasta. Someone had clearly just read C.S. Lewis' *The Horse and his Boy*! She was in hog-heaven or horse-heaven, as the case may be. She loved horses and looking after those animals was the highlight of a childhood full of highlights. It was also an answer to prayer. Like a lot of young girls, she asked her Mother for a horse. She wanted a horse so badly. Not wanting to crush her dreams, but knowing they'd never be able to afford it, her mom encouraged Dianne to pray about it. And she did, every day for the better part of a year, she prayed for a horse and when she got home and was invited to work on that farm, God gave her three! Too young to get paid, she worked all summer for her choice of a saddle and bridle and loved every minute.

One day, she was up in the hayloft, throwing down hay for the horses, when she noticed a most unusual sight. Three huge bulls, who must have been in the pasture with the horses, though Dianne never saw them, had walked through the open gate and were now lumbering slowly down the paved road that split the farm in two. Horrified, Dianne clambered down the ladder and ran after the bulls. Wholly unaware of the potential danger and feeling responsible for leaving the gate open, she approached the lead bull, took hold of its prodigious horn and pulled it to one side, encouraging the bull to turn around. To her surprise and under her gentle touch, the bull turned and headed back up the road to the pasture, followed dutifully by the others — three huge behemoths led by an audacious twelve-year-old girl! They were probably just as shocked as she was! This was a time before cell phones or this video, once captured, would have gone viral instantly. This is what I think of when I think of the gentle way Jesus often draws us through life. Are you drawn or are you driven?

The following prayer has become a regular part of my life. I cobbled it together in a season when the Lord was increasing my desire for deeper water. I'd encourage you to pray it daily as an expression of your own desire to be drawn, not driven. Pray it slowly as a kind of breath prayer, savoring each phrase. Allow the ideas to become a part of you, as you purposefully align your desire with God's desires for you.

Dear Jesus,
With all of my heart...

I choose an unhurried life.
I choose the road less traveled.

I choose to walk with you in the cool of the day.

I choose to float on the unforced rhythms of your grace.

I choose to be present in the present with the ever-present One.

I choose the easy yoke and the light burden.

I choose the journey, not simply the destination.

I choose to be with you, not simply do for you.

I choose to live freely and lightly.

Amen.

Training, not just trying and drawn, no longer driven, were important steps in my journey out of the shallow end of the pool. But it wasn't just about leaving where I'd been for most of my life, it was the joy of discovery, the mystery of what awaited me, the promise of the life Jesus said I could have. What follows is some of what I discovered or rediscovered in a fresh, new way as I responded to Jesus' invitation.

four
———

You are Always and Everywhere with God

"You make known to me the path of life; in your presence there is fullness of joy; at your right hand are pleasures forevermore."
~ Psalm 16:11 ESV

"We have a formula of the spiritual life: a confident reliance on the immense fact of His Presence."[50]
~ Evelyn Underhill

One Sunday morning, some forty years ago, I stood up to teach the Bible. The summer sun, streaming through the floor-to-ceiling windows on one side of the sanctuary, illuminated a dense cloud of dust that hung in the air like the product of a low-tech fog machine. A rosy-cheeked, twenty-three-year-old with more passion than sense, I preached my heart out every week, full of fire and optimism on the outside while

73

inside, I couldn't have been more discouraged. Nothing I did was working. The church, averaging fewer than twenty on a weekly basis, was hanging by a thread and I was out of ideas.

Nevertheless, my first congregation was an interesting collection of characters. There were the three elderly couples who clearly didn't want to be there but preferred their sermons short and I had so little to say, I could reliably be counted on to oblige. There was the forty-something man who lived across the street with his parents, nephew and a variety of household pets. There was the kindly farmer and his wife who lived in one of those houses buried in the earth on three-sides as a bulwark against high energy bills. They were incredibly creative and self-sufficient, though a bit preoccupied with the coming apocalypse, and would often invite Dianne and I to their home for dinner after church. Grateful for their generosity, I was less grateful when he insisted on cutting his nails practically every Sunday while I taught. I'd start a sentence, and he'd go to work with the nail clipper, spraying discarded cuticles all over the knotty-pine floor. Click, zing, click, zing, was the unrequested soundtrack of my early days in ministry. Think I'm exaggerating? On special occasions, he would take off his shoes and socks and go to work on his toenails, seemingly without a care in the world. Those were heady days.

But that Sunday was special and would remain so for the rest of my life. We had a visitor! "O frabjous day! Callooh! Callay! [I] chortled in [my] joy!"[51] As I started my sermon, a comfortably dressed man with gray hair and an unruly mustache — think Wilford Brimley — shuffled down the center aisle and took a seat in the second row on my left. I remember it like it was yesterday. As he settled in, I could hardly contain my excitement. Finally, a visitor, a positive sign of church growth. I had never seen him before but I have to tell you, he had some of the best attending skills of anyone who's ever listened to me preach. He opened his Bible, looked up hopefully and smiled warmly throughout the entire message. I was so encouraged!

When I finished, wrapping it up with a flourish and an over-the-top closing prayer, I said, "amen" and bounded off the platform to make his acquaintance. Extending my hand while flashing my friendliest grin, I said, "Mark Warner, pleased to meet you." If that seems like an odd thing to say, you probably haven't spent much time in the beautiful state of Georgia. In Georgia, there's no need to clutter up a simple greeting by being all formal and flowery. Why say, "Hello, my name is Mark Warner," when you can just say your name and wait for them to respond in kind? But he didn't respond, at least not in the way I expected. He didn't take my hand, and he didn't share his name. He simply looked me in the eye, with the kindest smile, and said, "I know." "You know?" I replied, a little off balance, wondering if we'd met before. "Yes," he said. "I know you, Mark. God sent me here with a message."

Now, I've heard *that* one a lot over the years, "God sent me here with a message" or "I have a message for you from God." If I had a dollar for everyone who's come up to me after a sermon with a message from God I'd... have a lot of dollars. But this was the first time anyone had ever made such a pronouncement and it was, by far, the most memorable. Frankly, I was speechless. It wasn't that I didn't know how to respond. I knew I should say something. It was my turn, after all. But what he said and the way he said it threw me for a loop. I was sputtering, like my brain had slipped a gear or the chain had come off the sprocket. He, then, smiled kindly and said, "God wants you to know that he sees you, Mark, and he loves you." The words were like a warm embrace, enveloping me but also penetrating deeply into my heart. I felt them as much as heard them and it took my breath away. *"He sees me and he loves me?"* I repeated to myself, looking vacantly into his eyes. "That's it," he said softly as he put his hand on my shoulder. Then, brushing lightly by me, he started for the door.

That moment, for me, has always been oddly suspended in time, like a gossamer dream only it wasn't a dream. Even as I write this, I'm bodily transported. It's like I'm standing there still in that tiny wooden church in

Homer, Georgia. I can feel the warmth of the sun in the windows, the gentle breeze of the single ceiling fan turning lazily over my head. I can still hear the muted conversations of post-service lingerers around me and I can see his face — those eyes, that smile.

Coming to myself, in that moment, I suddenly realized I hadn't gotten his name. For a young pastor, in a tiny church of less than twenty souls, that was an epic fail. *"We finally get a visitor,"* I thought, *"and you don't get his name and number? What kind of pastor are you?"* Jolted into action, I rushed to the door, fully expecting him to be on the front porch, or maybe in the yard. I was hoping for an opportunity to redeem myself. He couldn't have been more than thirty seconds ahead of me. But as I stepped out into the light, he was gone. He was not on the porch or in the yard or in our tiny parking lot. I checked. I checked both sides of the building. *"How could he be gone? People don't just evaporate into thin air."*

Disappointed, I went back inside and asked my wife, "Did you talk to him?" "Who?" she replied. "The visitor," I responded. "What visitor?" "The one in the second row," I said, a bit exasperated. "He was sitting right in front of you. Did you talk to him?" "Mark," she said evenly, "there was no one in front of me. What are you talking about?" Annoyed, I shook my head and went over to a small gaggle of folks making their way to the door. It was such a tiny town, such a close-knit community. Surely someone would know him. "Good morning," I said. "Did any of you know the man who was sitting in the second row? I didn't get his name, and I want to be sure to follow up." They looked at one another oddly and one of them replied, "What man?" "The kindly looking man in the second row," I said pointing, "with the mustache, big smile on his face. Do you know him?" There was a pregnant pause. "There was no one sitting in the second row," one of them said. I half-nodded while thanking them. *"Was no one paying attention this morning?"* Turning to another couple who had cued up behind them, I asked the same question and got the same reply. That's when I realized, *"Could it be? Was it possible? Did I just have a conversation with an angel?"*[52]

God With Us

Now, before you start feeling sorry for yourself — "Mark was visited by an angel…twice! What's wrong with me?" — you need to know my working theory on unusual things like God speaking through dreams, visions, angelic appearances and the like. Without wanting to minimize such things or limit God in any way — I've had a number of profound encounters with God in these ways! — I have always wondered if God sent me an angel that day because all His more conventional methods of communication were falling on deaf ears. It was my first church. I was twenty-two years old. I wasn't exactly a man of prayer or someone who spent a great deal of time in the Word. I wasn't practicing His presence, as Brother Lawrence wrote, through contemplation or meditation, listening for the voice of the Spirit inside me. I was a novice pastor fresh out of Bible College. I would invoke His presence at mealtime, acknowledge His presence on Sunday mornings, but I wasn't actually attending to His presence in my daily life. I hadn't yet learned how to simply *be* with Him moment-to-moment or abide in Him. I had a very limited view of what A. W. Tozer called the Universal Presence.[53] I saw the presence of God as a dusty theological truth, an attribute of God, His *omnipresence* to use the reference — which makes Him sound even more inaccessible — not something tangible or wonderfully experiential. I emphasized "God is everywhere" over "God is here" and I often felt alone. I wondered, in difficult times in those early years and for many years thereafter, if God was there, with me, or simply everywhere or somewhere else. Perhaps you've felt that way as well.

Yet, everywhere you look, the Scriptures seem to emphasize the manifest presence of God. God *with* us in every sense of the word. He was with us in the Garden of Eden. He was with us in the Old Testament tabernacle, present in the Holy of Holies. As Jan Johnson wrote, "God was so determined to be with us [when the Israelites were wandering in the desert] He was willing to live in a tent for forty years!"[54] So true! He was with us in the birth of Christ. This is the wonder of Christmas. The wonder of Christmas is not us being nice to each other or the fact that many of us take our loose change and deposit it in a Salvation Army pot. The wonder of Christmas is not that Christmas shopping provides a needed boost to our ailing economy or that we get to decorate our houses with lights and eat more than we should. The wonder of Christmas is that God Himself took on human flesh and entered this world through the womb of the virgin, Mary.

The theological term for God taking on flesh is "incarnation" which comes from the Latin word, *in carne,* meaning "in flesh." God manifested Himself in the flesh. Think about that for a moment. In Jesus, the invisible God became visible and walked among us. Quoting a 700-year-old prophecy about a virgin-born Messiah, the Apostle Matthew wrote, "The virgin will conceive and give birth to a son, and they will call Him Immanuel (which means 'God with us')."[55] Do you know what that means? As Paul Stevens wrote, "If God has come in the flesh, and if God keeps coming to us in our fleshly existence, then all of life is shot through with meaning. Earth is crammed with heaven, and heaven (when we finally get there) will be crammed with earth. Nothing wasted. Nothing lost. Nothing secular. Nothing absurd…All are grist for the mill of a down-to-earth spirituality."[56] Do you have a down-to-earth spirituality, a faith rooted in an ever-present God? God is with you. He's not just everywhere, He's here.

I have a memory from early childhood that has never left me. My Sunday School class met in the furnace room, a small, out-of-the-way, window-less space in the basement of my home church. It was austere in the extreme, a single light bulb casting shadows on hospital-green walls and a bare concrete floor. It was all we had and meeting there was perfectly normal. Our teacher, every week faithfully without fail, was a sweet, thirty-something single woman named Sally who we adored. I remember her, dressed in a snappy orange and brown pantsuit, and I remember the sound of those furnaces in winter as they roared to life on regular intervals. I also remember a solitary framed painting, too small for the far wall, of a young boy lashed to the helm of an old ship bouncing violently on turbulent seas. He was in earnest, staring straight ahead into the darkness, clinging to the wheel, but despite his circumstances — and the artist captured this beautifully — he was oddly at peace. The reason was immediately obvious. Jesus stood behind him, not ethereally or spiritually but bodily, His powerful arms wrapped around him, His large carpenter's hands covering the boy's hands on the wheel, His cheek pressed gently against the boy's cheek. And oh, the look on His face. I haven't bothered to find it on the internet because I love the memory so much I'd hate to ruin it. But His face, in the painting, as I remember it, was full of a confident reassurance and joy. Think of it as a visual version of the country song, "Jesus, Take the Wheel." That song is memorable for the same reason I remember that painting from long ago. We all want to know Jesus is there for us in difficult circumstances, gently guiding us through the hard things in life. But the truth is, you're never out of His presence. He's not just there for you in the hard times, but all the time. He's not just there when you need Him, He's there, full stop. You are always and everywhere with God.

Why so Lonely?

A moment ago, I mentioned how lonely I felt in my early years as a pastor as I leaned by default into the omnipresence of God — God is everywhere — over the manifest presence of God, God is here, with me, right now. It stands to reason. I had an embryonic knowledge of His omnipresence, rooted in my original study of theology, but very little experience with Immanuel, His manifest presence. Therefore, I often felt I was on my own, that God was there but not fully present, not all the time.

That feeling, once firmly established and reinforced through heartache, failure and pain, large and small, was hard to shake. "God is there for me sometimes or God is there but He chooses not to intervene," left me with a sense that I was working for Him, not with Him. That loneliness remained a persistent theme into my early fifties and contributed to the hopelessness I've already written about.

Paradoxically, loneliness has nothing to do with being alone. One of the most common human experiences is to feel lonely in a crowd. Singles often believe that marriage will cure feelings of loneliness, but some of the loneliest people I've ever met are married people. You can feel terribly lonely in your marriage. You can feel terribly lonely in a big family. Talk with kids who grew up in a family of seven or eight children, they often feel lost in the crowd. Loneliness has nothing to do with being alone. It's a feeling of being unrelated, isolated, and cut off from the people around you.

And how do people try to relieve their loneliness? They join groups. They try to meet people through dating apps. They take up various hobbies and get involved in sports. They fight with others in the comments section and call out total strangers under the protection of a fictitious name. Loneliness drives a lot of self-destructive behavior. It's not curiosity that fuels the growing porn industry or the desire for prostitutes or the number of extra-marital affairs. It's loneliness. Drinking in bars is still popular despite the five-hundred percent markup because "everybody knows your name. And they're always glad you came" to pay the five-hundred percent markup. Jesus understands that at the root of our loneliness is something truly unexpected. At the root of all loneliness is homesickness for God. He said, "My Father's house has many rooms; if that were not so, would I have told you that I am going there to prepare a place for you? And if I go and prepare a place for you, I will come back and take you to be with me that you also may be where I am (John 14:2-3)."

Loneliness, at the root, is homesickness for God. We want to feel like we belong to someone, that we're a part of something, that we're loved.

Are you familiar with the word *nostalgia*? Today, when people talk of *nostalgia,* they mean remembering old TV shows, songs or movies. We get nostalgic about the shows we watched as children — "The Brady Bunch," "Happy Days," or, if you're a little younger, "Seinfeld." We get nostalgic about the music we grew up with. I still know all the lyrics to *All Shook Up*. Sometimes certain smells can make a person nostalgic. If your mother baked and you smell cookies coming out of the oven or you catch the scent of honeysuckle as you take a walk or the smell of clothes that have been dried outside — yes, people still do that — it can produce feelings of nostalgia.

But nostalgia has nothing to do with the remembrance of old TV shows or music or smells. The word *nostalgia* comprises two Greek words, *nostos,* meaning "to return home" and *algos*, meaning "severe pain."[57] And I know what you're thinking. "That sounds about right. Every time I go home for the holidays, I often experience severe pain." But that's not what the word means. Nostalgia literally means the experience of severe pain that comes from a *desire* to return home. Jesus recognizes that desire in us, that our loneliness is rooted in something deeper than a desire to return to an earthly home. It's fundamentally homesickness for God. We're feeling true nostalgia. So Jesus says, "My Father's house has many rooms; if that were not so, would I have told you that I am going there to prepare a place for you (John 14:2)?"

A century ago, novelist Thomas Wolfe wrote what would become an oft-quoted line. It's the title of a celebrated novel published after his untimely death at the tender age of thirty-seven. It's called, *You Can't Go Home Again*. I'm sure you've heard of it, if you haven't read it. If you have, congratulations! Like *War and Peace*, it's one of those books people often start but rarely finish. I certainly never have, started or finished it but I know, thanks to the review on *Goodreads*, that it's seven-hundred and four pages of densely packed prose about a man named George Webber who wrote a highly successful novel about his hometown. He, then, returns home for a visit and is shocked by the hostility of the home-folks "who feel naked and exposed by the truths"[58] revealed in the book. Wolfe's conclusion is that having left home, you can never really return. You can go home, but you can't go back because your memories and the feelings you had growing up can never be recaptured. Even if things at home haven't changed all that much, you've changed. We've already talked about that.

But Jesus says you *can* go home again. He left to prepare a home for you, your true home. He says, "And if I go and prepare a place for you, I will come back and take you to be with me that you also may be where I am (John 14:3)." The feelings of nostalgia you have in this life are signposts pointing to a deeper need within you, a need to be reunited with God, your Father, a need to return home. Your true home is with Him. Underneath all our loneliness is this homesickness for God.

The Way Home

It's amazing how much of creation has a homing instinct. Not long ago, Dianne and I made the long trip home to celebrate Thanksgiving with my mom, my two brothers, and their families. It was a wonderful time, full of laughter and shared memories. The day after, my brother Dave, an avid angler, invited his new son-in-law to come and check out a couple of local spots where the Steelheads are known to congregate and run. Despite the cold, the wind off the lake, and the fact that I'm an *indoorsman*, Dianne and I tagged along. And it was fascinating watching these massive fish gather their strength to try, time and again, to leap up waterfalls in an all-out-effort to return home to the place where they were spawned. Swallows do much the same thing, traveling literally thousands of miles to return to the place of their birth and it's a spectacle, a tourist attraction in places like San Juan Capistrano. Every once in a while, you'll read a story about a family who lost a dog just before they had to move hundreds of miles away, and somehow, six months later, a year later, the dog will show up on the doorstep of their new house. It's amazing how much of creation has a homing instinct. I believe every human being has a homing instinct built into them by God, a desire to return to our true home with Him. Our feelings of loneliness are mere reflections of a deeper pain within, our homesickness for God.

Jesus claims to be the way home. And, one day, if you're a follower of Jesus, those persistent feelings of loneliness and homesickness will fade as you enter your heavenly home. That's part of what he's saying here when He says, "I will come back and take you to be with me (John 14:3)." It's something to look forward to but there's more. There's also a cure for homesickness *now!* Jesus says, "I will ask the Father, and He will give you another advocate [counselor, helper] to help you and be with you *forever* — the Spirit of truth. The world cannot accept Him, because it neither sees Him nor knows Him. But you know Him, *for He lives with you and will be in you.* I will not leave you as orphans; I will come to you (John 14:16-18)." He hasn't left us as orphans in this life. The Spirit of God has come to help us and be with us forever. You are not alone. In truth, you are never alone. He is with you.

Jesus explains further in verse 23, He says, "Anyone who loves me will obey my teaching. My Father will love them, and we will come to them and *make our home with them.*" Do you know what that means? If you're a follower of Jesus, not only is a home being prepared for you in the future, a home has been prepared *in you* in the present. The Spirit of Truth, the Spirit of God, has come to live with you. Your heart is now his home. A home in heaven. A home within. A home in the future. A home right now. This is the part of our inheritance as believers that we tend to forget. God is with you, now and always, ever-present! He goes before you. He's behind you, beside you, beneath you, above you and especially within you. Wherever you go, He is there. He's inescapable. You are always and everywhere with God.

No Time Like the Present

And God is present *to* you, not just *with* you. He's attending to you moment-to-moment, always near at hand, available, accessible. If that's true — and I know now that it is — why, then, did I struggle so to discern His will? Why, over thirty years of ministry, did I so often feel His absence? Why did I feel so desperately alone? Why, at fifty-two, was I sitting in my office in tears? Why was I so depressed? The problem was certainly not on His side. The problem, my problem, was a lack of *awareness*. As David Benner wrote, "We cannot attain the presence of God. We're already totally in the presence of God. What's absent is awareness."[59]

At that point in my life, I was only vaguely aware of His presence and not self-aware enough to know how unaware of the presence of God I actually was. I had no real sense that He went before me, behind me, beside me, let alone within me. If you asked me, I could teach the concept. I could point you to chapter and verse and defend it as truth. But the manifest presence of God wasn't a daily, lived reality for me. That began to change as I worked my way through the *Ignatian Exercises*. The *Exercises* provided ample opportunities for self-reflection, a practice that was largely foreign to me. I mean, how many of us regularly take the time for contemplation, reflecting on God? How many of us engage in self-reflection before the Lord, asking Him to help us see ourselves are we are?

I remember being flummoxed by a simple reflection and accompanying questions early in my journey. Larry Warner wrote, "Take time to think about God. What images of God come to mind? Come up with three to five images of God and write them down. Now explore each of these images. Do they seem to have a predominantly positive or negative sense to them? Why?"[60] Well, I had no idea. I had a hard time coming up with three images of God. This way of being with God or thinking about God was just so alien to me. I'd spent years having my devotions — read a little, pray a little, write a little then check the box. I was drawn to resources that promised I could spend one minute with God and still fulfill my devotional obligation. *This* was something else. The next question didn't exactly give me a breather. "What is your internalized sense of God's love for you? Do you believe (not just give theological assent) that God loves you and accepts you just as you are in this moment? Why, or why not?"[61] Okay. I'll get into my struggles with letting God love me in the next chapter but, that aside, you can see my dilemma. How was I going to learn to be present when I hadn't truly kept company with Him? What was robbing me of His presence? The answer goes back to a lack of awareness. I simply didn't know any better. I'd spent my whole life in the shallow end of the pool having my devotions instead of attending to the presence of God.

Why is cultivating an awareness of God's presence so important? "Being aware plants you in the present moment — the only place one can experience God. While we can see God's hand in the past and pray for spiritual intervention in the future, we can only actually *be* in the present. To live in the present moment takes awareness, the ability to be present to the Presence that surrounds you (in God we live, move, and have our being), indwells you, and opens you to God's leading and the Spirit's prompting."[62] That was revelatory for me!

"Being aware plants you in the present moment — the only place one can experience God." Pause and think about that. God worked in the past and He'll work in the future but He only works in the present. He was present in the past and He'll be with us in the future but He's only actively here now. Now is the time for fellowship. Now is the time for conversation. Now is the moment of transformation. "There's no time like the present," they say and I couldn't agree more. The present is precious, the leading edge of our lives with God. No moment with God is wasted if you can learn to be present in the present with the ever-present One.

I had a hard time being present in any situation for years, let alone with God. Besides my lack of awareness, the past, my past, acted like a boat anchor, impeding my progress. I was constantly distracted, weighed down by regrets and recriminations, things I'd said or hadn't said, done or hadn't done. I was often in mourning, grieving the loss of my youth, the unexpected death of my father, the growing host of people who used to attend my church. The past, with all its wonderful memories, simple joys and "best days ever," is, nevertheless, sprinkled with regret. I know people love to say, "I have no regrets" but it's just not true. Everyone has regrets. Is it possible I might have spent my whole life living in the past, a slave to the past, never able to enjoy the moment or be fully present to God?

And what of the future? Fear of what might happen or what could happen, stoked by those who make their living peddling fear, along with the anxiety associated with yet unrealized hopes and dreams can be paralyzing! The future can hold as much foreboding as promise when you're single and you want to be married or your children are making self-destructive choices or you're forced to watch a loved one fade away to Alzheimers or you wonder if you'll actually be able to retire. Living in the past is exhausting. The fear of the future is exhausting. I was dragging anchors and making chains, preoccupied with the past and wringing my hands about the future, unaware and rarely present. What's the answer? How do we trade a life weighed down by the past and obsessed with the future for an ever-present life with God? How do we cultivate a deeper awareness of God?

Find God in All Things

As a beginning, Ignatius of Loyola would encourage us to "find God in all things," an idea that's rooted in a growing awareness that God can be found in everyone, in every place and in everything.[63] I really wrestled with this idea when I first heard it. How can God be found in all things? Is He present in pornography or human trafficking? Is He present in abusive marriages and government corruption? Is He present in the drug dens and houses of prostitution? The answer, I've discovered, is "yes." You are always and everywhere with God. He's ever-present, everywhere *and* here. Here with you and there with them. Sometimes, He's present and rejoicing, present and comforting, present in power and in other cases, where He's not welcome, He's present but not approving, present and mourning, present in protection, present to attend to those He dearly loves. Nothing escapes His attention. Some things make Him glad and some sad, but He's present, nonetheless.

This came home to me several years ago when Dianne and I were visiting a sister church in Mexico City. We had worked among the poor, serving the homeless in our church-planting days, but our sister church's heart for young girls held captive by prostitution was truly wonderful. One night, on a mission to a red-light district, we gathered in a small room, pulled on matching pink t-shirts, gathered supplies, and prayed. They, then, told us to remember what Jesus did with the woman caught in adultery and what He didn't do. Do you remember that story?

Once, when Jesus was teaching in the temple courts, the Pharisees and teachers of the law brought a woman to Him, forced her to stand there in front of everyone and said, "Teacher, this woman was caught in the act of adultery. In the Law, Moses commanded us to stone such women. Now what do you say (John 8:4-6)?" What Jesus did next was powerful. He bent down, and without saying a word, wrote something on the ground. When they continued to question Him, He straightened up and said, "Let any of you who is without sin be the first to throw a stone at her (John 8:7)." He then bent down again and continued writing. And, one by one, starting with the oldest among them, her accusers just walked away. When only she and Jesus were left, He straightened up again and said, "Woman, where are they? Has no one condemned you?" "No one, sir," she said. "Then neither do I condemn you," Jesus declared. "Go now and leave your life of sin (John 8:10-11)."

What Jesus did that day will never be forgotten, but it's what He didn't do that blows me away. He didn't look down His nose at her or shake His head in disgust. He didn't compel her to explain herself. He didn't moralize or pontificate or lecture or sermonize. He didn't use the occasion as an opportunity to remind His listeners of the consequences of sexual sin. He didn't make an example of her. He didn't use her to His own ends, to further His cause or quiet His critics. And He didn't condemn her, but He also didn't affirm her in her sin. "Remember that," our hosts said that night. "We're not there to condemn the girls or affirm them. We're there to care for them."

We set up on a dingy side street somewhere in the city, surrounded by pimps, prostitutes and dozens of prospective clients, the specter of heavy drug use and cheap alcohol floating in the air. We put out tables and folding chairs, strung lights on poles to illuminate the darkness, and fired up the music. There was plenty of food, face-painting, a group of folks from the church were giving manicures. It was a bit like setting up a carnival on the outskirts of hell and I was honestly overwhelmed. Dianne and I were assigned to a team serving hot tacos on paper plates. We'd take a plate and, with the help of interpreters, walk up to a prostitute standing along a fence line. The girl, and I do mean girl, was surrounded by a group of men, which was more than a little intimidating. I swallowed and looked at my interpreter. He smiled and nodded gently, encouraging me to engage her.

Summoning my courage, I stepped through the crowd and spoke to her, Dianne handing her the plate of food. It was hard at first. She was stiff and unresponsive, wary of our motives. But then something dramatic happened. As the conversation continued and the surrounding men slipped away, she dropped all pretense and realizing we had something for her and wanted nothing from her, her countenance changed and there, in that moment, she was a little girl again. It broke my heart and took my breath away. One minute, she was standing there provocatively, playing a part she'd been trained to play, and the next, in response to a simple act of unconditional love, everything changed. God was with us that night as He always is, present in us, but He didn't arrive with us. He was already there! The candle of His love had already been lit. He had prepared her heart to receive us. He had prepared the ground we walked on. He had given us favor in the community, no one challenged or abused us. He can be found in anyone, any place and everything. You are always and everywhere with God.

As I journeyed through the *Exercises*, I was encouraged to be more mindful of the presence of God, to look for God in my everyday life. I have wonderful memories of taking walks with Jesus in the village near the church, looking for His presence in the rustling leaves, the greeting of a neighborhood dog and the furtive chatter of a thousand squirrels dodging cars on the street. I can remember eating a meal with Jesus, inviting Him to join me while I focused on His presence and savored the food. And I have to tell you, you haven't eaten a bowl of strawberries and truly appreciated them until you've eaten them with Jesus. Strawberries are wonderful any day of the week, who would disagree? But even strawberries are better with Jesus than without him. You simply have to invite Him to join you. Will you do it? He so wants to be included. He wants to be included in every aspect of your life. If we could just fix our minds on the truth that God is not just everywhere, God is here and learn to attend to His presence, the mythical sacred-secular divide that often dominates our thinking where we're with God in one context — church, worship, devotions — and without Him at other times — work, family, leisure — would simply melt away. That's what happened to me. As I grew more aware of God's ever-presence, I came to the realization that every moment is sacred, that I am truly never alone and my connection to God, my relationship with God, grew exponentially. His presence became a felt reality. Even now, as I write this, I feel Him near and I'm at peace. How are you doing with that? How aware are you of His presence? How mindful are you of Him in the mundane, humdrum, ordinary things of life?

Be Open, Walk Slowly, Bow Often

Over time, my desire to "find God in all things" found fresh expression in three simple phrases — "Be open. Walk slowly. Bow often."[64] For me, they became a kind of mantra, an oft-repeated reminder of my desire to grow in awareness of the manifest presence of God. "Be open," mindful of God, on the lookout — watchful and observant. As the Apostle Paul wrote, "Fix your eyes not on what is seen, but on what is unseen, since what is seen is temporary, but what is unseen is eternal (2 Corinthians 4:18)." "Walk slowly," unhurriedly, at a leisurely pace, taking your time. "Hurry is the great enemy of spiritual life,"[65] a quality too often celebrated in the shallow end of the pool. "Bow often," when you see Him, get a glimpse of Him, when you sense His presence in a brief interaction, a conversation, a moment of reflection, a picture, a memory, a sunrise or sunset, acknowledge Him, welcome Him, worship Him. "Help me be open, walk slowly and bow often," I prayed every day as I finished my time with God. I prayed it for years. I framed it and put it in a prominent place on my desk. It's the little things that sometimes make the biggest difference.

Let me take it a step further. How can we turn our desire to be present in the present with the ever-present One into practices that might help us grow in God-awareness? Well, some things bear repeating. Here are three practices called, "The Three S's of Awareness." They've been incredibly helpful to me.[66] I'm not saying I'm good at these things but the Lord is using them to help me attend to His presence, miss Him less often and find His voice amidst all the clutter of daily life.

The first "S," the first thing you need to do, is *Slow Down*.[67] This is very hard for us, slowing down. In Psalm 46:10, the psalmist addresses our need to slow down, connecting it to a deeper knowledge of God. It reads, "Be still and know that I am God" (NIV) or "Cease striving and know that I am God" (NASB) or "Step out of the traffic! Take a long, loving look at me, your High God" (MSG). "Be still, cease striving, step out of the traffic" — He's encouraging us to regularly extricate ourselves from the busyness of life in favor of a fuller experience of Himself. Yes, you can encounter God as you are going, amidst the noise and activity, at full throttle, in the rush of the current, but He's more often found, more consistently heard, more readily available in the margins, apart from the crowd, in the quiet moments, in the gentle ebb and flow of a tidal pool, more easily heard on a quiet stroll than at a dead sprint. If you want to know and follow Jesus, if you want to hear His voice and know Him, not just know about Him, you need to learn to match His pace and find His rhythm, aligning your heart with the metronome of the Holy Spirit inside you.

Seasons of busyness, activity and engagement need to be sprinkled with stolen moments of rest and repair. We see this in God's creation, day inexorably gives way to night, fall and winter give birth to spring and spring to summer, even God Himself took a day to rest and encouraged us to do the same. We see it in the life of Jesus — periods of intense ministry and activity supported by, fueled by extended times of rest and repair. Jesus' rhythms are not often our rhythms. Our culture doesn't lend itself to living at Godspeed.[68] We often go out of our way to create activities that keep us going no matter what, trying to squeeze the most fun, excitement, entertainment, whatever out of every available minute. How many times have you gone to a restaurant where practically everyone at every table was glued to their phones? They were supposed to make our lives easier, provide margin, and increase our connection to one another. I can't help but wonder if they've simply given us more to do. We're more disconnected than ever, more distracted than ever — answer this call, listen to that voicemail, read this email, respond to that text, watch this video, find the perfect meme and if you want people to keep you in the loop, like things, love things, tweet things, retweet things, slap a thumbs up or thumbs down on every post, add a hashtag, review, check in, worried face, sad face, happy face, clown face — we need a vacation from our devices!

Larry Warner wrote, "One way to slow down is to walk more slowly. This leading with your body is powerful. It takes concentration to slow our walking, as we are always on our way to the next important place. But to rush to the next destination is to miss God in the present."[69] Don't I know it? I am, by nature, a fast walker. The old me would routinely hit the door at Walmart like a heat-seeking missile, determined to get what I need and get out the door as quickly as possible. I don't know if the thought has ever possessed you, "I need deodorant and I need it now," but that pretty much sums up my old approach to shopping. "Get in, get what you need, get out. I must have my Old Spice Swagger. Nothing else will do." Having achieved my objective, I'd angle my way to the front, zip my card through the card-reader at self-checkout then launch myself into the parking lot hitting the "open" button on my key fob multiple times to help me find my car. Why did I need to do that? Didn't I know where I parked? No, when I arrived, I wasn't paying attention. I was on a mission and not present in the parking lot. I always used to be more about the destination than the journey.

When I was growing up in the 1960s, one of our regular family entertainments, if you could call it that, was the Sunday afternoon drive. Despite the fact that those were simpler days, I never understood the appeal. My mom and dad would load us three boys into the car after lunch and we'd just drive around town for a couple of hours, "seeing," as my dad would often say, "what we could see." What was there to see that we hadn't seen countless times before? The town I grew up in was home to less than a thousand folks, most of whom I knew, many of whom were related to me. Besides, we lived on a dead-end street. There was only one way to go, so the first several minutes of every Sunday drive was exactly the same. And it wasn't like riding in the car was a novelty. Cars had been around for years. I mean, the very idea of taking a drive with your family, looking out the window and talking while we crawled around the countryside for two hours. Who does that? What are we trying to achieve? But that's the point.

For two hours, we weren't trying to achieve anything. We were just being together. Those Sunday conversations with my parents from the backseat of our Ford Rambler are some of my most treasured memories. Are you slowing down? Finding Jesus' rhythm of life, so you don't miss Him in the moment, is critical to an eyes-wide-open life with God.

Practice Solitude

That leads me to the second "S." To cultivate a deeper awareness of God, you need to practice *Solitude*.[70] "Solitude does not just happen; it involves a choice and intentional actions on our part, as the world seems to conspire against it."[71] It's true. Anyone raising toddlers, anyone taking care of an ailing parent, anyone who's looking for work, anyone who simply has too much to do knows how true that is. "I haven't had a moment to myself," is a common complaint in our culture. Everyone and everything seems to conspire against our desire to steal a few quiet moments with God. Ruth Haley Barton calls this "the push-pull phenomenon." She writes, "It seems no matter how well I understand the necessity of solitude, no matter how much I feel drawn to it, no matter how well I plan for it, there are forces working against it both externally and internally."[72] And yet our hearts long for it, they pine for a space among the trees (no pun intended), a moment away from the crowd, a hot minute, however brief, when we can "step out of the traffic" and be present to the ever-presence of God.

You can almost hear His gentle invitation, "Be still and know that I am God" (Psalm 46:10). I was invited to meditate on those words for a season not long ago. A slow reading, emphasizing and resting on each word is especially helpful. Close your eyes, take a deep breath and say aloud, "Be still and know that I am God." Sit with it. Let it wash over you. Then, after a few moments, take another breath and say, "Be still and know that I am." Meditate on the person of God, the great I Am and invite His presence.

Invite Him to reveal Himself to you. Then, take another breath and say, "Be still and know." Then, "Be still." Then, finally, "Be." Sit with these things, feel the longing of your heart to simply be with God. Resist the urge to rush through the steps. It's not about finishing the exercise. It's about practicing the presence of God.

Ruth Haley Barton helpfully points out that the Hebrew word translated "be still" literally means "loosen your grip." She writes, "Let go of your grip on your own understanding. Cease striving at the level of human effort, and in so doing open yourself to a whole new kind of knowing."[73] It reminds me of when I was first learning to play golf. I'd stand on the tee box looking out at a six-hundred yard par five then, with steely resolve, I'd take a deep breath, grip the club until my knuckles turned white and swing with all my might trying to muscle it down the fairway. The results were predictable. One time, I swung so hard I missed, spinning like a top before falling to the ground. Another time, I swung so hard I hit the ball off the toe of the club sending it screaming into an electrical transformer to the immediate right of the tee box. There was a resounding clap, sparks flew in every direction and my ball, now supercharged, was launched more than one hundred yards in the opposite direction! Once I hit a ball off a tee marker fifteen feet in front of me that bounced back and nearly knocked me unconscious. Who knew golf could be so dangerous? I, once, duck-hooked a ball onto the deck of a nearby house that wasn't even close to the fairway. The people on the deck never saw it coming until it was too late. I shouted, "Fore," but they would have been better served if I had shouted, "Incoming" or something helpful like, "Duck and cover." A "For Sale" sign went up in the yard the next day. I'm kidding. I didn't go back to that course to check.

One day, a few years later, I was playing with a friend who, after observing my take-no-prisoners approach to striking a golf ball, offered me some friendly advice. "Loosen your grip," he said. "You're gripping the club like you're trying to strangle it. Let the club do the work." Well, at first, I thought he was crazy. I knew all the golf lingo. Whatever happened to "grip it and rip it?" But he was a good golfer, a scratch golfer who could really spin it. I don't know why he agreed to play with me all those years ago, but I'm glad he did. When I loosened my grip, settled my stance, drew the club back slowly and smoothly followed through, I was in awe at the results. It didn't always go straight, but at least it went forward, which was a step in the right direction. Golf, once an exercise in self-flagellation, became an enjoyable walk with friends. Are you trying too hard? What would it be like for you to loosen your grip and relax into God's presence? What would it be like for you to step out of the traffic and be with God in a place beyond wordy prayers, another Bible study, radio preachers and endless fill-in-the-blank devotionals? What would it be like for you to be still and stay there long enough for the troubled waters of your soul to run clear? Do you think you'd be able to hear Him? Do you think you'd find rest for your soul?

Choose Silence

The third "S" is *Silence*.[74] I wrote about my early experience with silence in chapter 2. Let me just say here that this one spiritual practice, sitting in silence with God, has meant more to me than a thousand devotional guides. "It is in silence that we habitually release our own agendas and our need to control and become more willing and able to give ourselves to God's loving initiative. In silence we create space for God's activity rather than filling every minute with our own."[75] Are you finding time for God? Have you made space for His activity? Are you practicing His presence?

The three S's — slowing down, silence and solitude — are deep water skills, the practice of which helped me escape the noise in the shallow end of the pool but it wasn't easy. Slowing down was hard enough, but the practice of silence and solitude — sitting quietly and attending to God, listening for His voice — was even more challenging. Why? Why is this so hard for us? It's hard because the enemy wars against it. It was hard for me because I needed to train and develop this seriously underdeveloped dimension of my life. It was hard because, at first, I was really uncomfortable in God's presence. I felt a bit out of place. It didn't feel like home because I hadn't yet learned to live in the truth that I was His beloved. In the practice of the three S's, I saw myself more clearly and much of what I saw I didn't like. It left me feeling vulnerable, unlovable. My understanding of God's love for me wasn't adequate to address my shortcomings or allay my fears. I needed to go deeper, and that is where He took me next.

five

___

You are Dearly Loved by God

And so we know and rely on the love God has for us. God is love.
Whoever lives in love lives in God, and God in him.
~ 1 John 4:16

"Divine love is absolutely unconditional, unlimited
and unimaginably extravagant."[76]
~ David Benner

My dad died in a car accident in 2007, and we were devastated. I felt unmoored, like an anchor had been cut away from my life, setting me adrift. He was idling at a stop sign not more than a quarter of a mile from his home, up, bright and early, one morning to run an errand, when the driver of a passing car lost control, veered off the road and hit him broadside. Several hundred miles away, in Kansas City, I was getting ready for work, gathering some things in my home office

97

before setting out for the day when the phone rang. It's odd how you can remember exactly where you were and exactly what you were doing when something you never dreamed would happen happened. I took the phone from Dianne, a concerned look on her face. It was my little brother, Eric. "Mark," he said urgently with no preamble, "you need to pray. Dad was in a car accident and it doesn't look good." He then briefly explained what had happened, most of my questions, spoken and unspoken, going unanswered. "The EMTs are working on him right now," he said gravely. "I'll call you back when they get him in the ambulance."

Stunned, I stood there staring at the phone after he hung up, my heart in my throat, my world teetering off its axis. "Let's pray," Dianne said softly, and we did, our two youngest daughters joining us in tears. The weight of time pressing down on me with increasing force magnified the agony of each passing second as I asked God to intervene. When the phone finally rang, some twenty minutes later, I quickly hit the button while drawing the phone to my ear. "Tell me what's happening!" I spluttered. There was a brief pause, then, choking out the words between sobs, my brother said, "We lost him, Mark. We lost him." Three simple words and just like that, he was gone. My dad died that day at the age of seventy-seven and, a few days later, more than twelve hundred people stood in line for hours outside a funeral home in my hometown for the chance to pay their last respects.

Standing there greeting folks, thanking them for coming, my brothers and I were amazed at all the things we didn't know about my dad. We knew that he and my mom had taken in her youngest sister, a wild child at sixteen, because her mother had died and her dad was an alcoholic. We knew together they had cared for my great-grandmother. She also lived with us for a time near the end of her life, standing at the screen door cheering us on well into her eighties as we played ball in the backyard. What we didn't know was that my father had been a mentor, a Barnabas-like encourager, to several other young men in the years after my brothers and I were out on our own. He didn't try to fix them; they told us in so many words. He took them fishing and listened. We were moved to by their stories, by the stories of all the lives he had touched.

But the story I won't forget is the one no one knew about but me. When I was five or six years old, I was playing alone on the floor in the living room on a Saturday morning when my grandfather, who I mentioned earlier, showed up at the front door after an all-night, alcoholic binge. I could see him through the front porch window and he was barely recognizable. He was covered in vomit. He had soiled himself. He looked like he hadn't slept in days. He reeked of smoke. His fingernails were so long they'd curled around to touch the underside of his fingers. He could barely stand up and I still can't believe he could walk the few blocks from the bars on Main Street to our house.

When my dad heard the doorbell, he dropped what he was doing and went through the dining room to the front porch. Seeing my grandfather in that awful state, he glanced around to see where I was and, not seeing me, rushed to the door. I was hiding behind a chair, peering out a small window with a view of the porch, and I watched the whole thing. The first thing out of his mouth was, "Oh, Charlie, what have you done?" He, then, tenderly wrapped his arms around him, picked him up bodily and practically carried him through the porch into the house and up the stairs to the bathroom. I crawled silently up behind them and watched through a crack in the door as my dad ran a bath, undressed his barely coherent father-in-law, washed him, dried him, trimmed his finger and toenails and dressed him in a pair of his own pajamas before putting him to bed. My dad never talked about it, at least not around me, and I don't think he ever knew I watched the whole thing, but that moment had a profound impact on my life. It's hard to plumb the depths of God's love for us but, now and then, we get a glimpse, a brief earthly example, of "the absolutely unconditional, unlimited and unimaginably extravagant" love of God.

God's Perfect Love

"Knowing, owning and internally embracing God's perfect love is the only soil within which our relationship with God can grow."[77] I have always known God loves me. The thread of God's unconditional, unlimited, and unimaginably extravagant love is woven throughout the Bible. It's unmistakable, showing up on practically every page. But knowing God loves you is not owning. Knowing is not internally embracing. Knowing alone is not enough. We know He loves us. We can produce biblical proof upon biblical proof, quoting chapter and verse, where God says unequivocally that He loves us — without caveat, reservation, or limitation. We know it! Many of us sang about it as children in church, "Jesus loves me, this I know, for the Bible tells me so." For most of us, knowing is not the problem. Knowing has never been the problem. It's believing, accepting and resting in his love — allowing ourselves to be loved by God — that's where we often fall short.

This began to change for me as I worked my way through the *Ignatian Exercises*. I always knew God loved me. I knew it because the Bible told me so. And, over the course of my life, I came to take the truth of His love for granted because I had never actually experienced it. I had a transactional relationship with God, rooted in a bargain kind of faith. "I'll do this for you if you do this for me." It was, I used to flatter myself, a "mutually beneficial relationship" though, in retrospect, I'm not sure what God was getting out of it. For my part, I can tell you, I never felt loved, not really. I wasn't relying on His love or secure in His love. I wasn't, as Paul wrote, rooted like an oak tree or grounded like a skyscraper in God's perfect love (Ephesians 3:17). I didn't have the power to grasp the width, length, height or depth of God's love, nor had I tried (Ephesians 3:18). Paul prayed that the Ephesian church might "know the love that *surpasses* knowledge (Ephesians 3:19)." The love I knew was based entirely *on* knowledge. I hadn't internalized it in any other way.

As a result, I was untethered, miserable, hoping some person, thing or event would come along and give me the feeling of satisfaction, contentment and validation I was so desperately seeking. Do you know that feeling? Do you ever secretly hope that a book, trip, course, job, accomplishment, purchase, role, title, person, place, or thing will satisfy your deepest desires? Here's what I've discovered. As long as you're counting on someone or something other than God to fulfill the deepest longings of your heart, you will go on running helter-skelter, always anxious and restless, always impatient and angry, never fully satisfied for the rest of your life. The same compulsive drivenness that kept me going and busy all those years also made me wonder if I was actually getting anywhere in the long run. This is the way to spiritual exhaustion and burnout. This is the way to spiritual death. Living outside the love of God! But, as Henri Nouwen wrote, "[We] don't have to kill ourselves. We are the Beloved! We are intimately loved long before our parents, teachers, spouses, children and friends loved or wounded us. That's the truth of our lives. That's the truth I want you to claim for yourself. That's the truth spoken by the voice that says, 'You are my Beloved.'"[78] When was the last time you heard Him say that? When was the last time you actually felt, deep down, that God loved you?

God Loves You

Given my circumstances, all those years ago, you can imagine my surprise when my time in the *Ignatian Exercises* began with three weeks on the love of God. "I already know this," I confidently informed my spiritual director who was leading me through the *Exercises*. "Is this really necessary?" I was hoping I could skip it and move on to something I didn't already know. Besides, it felt like overkill. The first section was entitled, "God loves you." The second section was entitled, "God really loves you." And the third section was entitled, "God really, really loves you!" Why would you do that? Why the repetition on something so basic? Working my way through it, over several weeks, I discovered the answer. Knowing, as I've said, is not enough. The truth of God's love needs to become a part of you. The idea is to internalize the love of God, "transforming it from a theological construct you mentally assent to into a heart-felt reality that pulsates through the veins of your being."[79] For most of my life, God's love was nothing more than a theological construct, nowhere near a heart-felt reality that pulsated through the veins of my being.

As the truth of my limited experience came home to me, I lowered my head in quiet contemplation. I remember feeling empty. I became acutely aware of the poverty in my soul and my resistance to immersing myself any deeper in the Father's love quickly gave way to longing. *"Are you telling me there's more?"* I wondered. That thought had honestly never occurred to me. After thirty years in ministry, I flattered myself that I was a master of the deep, equipped to lead and counsel others when, in truth, I had spent my whole life in the deeper end of the shallows never dreaming there was more. For the first time in a long time, I was filled with holy desire. I wanted the more, wherever that might lead me. I wanted to experience life with God beyond the buoys. I wanted a deeper awareness (there's that word again) of God's love for me, a deeper connection to God. Yes, God is love and He loves everyone. But what I needed, what I desperately wanted, was to live, rooted and grounded, in His love for me.

Well, I have to tell you; I was not prepared for what God had in store. Three weeks on the love of God in the *Exercises* turned into four, four turned into six, six turned into twelve. I simply couldn't move on. As the weeks went by and I immersed myself in what the Bible says about God's love for me, I was undone. I cried. I cried and cried, tears of joy and sorrow. *"Do you mean this has been available to me my entire life, and I somehow missed it?"* I simply couldn't believe how personal it all was. God really, really loves me! God really, really loves you! As David Benner wrote, "Neither knowing God nor knowing self can progress very far unless it begins with a knowledge of how deeply we are loved by God. Until we dare to believe that *nothing* can separate us from God's love…we remain in the elementary grades [the shallow end] of the school of Christian spiritual transformation. Genuine transformation requires vulnerability. It is not the fact of being loved unconditionally that is life changing. It is the risky experience of allowing myself to be loved unconditionally."[80] Do you dare to believe? Are you allowing God to love you unconditionally?

God Really Loves You

Those twelve weeks meditating on the love of God birthed a turning point in my life. As I was learning to internalize the love of God and his love was beginning to pulsate through my veins, I eventually reached a place of unguarded vulnerability where I finally let God love me. How do I describe that moment? How can anyone put into words what it feels like to be loved so thoroughly by the God who *is* love with what the Apostle John called "perfect love?" I can tell you this, it's not that God suddenly decided to love me after years of not loving me or that His love was simply a response to my love for Him. He has loved me (and you) with an absolutely unconditional, unlimited and unimaginably extravagant love from before time began! That's what I discovered. "God loves each and every one of us with depth, persistence and intensity beyond imagination."[81] More than anything, He wants intimacy — a close, transcendent connection — with His beloved, a togetherness or attachment that's so immersive, where we're so intertwined with Him, that His thoughts eventually become our thoughts, His desires, our desires. The love of God should never be described as casual, companionable or even familial, as wonderful as that is. It's not warm feelings or kind thoughts or a general sense of well-being — all here today and gone tomorrow. No! The love of God is God Himself! And He loves us, as Tom Ashbrook wrote, "by extending Himself to us in life-giving connection that brings us into relationship with Him."[82] This relationship or connection with the Trinity

— Father, Son and Holy Spirit — is the greatest gift anyone could ever receive. It is the pearl of great price, the treasure in the field, a gift of such inestimable worth that God, the Father, sacrificed His one and only Son to make it available to us. It is the ultimate gift of love — true intimacy with the Eternal God by which we come fully alive.

How, then, do we learn to rest in Him? How do we reach a place of vulnerability and finally receive the fullness of God's love for us? I can only share with you the steps I took, hoping they'll be helpful to you in your own journey. I wouldn't recommend you wait until you come to the end of yourself like I did, though I suspect that's what it will take for many of us. It was in desperation that I started down this path, submitting myself to a process that drew me into a daily time of reflection, meditation on the Word and prayer, a process that put me in a place where God could get at me and I could simply be with Him. How desperate are you to be touched by love? How willing to let God love you? How far are you willing to go in your quest to rest in God Himself?

One day, in the middle of my investigation into the love of God, I decided to try one of the optional exercises in *Journey with Jesus*. I'd already been way outside my devotional comfort zone, drawing pictures, taking walks with Jesus, even blowing bubbles and watching them float freely on the wind. I was so proud of myself, a dyed-in-the-wool activist being all artsy, creative and contemplative, like I'd been doing it all my life. Even so, I was resistant to the idea of the "blanket exercise" and the fact that it was optional gave me permission to skip it. But, when I met with my spiritual director that week, he asked me about it. I knew he would. "Did you do the optional exercise?" he asked. "No," I said dismissively, "I thought about it but I'm good." "I really think you should do it," he replied with a wry smile. "I think it would be good for you." Sighing internally, I grudgingly agreed, and the next day I sat down in a comfortable chair in my office and wrapped myself in a blanket.

Opening the book, I read, "The blanket exercise is designed to give you a tangible reminder of how God's love surrounds you and embraces you every moment of every day…The only thing you'll need for this optional exercise is a warm, cozy blanket. As you sit down to do your daily preparatory exercise, imagine that your blanket is God's love. Simply wrap yourself up in the blanket as you imagine it to be God's love wrapping around you…When you finish, journal about your experience…"[83] It sounded simple enough, and it was. I closed my eyes and imagined the love of God surrounding me, holding me, embracing me. Tears flowed as the Holy Spirit met me in that moment. I felt His loving arms around me, the warmth of His presence and His gentle touch. But it was more than a feeling, more than just feeling loved, which is no small thing. In that moment, I was connected to Him and that, my friends, is everything.

The book goes on. "Another way to use this optional exercise is to wrap the blanket around you and take a walk, once again reminding yourself that God's love surrounds you."[84] My first thought? "Okkkaayy. That's where I draw the line." I didn't mind wrapping myself in a blanket in the privacy of my office but I wasn't yet comfortable wrapping myself in a blanket like a cape-wearing crusader, waltzing through the neighborhood looking like the guy from *Assassin's Creed* or a poncho-wearing child of the sixties. *"What if somebody sees me?"* I thought. I was consumed with things like that in those days. I'm not so concerned about that now — the good opinion of others, keeping up appearances. I'm happy to say I'm more secure in the Father's love than I was then, more connected to Him than I have ever been. As the Apostle Paul wrote, "If God is for us, who can be against us (Romans 8:31)?" And I would add, if God really loves us, who cares what other people think? Does it really matter? How far would you go to get in touch with God's unimaginably extravagant love for you? Would you go so far as to wrap yourself in a blanket and walk around your neighborhood?

Surrender to Love

Here's another thing that helped me rest in the Father's love. The Apostle John, in his beautiful opus on divine love, wrote, "We know and rely on the love God has for us (1 John 4:16)." The word *rely* here is rendered in the perfect tense in the original language. It means you can rely or depend on God's love for you "over time and through experience." I believe the only way you can come to rely on the love God has for you is over time and through experience.[85] He will prove His love to you over and over again. You can learn to trust His love. That said, the question comes, how is it done? How do I learn to rely on God's love? I'll give you the answer, though you may not like it. Learning to rely on God's love requires *surrender*. "The English word *surrender* carries the implication of putting one's full weight on someone or something. It involves letting go — a release of effort, tension and fear. And it involves trust. One cannot let go of self-dependence and transfer dependence to someone else without trust."[86] We have a hard time letting go. It's counterintuitive for us as a culture. Propelled by fear, we want to be in control. We don't easily yield to others, let alone God. But, when it comes to experiencing God's love, that's precisely what is required of us: surrender and, with surrender, trust.

In the halcyon days of my childhood, my mom would often take us to the swimming hole under the bridge on Elk Creek. It was a magical place, just deep enough for a boy of seven to touch the bottom, but not so shallow that you couldn't cannonball into the water from a rock ledge near the surface. It was there, in the gentle current of Elk Creek, that my mom taught me how to float.[87] I can still see her in her stylish 1960s bathing suit with the flowery, white, rubber swim cap snapped securely under her chin, encouraging me to breathe, relax, lay my head back and let the current carry me. It was, at first, terrifying! Only a year or two removed from the near-death, deep-end-of-the-pool experience I wrote about in Chapter One, I was rigid as a board, afraid of sinking under the surface, not believing the water would support me. I kept sticking my head up, looking around, afraid of running into something, or looking down at my feet to see if it was working. "Am I floating?" I would ask excitedly. "Relax, Mark," she would reply in a soothing voice. *Relax?* Easy for *her* to say. She made it look effortless. She'd roll onto her back, gaze up at the sky and just be still. It was like she wasn't even trying. I, on the other hand, was trying, struggling. I wanted to believe her, but I just couldn't let go. Then, finally, somehow, I was able to settle myself for a few seconds and, for the first time ever, I floated. It didn't last long as I immediately started rejoicing, "Look, look mom, I'm floating!" And then, suddenly, I wasn't, but it didn't matter. I'd had a break-through and what an incredible feeling. Supported by the water, carried along by the current, I was completely at peace. But I had to surrender. I had to stop trying to make it happen on my own. I had to trust the water to hold me, lift me, support and carry me. I had to let go.

Some people have a hard time letting go. I was certainly one of those. I simply wasn't willing, for the longest time, to trust in God's love and allow myself to be carried along by the current of His love wherever He wanted to go. It was like I believed God's love was unreliable, like it wasn't enough, like He somehow couldn't be trusted. As a result, I regularly tried to make things go the way I thought they should go and, as I've said, I was never at peace. This is not what God has in mind for His children. He wants to support you, to carry you along enfolded in His loving arms, but you have to surrender to His love. Like learning to float, surrender takes practice. You surrender all the little things so you can learn to trust Him with the big things. So let me ask you. Do you see His love as reliable or changeable? Has He proved His love to you over time and through experience? Would you like to learn how to float? These are questions we have to answer if we want to trade the shallows for the deep end of the pool.

When God Thinks of You

What do you think God thinks of when God thinks of you? "God likes you. God loves you. And God loves loving you."[88] That's what one speaker said at a pastor's retreat I attended in 2015. He, then, had us break into groups, turn to one another and say it aloud, "God likes you. God loves you. And God loves loving you." My first reaction was a sudden desire to go to the bathroom. I'm essentially an introvert who's been traumatized by well-meaning extroverts in a number of group settings over the years. *"Come on,"* I thought, *"This is so awkward."* It reminded me of a time in my home church growing up when the pastor thought it would be amazing to have everyone stand, turn to a total stranger and say, "I love you with the love of the Lord." I know you extroverts love that stuff, but it makes my skin crawl. Nevertheless, I didn't go to the bathroom. I stayed. I was the Regional Leader, after all, and I had invited our keynote speaker. There was no getting around it. I *had* to do it.

Standing there in my group, I turned to the pastor next to me and mumbled half-heartedly, "God likes you. God loves you. And God loves loving you." And I must not have been the only one going through the motions because the speaker said, "No, no, I want you to take your time, look them in the eye and say each phrase slowly." There was that urge again, the bathroom calling my name. *"Look them in the eye?"* But, in the end, despite my internal protestations, I did it. What's more, someone else did it for me and it was powerful, the truth sinking in slowly, evoking desire mingled with resistance. *"Resistance? Where was that coming from?"* I wondered. "Now I want you to close your eyes and repeat it aloud to yourself," he continued, "paying attention to the internal reactions of the heart." Dutifully, I closed my eyes, took a deep breath, and softly repeated the refrain, savoring each phrase, "God likes me. God loves me. And God loves loving me." You might want to try it. I did it with my church. It was harder than I thought.

Do you know how many people struggle with the idea that God likes them? I think more people struggle with the idea that God likes them than that He loves them. This goes back to what I said about the love of God being nothing more than a theological construct in our lives. God *is* love. He loves everyone because He has to, or so we believe. It also has to do with the fact that many of us don't like ourselves. "If God only knew me, He wouldn't like me?" I've heard people say. And I always reply, "Really? Are you listening to yourself? 'If God only knew you?' Who knows you better than God?"

I think this is a test — God likes me, God loves me, and God loves loving me — a measure of where we are on the continuum of God's love as a theological construct on the one hand and God's love as a heart-felt reality, pulsating through our veins, on the other. Where our willingness to surrender (float) tests what we believe about the reliability of God's love, believing God likes us, loves us and loves loving us tests what we believe about His constancy, that His opinion of us and feelings for us never waver. Throughout my life, I've heard God's love described as unconditional, that He loves us without strings attached. And it's true! God loves us without condition. Before we ever decided to love Him, He loved us. Before we were born or could do anything for ourselves or Him, He loved us. His love is not dependent on a response of any kind. You don't have to follow Him, obey Him, listen to Him, honor Him or worship Him for Him to love you. On the contrary, you can ignore Him, doubt Him, curse Him, deny Him and flagrantly disobey Him your entire life and it won't make a dent in His constant, dependable love for you. He simply won't stop loving you.

God Knows the Real You

God not only knows you, He knows the real you. He knows the you you rarely reveal to others, and He loves you still. As Dallas Willard said, "God only loves the real you, not all your false selves."[89] It's funny. We spend so much time, years in fact, crafting our false selves, not just what we want others to see and how we want them to think about us but what we want to believe about ourselves, the me we want to be.

Uncomfortable with who God says we are, we go searching for identity, some form of validation that we matter, that we're special. We build a preferred image, at work, at home, at church, in the world, one brick at a time, putting ourselves out there, ninety feet high and nine feet wide like King Nebuchadnezzar's image of gold,[90] wanting desperately to be appreciated, celebrated, even worshipped for our accomplishments. It's exhausting! Do you know how it could change your life if you could come to accept and experience the truth that God fully knows and yet constantly loves you? I love the way Debbie Swindoll puts it in *Life with God*. She writes, "There are two essential things. 1. We need to understand and experience that God knows us fully, which includes the extent of our sin. There is nothing that we discover about ourselves that God does not already know. He occupies the places where we are hiding from ourselves and others."[91] He will always know more about us than we do. And, "2. We need to know and experience that God loves us constantly even in light of our sin."[92] Describing God's love as unconditional is fine. I love that, it's true, but I love the unshakeable constancy, the dependable faithfulness of His love even more.

An Important Question

Part way through the *Exercises*, my wife encouraged me to read *Mansions of the Heart* by Tom Ashbrook. Covered up with one thing or another, I kept putting her off. I put her off for months. Our vacation finally came, and we jumped in the car to go visit the family. Sensing she finally had my undivided attention, Dianne said, "Would you like to listen to an audio book?" "Sure," I replied. Smiling, she connected her phone to the car and hit the button for *Mansions*. I was immediately enthralled. It spoke to me on so many levels, making sense of things I'd long wrestled with and raising questions I'd never even thought about. One such question wouldn't let me go. "What do you think it's all about?"

I talk to a lot of young pastors who're looking for a track to run on. They want to know where to put their resources, how to structure their church, where to focus their efforts. So I ask them, "What do you think it's all about?" And they invariably reply, "I'm not sure what you mean." "The whole redemption story," I explain, "the overarching meta-narrative of the Bible, the ravages of sin and the Fall, God sending His Son, everything Jesus said and did on earth — dying on the cross, rising from the dead, ascending into heaven, putting His Spirit in us, the Kingdom of God! — what do you think it's all about?" After a bit of reflection, some will say, "I think it's all about evangelism, winning the lost, the Great Commission." That's the most common reply. It would certainly have been my knee-jerk reply if you asked me that question in the first thirty years of my ministry. Others might point to inner healing or social justice, ministry to the poor, or even signs and wonders. Here's why what you think it's all about matters. The root determines the fruit. Let me explain.

Jesus offers us a fruitful life. He said, "I am the vine; you are the branches. If you remain in me and I in you, you will bear much fruit; apart from me, you can do nothing (John 15:5)." *Fruit* is not defined here, but it almost certainly would include a changed or transformed Christian character. The Apostle Paul picks up on the idea in Galatians 5. He writes, "But the fruit of the Spirit is love, joy, peace, patience, kindness, goodness, faithfulness, gentleness, and self-control (Galatians 5:22-23)." Instead of an out-of-control life or a life characterized by hatred or outbursts of anger, anxiety, impatience, unkindness, grouchiness and the like, imagine if the basic characteristics of your life were love, joy and peace. Imagine a life where you're not up nights fretting over one of your children or a situation at work. Imagine your heart completely at peace regardless of your circumstances. Imagine, whatever your temperament, if the one thing people said about you is that you're a very kind person, a good person, a faithful person, that you're gentle or humble of heart, a person of blessing who walks through life with a kind word and a light touch. The fruitful life is the Spirit-filled life. The fruitful life is the Jesus-centered life. Because God is love, the fruitful life is the love-filled life — permeated, soaked through with His loving presence.

Look, every life bears fruit, intentionally or unintentionally, some good, some not. Some fruit we bear actually looks good. It *is* good. It's just not much. It cannot satisfy. There's not enough to go around and it simply doesn't last. The effects are short-lived; they have no eternal value. That's what Jesus meant when He said, "You did not choose me, but I chose you and appointed you so that you might go and bear fruit — fruit that will *last...* (John 15:16)." The fruit we bear in our lives as believers is meant to have a lasting impact. A truly fruitful life produces fruit that lasts or endures in this life into the next. Where does lasting fruit come from? It comes from a life lived with Jesus, in concert with Jesus, in total dependence upon Jesus. You have to remain or abide in Him and if you attach yourself to Him in this way, to the God who is love, you'll bear much fruit and it will last. Lasting fruit comes from your attachment to the God who is love.

If, on the other hand, you go it alone; you choose to live a largely autonomous life apart from God, only occasionally reconnecting to the Vine, you might bear fruit, but it won't be anything to write home about. It won't have a lasting impact or make a lasting impression. It's more like "here today and gone tomorrow." I've thought a lot about the fruitful life in the last several years and I've concluded that whatever is at the root determines the fruit. It stands to reason. You wouldn't expect to get apples from an oak tree or chestnuts from a pear tree, with or without the partridge. The root determines the fruit. Are you attached, connected, rooted and grounded in the God who is love?

Reverse Engineering

A little reverse engineering might be helpful here (See Figure 1). Let's say you want to live a fruitful life. Where does this fruit come from? The fruit comes largely from the myriad of *choices* we make, both big and small, every single day and our *behaviors*, the things we do and say, the way we engage the world around us. These choices and behaviors have consequences. They produce fruit, some good, some not so good, some that provide lasting nourishment and some that fall to the ground uneaten. Where do these choices and behaviors come from? What compels us to do what we do and say? Well, our choices grow up out of our *values*, the things we think are important, the things we hold dear. These values, then, emanate from our *deeply held beliefs*. So our beliefs help form our values, our values guide our choices and behaviors, which, in turn, produce fruit in our lives. Again, whatever is at the root determines the fruit.

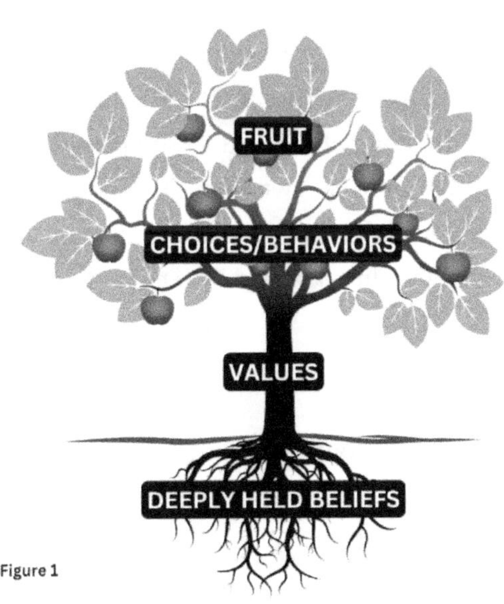

Figure 1

For example, if you believe life is all about the pursuit of happiness then you'll value the things that serve your need or desire to be happy and you'll choose friends, partners, careers, and churches based on their ability to add to or increase your sense of happiness and well-being. When Jerry Maguire famously told Dorothy, "You complete me," he was stating his belief that she would, in fact, make him whole, that she would be the cure for the homesickness in his soul, that she would fill the God-shaped hole inside of him. I know it's fiction but, if you ask me, the relationship was doomed from the start. No one, other than God Himself, could ever measure up or be enough to complete someone else. And, from Dorothy's perspective, who wants to complete someone else's life, like you're the missing piece to their thousand-piece puzzle? Instead of saying, "You had me at hello," she might have said, "Complete you? What about me? Who's going to complete me?" This is where you end up if you believe life is all about the pursuit of happiness.

If you believe life is all about what you can achieve, you might value things like an Ivy League education, an internship at a Fortune 500 company, a seven-figure income, a corner office, a house in St. Moritz and the respect and recognition of your peers. These values will inevitably drive your choices, potentially compelling you to see people as expendable, as a commodity to be used for your own ends. You might even become one of those people who, as Charles Colson confessed years ago, "would walk over your own grandmother to get ahead."[93] The root determines the fruit.

The One Thing

What do you believe it's all about? What is at the root of your life? It can't be all about several things. It can only be *all* about one thing. What is that one thing? Why did God create us? Why, after the Fall, did He eventually send His Son to redeem us? Why did He suffer what He suffered? Why die on a cross? Why the resurrection, ascension and the gift of the Holy

Spirit? I've been down all the other roads. For a time, as I said, I thought it was all about evangelism, "win the lost at any cost," and I reordered my church around getting people to decide for Jesus. For a time, I thought it was all about inner healing, so I trained a bunch of folks in various forms of prayer aimed at healing past hurts. I had a season where I thought it was all about joining God in His work and I encouraged folks to get in the game, underlining the value "everyone gets to play." I thought it was all about social justice, ministry to the poor, and I launched several programs to help the homeless, the marginalized and the oppressed. I also came to believe it was all about Kingdom ministry, proclamation and demonstration, signs and wonders. Each time, my deeply held beliefs helped form my values as a believer. My values influenced my choices and my choices produced fruit, good fruit, but I was still unsatisfied. Here's what I discovered. Evangelism, inner healing, joining God in His work, social justice, power ministry, church growth, even the pursuit of happiness, is *not* what it's all about. Jesus didn't simply come to save us. He didn't die on the cross solely to heal our past hurts. He didn't do what He did to recruit a bunch of co-workers or help us grow bigger churches. All of those things are fruit, not the root. They're not what it's all about. They're what happens when you root your life in what it *is* all about!

What is it all about? Well, I've searched the Scriptures and I have to tell you, I think it's all about *love*. It's all about a love relationship with Jesus, a connection to the God who is love. Love is the central theme of the Bible. We were made for love by a God who is love and He will stop at nothing to restore that relationship. "For God so *loved* the world that He gave His one and only Son...(John 3:16)," it says in the verse they still put on banners at football games. As the Apostle Paul wrote, "And now these three remain: faith, hope and love. But the greatest of these is *love* (1 Corinthians 13:13)." The word, as I'm sure you're aware, is *agapē* in the original language. It refers to the highest form of love, the love of God for humanity — unconditional, selfless, unlimited and unimaginably extravagant love — and the life-giving connection that He offers us. It's greater or more valuable than faith. It's greater or more valuable than hope. Wow! Think about that for a moment. Faith and hope are pretty valuable, right? But Paul says it's no contest, "the greatest of these," the greatest by far, is love. It's at the top of the list and whatever is second is so far down the list, it's not even on the same page. For the Apostle Paul, there was nothing more important than this life-giving connection to God. God is love. But it's more than just a beginning.

Never Leave Love Behind

Jesus told His followers that they should never leave love behind. He said, "As the Father has loved me, so have I loved you. Now remain in my love (John 15:9)." As pastor and author Rich Nathan, said, "Love is not in first place in the sense that we first have to go to the kindergarten of love and then graduate and move on to more substantial subjects in higher grades. Love is not in first place as a starting block for sprinters that we leave behind in our race for the finish line. Jesus says: 'I want you to remain in my love.' You never get beyond this. Love is not an airport you fly out of in order to get to where you're really going. Love, for the Christian; love for a human being is the soil a tree is planted in without which the tree will die. Love is the water a fish swims in. Love is air for our lungs. Divine love is the environment, the atmosphere, and love is our eternal destiny! What is heaven if it's not to be embraced by the love of God forever? You start your life with God in love and you never leave that love behind [Because God is love]! No matter how much you grow, you never outgrow God's perfect love."[94]

Jesus told us to *remain* in His love if we want to live a fruitful life. The word, in the King James version, is *abide*. J. C. Ryle, a 19th century preacher and Bible scholar, tried to capture the full meaning of the word in John 15. Assuming the voice of Jesus, he writes, "Abide in Me. Cling to Me.

Stick fast to Me. Live lives of close and intimate communion with Me. Get nearer and nearer to me. Roll every burden on Me. Cast your whole weight on Me. Never let go of your hold on Me for a moment. Be, as it were, rooted and planted in Me. Do this, and I will never fail you. I will forever abide in you."[95] Can you imagine such a life, a life rooted in God's perfect love? This is what Jesus offers you in the shallow end of the pool that's there in abundance in the deeper end of the pool. It's what He came to make possible for you. Do you believe it's all about love?

Prayer as a Gateway to Intimacy

Let's take a moment and explore how a love relationship with Jesus works itself out in a spiritual practice like contemplative or abiding prayer. Jesus said, "If you remain in me and my words remain in you, ask whatever you wish, and it will be done for you (John 15:7)." He explains further in verse 16. He says, "You did not choose me, but I chose you and appointed you so that you might go and bear fruit — fruit that will last — and so that whatever you ask in my name the Father will give you (John 15:16)." Whatever you wish? Whatever you ask in my name? These are sweeping promises. He's saying, in effect, if you remain in me, abide in me, cling to me, more than the desires of your heart, I'll give you what your heart should desire. I'll give you what you a should wish for. Imagine it! Imagine what it would be like to ask God for whatever you wish and it would be done for you. Imagine if your prayers were regularly answered, that you didn't constantly feel that you were praying in vain, that it was entirely hit or miss. Imagine having the confidence that you would receive whatever you ask for in Jesus' name and that in seeking, you would find. Jesus is describing a very mature prayer life here, rooted in perfect love. He says that those who're living in close communion with Him, who pray in His name, according to His will, praying His thoughts after Him, in accordance with all that Jesus is and stands for, are going to see answers to prayer. We see people in the Bible get their prayers answered. What if you had confidence that your prayers would be answered, that they'd actually make a difference? Imagine what that would be like. Imagine prayer coming from the overflow of this rooted, abiding, deeply interconnected life with Jesus. Imagine prayer as a conversation between intimate friends. Imagine prayer as a gateway to deeper intimacy with God.

I love how author Thomas Green describes a healthy prayer life. He says that there are basically three stages. Using the analogy of human love, he describes the three stages as…

Stage 1: Getting to know (the courtship period)
Stage 2: From knowing to loving (the honeymoon period)
Stage 3: From loving to truly loving (the long years of day-to-day married life after the honeymoon is over)[96]

In the initial stage, you're seeking knowledge. You cannot love what you do not know. Your conversations, then, are full of discovery, getting to know each other. When I first met Dianne, I was shocked that it took her over two months to ask me out! When she finally got around to it, I quickly agreed to go with her to the annual Sadie Hawkins Hayride. That night after the hayride, in a party with a few hundred folks from school, it was like everyone else just faded into the background and she was the only one in the room. We talked for hours about our families, about me growing up in Pennsylvania and her in Africa, about our favorite books. She grew up reading the classics — Dickens, Hugo, Dumas. I told her about my favorite comic books. We were getting to know one another. I'm still surprised she said 'yes' to a second date.

Now, when it comes to your relationship with God, it's really you getting to know Him and, in the process, getting to know yourself better as well. He doesn't need to get to know you. He already knows you as thoroughly as you can be known. And He certainly doesn't need to get to know Himself. He's already as self-aware as anyone could possibly be. He's ready, when you're ready, to move the relationship to the next level. He'd like to go from knowing to loving, but He wants you to want it, too. This first stage, the courtship stage, is an essential part of any eventual love relationship, though it is fraught with potential issues. For example, many people in the courtship stage are simply infatuated with the other person, with who they think they are or who they want them to be. They don't really know them yet. As a result, they're not really in love. They're more in love with the idea of love. Many relationships never survive this stage. Couples get to know each other, the rose-colored glasses come off, and they discover their partner is not who they thought they were.

It's even possible, I think, to be infatuated with Jesus, drawn to Him. I mean, who wouldn't want a relationship with Jesus? He said, "If you remain in me and my words remain in you, ask whatever you wish, and it will be done for you (John 15:7)." That's a pretty attractive offer. But infatuation is not love, precisely because we don't really know the object of our infatuation. In the early days, we see Him as we want to see Him. He is what we want Him to be — a Savior made to order, a benevolent dispenser of blessings, a get-out-of-hell free card, a four-leaf clover we hope will bring us luck, a pillow for our bottoms to make life a little more comfortable, a hopeful suitor who will fulfill our every wish.

Haven't you seen couples in this first stage of their relationship who were besotted with one another only to break up a few months later, disillusioned? They thought the other person was exactly what they were looking for, projecting their need onto that person, they saw them as the answer, the one who would fulfill their deepest need, only to discover, as they got to know them better, that they weren't everything they hoped they were. This happens with Jesus all the time. It's the problem of unrealized expectations. People hear about Jesus, about His offer of a fruitful life, a life without lack, a life with God rooted and grounded in love, and they fall head over heels in love with the idea. But the relationship that started with such promise never moves from knowing to loving because, as they get to know Him, Jesus isn't what they thought He was or what they wanted.

Maybe they wanted a sugar daddy who would fulfill their every wish or an ever-present therapist who would constantly affirm them or an enabler who would help them get what they wanted in life or a savior who would rescue them from their bad choices or a lover who would satisfy their needs without making demands on them. Many, many relationships with Jesus never get out of the courtship stage, they never move from knowing to loving because the more folks get to know Jesus, the more they come to realize He's not a cosmic genie there to answer the call every time they wish upon a star. He actually requires something of you. He says, "If you remain in me [Abide in me. Cling to me. Stick fast to me. Live lives of close and intimate communion with me. Get nearer and nearer to me. Roll every burden on me. Cast your whole weight on me] and my words remain in you, ask whatever you wish and it will be done for you (John 15:7)."

Jesus is so much more. He offers so much more than any of us could possibly imagine. He's what you truly need. He's what your heart should desire. And He's ready to take your relationship to the next level, but He won't force the issue. He won't force you to move from knowing to loving. He's waiting for you to make a commitment. He's waiting for you to abandon your independence, your self-reliance, your autonomous life and the slavery to self that so many of us think is freedom and cast your whole weight upon Him. Will you let Him love you?

Pursing and nurturing this intimate, life-giving connection or attachment to Jesus remains the central focus and joy of my life. It's as I've learned to cling to Him, abide in Him, cast my whole weight on Him and never let go of Him that He has helped me discover who I truly am. Are you living out of your true identity?

six
—

You are a Masterpiece of God

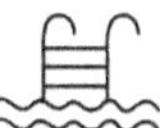

I praise you, for I am fearfully and wonderfully made.
Wonderful are your works; my soul knows it very well.
~ Psalm 139:14 (ESV)

"We are, not metaphorically but in very truth, a Divine work of art,
something that God is making, and therefore something with which
He will not be satisfied until it has a certain character." [97]
~ C.S. Lewis

I accepted the call to my first church as a newly married man at the laughable age of twenty-two. I laugh now, but it was no laughing matter. Three retired couples were meeting in a drafty, turn-of-the-last-century, clapboard building in rural Georgia. It was tough going for a man my age, made even tougher by my naiveté and lack of leadership experience. My wife, Dianne, and I were soon living hand-to-mouth, so poor we would dig through the couch cushions hoping to scare up enough change to go to Burger King and share a small fry while enjoying the air conditioning. We

121

were so poor I built a rickety bookcase to hold my fledgling library out of a discarded length of barn wood I found rotting in the crawl space under the church. It was so out of plumb I had to screw it to the wall to keep it from falling over. We used everything at our disposal and tried everything we could think of to help that little church grow.

My brother-in-law, a youth pastor at the time in Birmingham, brought his youth group over, out of the kindness of his heart, to give us a hand. Together, we canvassed the town on a Saturday morning, inviting all the young people we could find to join us for a party at the church that night. We set up a film projector, built a 50-foot banana split down the center aisle, and waited with great anticipation to see what God would do. When the appointed time came, only one young man showed up, accompanied by his grandmother, who clearly thought he needed to get out more. I drowned my disappointment that night in three to four feet of banana split.

Fourteen months later, I moved my young family across the state to our second posting, excited for a fresh start. Though the church was small, we loved the town and grew to love the people. I have many happy memories from there. Sweet tea and southern cooking, our first house, and Dianne, like a pioneer woman, up on the roof in the fall, sweeping away the pine needles. On Saturday's in the summer, I'd mow the grass around the church wearing dress pants, dress shoes and a tie. I was a *real* pastor, after all, and felt I needed to dress the part. Three years in, I had a dustup with a long-time elder. One of the young ladies in the church had accused him of inappropriate behavior. I felt it was my duty to confront him and the fallout split the church. We, then, spent a long and painful year trying to right the ship, to no avail. Our lives were threatened, though we never took it seriously. We were regularly harassed. We'd get phone calls in the middle of the night, waking up the baby, only for the person on the other end to hang up without saying a word. One older couple, who I visited faithfully for four years, told me in parting, "You've really torn up the church." The pain I felt at that moment was profound. Their words left a mark on me. Though my actions were justified, if not overzealous, I shouldered the full weight of responsibility. I was five years into my career as a pastor and I already felt like a failure.

Moving on to a larger church in my home state of Pennsylvania, I felt I had finally hit the big time. The best part was that I accepted the position two full years before what one pastor told me was "the age of marketability." "You can't get a big church until you're at least thirty," he said. "You're simply not marketable." "Marketable?" I thought. "What an odd thing to say," but that was the pool I was swimming in. Now that I think about it, it hasn't changed much. Pastors, like everyone else, can be incredibly competitive. I've been condescended to more times that I can remember by pastors whose churches were larger than mine. I've, no doubt, done the same thing to others. Bigger is always better, we're told, especially in our consumer-oriented culture. The measure of your worth, as a pastor here in the United States, is often based on what my friend, Marty, calls the three B's — Bucks, Buildings and Butts in the seats. It took years for me to learn that just because it's big doesn't mean it's God. Lots of things grow wholly apart from God, some without any reference to God. It took me even longer to discover that my sense of identity, worth, and value was based on roles and titles instead of God.

The church in Pennsylvania had an eighty-year history, which is a wonderful thing. Eighty years of ministry in the same community is something to be celebrated. What wasn't so wonderful was that it took me the better part of a year to realize I wasn't the leader. This was a board-run church, had been for years, and I was a hireling. It's not a criticism. It's just the way it was. Half of the twelve members of the board were from a single, prominent family. I would propose and they would depose, batting away my suggestions like one would dismiss a small child. Inexplicably, the church flourished. Young people were finding us, attendance swelled. We had some wonderful times together, but the growth introduced a new tension as the 'originals' worried things would change and they *were* changing. Though I would never have admitted it, I was completely out of my depth, over my head in the shallows of all places, and the stress started showing up in unexpected ways. I was angry inside, losing sleep, eating poorly, anxious all the time. Eventually, I found myself in the emergency room of a local hospital, so depressed I could barely hold my head up. The weight of expectations — those of others and my own — was tearing me up inside and I felt helpless, pulled along by *shoulds and oughts*. Three years later, under immense pressure, I left.

What now? Well, without the benefit of counsel or common sense, I planted a church. It seemed like the logical thing to do. I was done with established churches. I'd had my fill of boards, dysfunctional DNA, the keepers of the tribal legends and the ghosts of pastors past. I was sure I could do it better — church the way it was meant to be! — if I started from scratch. So I wrote a twenty-page philosophy of ministry full of grandiose ideas and deep convictions. I developed a strategic plan and, gathering a handful of friends from my last church, I launched the new church on January 1, 1993. I was not yet thirty-two years old, less than six months removed from the painful breakup with my last church. I was, as they say, on the rebound, still hurting over what happened. I had not taken the time to heal. I was not even aware of how deeply wounded I was, and my motives were anything but pure. I wanted to prove them all wrong, every naysayer at every church who had ever written me off.

Here's what I learned. Church planting is hard! Two years in, Dianne and I attended a Vineyard conference in Canada. That first night, as the meeting wore on and John Wimber spoke, I had this growing sense of emptiness in my soul. The church was struggling. Nothing was working. I was also secretly angry with God, so angry I went to the conference under protest. I didn't want to be around the annoying lovers of Jesus. I didn't want anybody to ask me about my church. I didn't want their advice or their sympathy or their prayers. I just wanted to be left alone. I was frustrated, fed up, ready to quit again, seething inside. It seemed like everything I touched in ministry turned to poo.

John stopped preaching, started the ministry time, and Dianne and I stood for worship. She immediately closed her eyes and raised her hands. I, on the other hand, was completely disinterested and couldn't wait to get out of there. After a few minutes, I noticed she was weeping and trembling. "Oh, great," I thought with mild irritation. "She's under the influence of the Spirit and we're going to be here all night." Several minutes passed and, gathering herself, Dianne slipped out and headed to the back of the auditorium to pick up our kids. Relieved, I sat down to await her return. When she didn't come back immediately, I turned around, wondering what was keeping her. To my surprise, I saw her lying on the carpet at the back of the room with our 10-year-old, 8-year-old and 5-year-old standing around her, staring wide-eyed in amazement. Jumping to my feet, I ran over and asked her what was going on. Softly, she smiled and said, "I can't move." Stupidly, I said something like, "Did you fall? Did you hear anything pop?" "No, Mark," she replied firmly, "It's the Holy Spirit. I can feel Him all over me. I was completely overwhelmed." Exasperated, I said, "Well, what do you want me to do?" "I want you to go get prayer," she said without hesitating. "Me?" I replied. "Why?" "Because," she said, "you need it more than I do."

Shaken, I mumbled something to a friend about monitoring my kids, and walked over to the line where people were getting prayer. I stood there with my eyes closed for several minutes, half-heartedly asking God for grace and before anyone came to pray for me, before anyone even came near me, the Spirit of the Lord wrapped Himself around me like the blanket I described in the last chapter. I instantly felt this exquisite heaviness, this profound Presence, and it was like all the wind was driven from my lungs. Struggling to take a breath, I started confessing sin rapid fire, begging God for forgiveness, while the downward pressure increased. Soon, my legs gave way, and I was on my knees and finally I was on my back, glued to the carpet, absolutely incapacitated, utterly unable to move. I couldn't even open my eyes. I know because I tried!

Then, I heard someone praying softly, blessing what God was doing, praying that God would go deep and did He ever. What followed was three hours of inner healing. The Spirit addressed my anger, He put His finger on my pride, He confronted my disappointment, bitterness and fear. He healed my broken past and gave me an early glimpse of my false self, the beta-version I'd present to others, my perfect pastor alter ego, the me I desperately wanted to be. The release and sense of peace was so wonderful, joy welled up inside me. I laughed. I couldn't stop laughing. People around me started laughing with me and at me, no doubt. I laughed for three hours and, as the heaviness lifted, I heard the Spirit say, "Mark, you are my delight. Don't ever forget that." "I won't," I said, choking it out through tears and laughter. "I won't."

Exploring the False Self

Well, I'm sorry to say, I did. I quickly forgot what He said to me that night. As blessed as I was by the encounter and as happy as I was to experience His delight, I eventually slid back into the familiar lead-lined suit of my driven, performance-oriented, false self, looking for identity, worth and value in roles and titles instead of simply who I am in Christ. Who am I? That's the question I was trying to answer, and I am not alone. Our culture has long encouraged folks to go on a journey of self-discovery — to eat, pray and love their way to a whole new way of life — particularly in middle age. And young people, like every generation before them, continue to rush unknowingly down one dead-end street after another — trying on personas, putting on masks, taking up causes, staking out positions, all to set themselves apart. Who can blame them? We all want to think we're special. We want to feel special. Well, the good news is, you *are* special, "fearfully and wonderfully made"[98] by a Creator who is head-over-heels in love with you. You are special to Him. No matter what you do, you will always be special to Him.

To paraphrase Augustine of Hippo, "He has made us for Himself, and our hearts are restless until they find rest in Him."[99] I was young and restless. Many people are young and restless. A lot of older folks are restless, too. This explains why our culture is such a soap opera! As Billy Graham noted at a 1998 crusade in Ottawa, Canada, "We live on a diet of up-to-the-minute news and 15-minute celebrities, while we ache for a transcendent, timeless touch. The information age may go down in history as the period when our culture forgot the most important thing: That our souls need to breathe and grow. We're separated from God. We're dead people walking."[100] Whether you agree with Graham's assessment or not, you have to consider the idea that technology and social media are simply the latest means by which folks are trying to satisfy the longing of their souls. Our souls need to breathe and grow, and they can't do that when they're separated from God.

Who am I? The answer varies. I'm a socialist, a communist, a capitalist. I'm a democrat, a republican, an independent. I'm pro-this or pro-that, anti-this or anti-that. We label ourselves. We label others. Labels are limiting. It's a way of minimizing and marginalizing while elevating self and our culture is addicted to it. We just can't help ourselves. One way to feel special is to identify others as less special. So we have the enlightened and the unenlightened, people like us and people like them. We call people fascists and racists when they simply disagree with us. Even as Christians, we often settle for labels and modifiers to describe who we think we are. "Tell me about yourself," someone might ask. And for years, I would reply, "I'm a pastor, teacher," or some variation on the theme. As David Benner wrote, "Although I have always wanted to avoid being defined by my professional role, when asked to introduce myself, I am likely to resort to the common social practice of trotting out vocational designations. But, even more telling, if my self-esteem is threatened and I feel my identity to be a bit vulnerable, my almost automatic first response is to think of accomplishments or present and future projects. What this tells me is that much more than I usually care to acknowledge, my identity is based on what I do, not who I am."[101] I call this sharing your verbal résumé. I did it for years. If you always lead with your verbal CV — the roles you play, the titles you've acquired, the labels people ascribe to you, your achievements, and successes — if that's who you think you are, you're living out of a false identity, separated from God.

The problem with "I'm a parent, a leader, a singer, a teacher, a doctor, an entrepreneur, a stay-at-home-mom, a business owner or a caregiver" is, what happens to your sense of worth and value when you lose your job, when your kids want nothing to do with you, when the people you thought you were leading start following someone else, when you retire? What happens when you get repurposed at work, when they assign you a new role, when they ask you to do something you weren't hired to do? The genesis of every mid-life crisis is a sense of dissatisfaction over your current lot in life. At the root of all of that is an identity crisis, not a mid-life crisis. It isn't chronological, it's that you spent your life cultivating a carefully crafted image and you suddenly don't know who you are anymore. You wonder what it was all for. You're off balance. The foundations of your life, who you thought you were, have been rocked. What you've always been and done you suddenly can't do and be anymore and if you're not that, you wonder, then who are you?

A Piece of Work

The followers of Jesus should never suffer from an identity crisis. Our true identity has already been established by virtue of our relationship with Jesus Christ. Do you want to know who you truly are? While the world searches for identity, significance, and validation, the followers of Jesus are invited to rest in the Father's love. Who am I? You "are God's handiwork, created in Christ Jesus to do good works, which God prepared in advance for [you] to do (Ephesians 2:10)." The word "handiwork" might bring to mind a number of things, both positive and negative. A straight line definition of the word would be the work of our hands, the result of our labors, something homemade. Your reaction to the word might have a lot to do with how you were raised.

When I think of handiwork, I think of something you might make in shop class or buy at a craft fair. Paint by number was popular when I was growing up. This is all handiwork, in my mind. The word became synonymous in my family, with something fairly crude, unprofessional, lacking in quality, inexpensive but fun to do. That's what I think of when I think of handiwork. When I think of handiwork, I think of a time when my dear mother discovered a mural I'd created with nothing but a box of crayons on a wall in the upstairs bathroom and, when my father asked her what happened, she replied, "This is Mark's handiwork." When I think of handiwork, I think of the countless ceramic dolphins, starfish and sea horses available at practically every store you might walk into while on vacation in Florida or the ubiquitous black bear figurine you absolutely have to have after you've spent a couple of days inhaling the mountain air in Colorado. The salesperson in me says, "They wouldn't sell them if they didn't sell," which brings up the whole idea of the things we buy while on vacation that we would never buy at home. Handiwork.

When I think of handiwork, I think about a time when I was seven or eight years old. It was a week before Christmas and I wanted to give my mother something special. Never one to think small, I decided to make her a dress. It was the late 1960s and I have fond memories of my mother going about the household chores wearing a day dress, pumps and the ubiquitous string of pearls. I have a very specific memory of her ironing, dressed in a light tan, sleeveless number with a full skirt, like she'd just come from a [fruit] cocktail party. Determined to add to her wardrobe, I went to the family rag bin, found an old sheet, laid it out on the floor of my bedroom, folded it in half and, using an El Marko marker, I traced the outline of a dress I thought would fit my mom. One arm was laughably longer than the other. The skirt, had I finished it, would have been scandalously short. I cut it out, put the two pieces of cloth together and, taking a needle and thread, I began sewing. The stitches were uneven to say the least, long looping swings through the fabric followed by an inch or two of manic detail. Imagine my surprise, after several minutes, when my handiwork didn't resemble the dresses my mother routinely wore. I was devastated at my incompetence. And that's how my mother found me — sitting alone on the floor of my room over a rumbled bed sheet, with a needle and thread in my hand, sobbing. Thus ended my promising career as a fashion designer. She still has it, by the way, tucked away in her cedar chest along with all her other "treasures." That's what I think of when I think of handiwork.

Then I met my wife, and my perspective on handiwork changed. Growing up in Africa with limited resources, she believed that the very best gifts are often homemade, the things that require thought, creativity, planning, and skill. For our first Christmas, she presented me with a small plaque upon which she had wood-burned a verse from Isaiah 43 in a flowing cursive that I treasure to this day. I treasure it because it's her incredibly beautiful penmanship. It brings her to mind every time I look at it because it has her stamp on it, an unmistakable echo of herself resident in it. We treasure handiwork because the hands that made it are precious; they mean something to us.

So, when the Apostle Paul writes, "You are God's handiwork," he's saying a lot! You were originally made in His image and remade the moment you trusted in Jesus Christ by the power of the Holy Spirit. If you're a follower of Jesus, His unmistakable signature, the imprint of His hand is on your life. No matter how far from God you might wander, there's still an echo, a watermark, however faint, that points to the one who made and remade you. That's good, but we can take it a step further. The Greek word translated "handiwork" sometimes refers to "a work of art."[102] As a result, the word "handiwork" could also be translated "masterpiece."

Art Appreciation

See if you can get your hands around this — if you're a follower of Jesus, you are a masterpiece of God! Not a piece of work, a masterpiece! Let me pause there a moment. As you think of yourself as a one-of-a-kind masterpiece of God, how does that make you feel? What is your initial reaction? Does it bring a smile to your face or do you sense some resistance? Perhaps it's your own internal voice saying, "That can't possibly be true." If so, I get it. I felt the same way. Until the transformative work God began in my life, as I responded to Him at the age of fifty-two, I had a very low opinion of myself. I simply couldn't believe it. Maybe it's because I was so intimately acquainted with my own weaknesses, so conscious of my own flaws and preoccupied with my besetting sins that, despite the miracle of new birth, I became convinced I was simply not that special and would probably never be special no matter how much Jesus puttered, dabbed and detailed or chipped, filed and sanded me over the years. But that's the thing. He wasn't finished with me yet.

I think it was C.S. Lewis who said, "God works on us over the course of our lives, patiently shaping us to be more like His Son, and when we die, we're about half done." When I heard that the first time, I laughed out loud. "That sounds about right. I'm loaded with half-baked ideas." But half-baked, when you think about it, is still a work in progress, especially when you're in the hands of God, the Master Baker. We need to "trust in the slow work of God. We are quite naturally impatient in everything to reach the end without delay. We should like to skip the intermediate stages. We are impatient of being on the way to something unknown, something new. And yet it is the law of all progress that it is made by passing through some stages of instability — and that it may take a very long time. And so I think it is with you; your ideas mature gradually — let them grow, let them shape themselves, without undue haste. Don't try to force them on, as though you could be today what time (that is to say, grace and circumstances acting on your own good will) will make of you tomorrow. Only God could say what this new spirit gradually forming within you will be. Give our Lord the benefit of believing that His hand is leading you and accept the [uncertainty] of feeling yourself in suspense and incomplete."[103] Can you accept the uncertainty? Are you willing to live in the tension between what you were, who you are, and what He is making you to be? Will you submit to the process, His ongoing work in your life?

Look. It's easy to see God as a Master, *the* Master, the genesis of all creation, who created from nothing, without precedent and without inspiration. For nothing preceded Him, before Him nothing else existed and apart from Him nothing was made that has been made.[104] The greatest painter who has ever lived, the most gifted sculptor, the most creative musician, the most visionary architect, the most brilliant mathematician, draw their inspiration from Him whether they know it or not. And though they try, their most breathtaking creations can't begin to match the beauty of His splendor. I see the handprint of God, whispers of Him, in every created thing. That's the easy part. It's easy for me to think of God as the ultimate Master. What's infinitely harder is the idea that I might be one of His masterpieces, one of His great works upon the earth. I always see myself as a work in progress, roughed in but hardly finished, and how can a work in progress ever be considered a masterpiece? Then again, I'm reminded that every great work of art was, at one point, a work in progress. And many artists, I have heard, never consider a work completely finished. There's always something more, something else that could be done.

An Impressionist's Delight

For example, though I'm not, by any stretch of the imagination, an art historian, I love Monet's Water Lilies. In 1893, Monet, a passionate horticulturist and French Impressionist painter, purchased land with a pond near his property in Giverny, intending to build something "for the pleasure of the eye and also for motifs to paint." The result was his water-lily garden, which he painted in great detail, assembling the forty large-scale panels in a "circular installation [meant] to envelop the viewer in an expanse of water, flora, and sky."[105] Several panels are on display at the Musée de l'Orangerie in Paris. It's an immersive experience. The paintings appear to change before your eyes, details emerging and disappearing as you move closer or further away. The first time I went, I stood for more than an hour in rapt fascination, turning slowly in the center of an oval-shaped room, trying in vain to take in the grandeur of the panoramic. It was simply captivating. I had a similar experience a few years later when one of the "Water Lilies" triptychs, separated in the 1960s — the three panels sold to three different museums — were reunited for a time at the Nelson-Atkins Museum here in Kansas City. It reminded me of why I love Monet. The paintings are evocative, but also peaceful. But here's where I prove that, when it comes to fine art, I'm still a neophyte. I left the prime viewing area and walked up to one of the panels for a closer look, the image of the peaceful pond disappearing in the busyness of a million seemingly unrelated brush strokes. I read, somewhere, that Monet was one of those artists who could get lost in his work, forever tweaking, and I could see how that was possible. My first thought was, "How in the world did he ever know the painting was finished? Surely, someone who loved him must have taken pity on him one day and said, 'Claude, you're obsessed. You need to stop. Put the brush down, my friend.'" Every panel remains a work in progress and yet still a masterpiece.

The point is, if you're a follower of Jesus, you are incredibly blessed. You're blessed to be the work of His hands, blessed to be molded and shaped by the Master, blessed by His flawless sense of beauty, His infinite perspective, His dogged attention to detail, His love of symmetry and irregularity, harmony and dissonance. You're blessed that, by the miracle of grace, God took a smashed and broken pot and is in the process of recasting it into the image of His Son. You're blessed because you're part of a grand mosaic, a painting of countless panels that stretches across time into eternity, the greatest single work of art in human history, the body of Christ! And He's not finished. He's not finished with me and He's not finished with you.

Finding your purpose, doing what God made you to do is *not* foremost about doing. It begins with being, with embracing your true identity in Christ. That's where you'll find significance, not in what you do for God, but in who you truly are. Before you can effectively join God in what He's doing, you've got to settle a few things, a few foundational things, or your gifts, abilities, personality, what you're passionate about, and your life experience won't take you very far. You won't find significance, you'll simply end up on a treadmill of performance like I did and you'll ultimately give up. Doing things for God, serving apart from a deep understanding of who you really are in Christ, is like trying to fire a cannon from a canoe. Without a proper foundation in who you truly are in Christ, you'll eventually capsize. You are not what you do. Your work does not define you. Your service does not define you. Your gifts do not define you. It's not about what you do, it's about who you are. What you do flows from who you are. "Instead of, 'You are what you do,' calling says: 'Do what you are.'"[106]

Your True Identity Revealed

Who are you? If you're a follower of Jesus, you are a masterpiece of God. But that's just one image, one descriptor of your true identity in Christ. The Bible offers so many more.

- You are *forgiven*. 1 John 1:9 says, "If we confess our sins, He is faithful and just to *forgive* us our sins and purify us from all unrighteousness."

- *You were chosen.* Ephesians 1:4 says, "He *chose* us in Him before the creation of the world to be holy and blameless in His sight."

- *You were adopted into God's family.* Romans 8:15 says, "The Spirit you received does not make you slaves, so that you live in fear again; rather, the Spirit you received brought about your *adoption* to sonship. And by Him we cry, 'Abba, Father.'" God is your Father and you are His dearly loved adopted son or daughter.

- *You contain Him.* Galatians 2:20 says, "I have been crucified with Christ and I no longer live, but Christ *lives* in me."

- *You belong to Him.* Romans 14:7-8 says, "For none of us lives for ourselves alone, and none of us dies for ourselves alone. If we live, we live for the Lord; and if we die, we die for the Lord. So, whether we live or die, we *belong* to the Lord."

- You are *loved.* 1 John 3:1 says, "See what great love the Father has lavished on us, that we should be called children of God! And that is what we are!"

He's talking about your true identity as a follower of Jesus. The things that never change. You're forgiven, chosen, adopted. You contain Him; you belong to Him, and you are loved. Say it aloud to your Father, "Because you forgave me, chose me and adopted me into your family. I contain you, I belong to you and I am loved!"

The choice of adoption was entirely the Father's, and it was motivated by love. Adoption, as you know, is a legal action by which a person takes into his family a child who is not his own, who has no rights within that family, in order to give that child all the privileges of their natural-born children. It's an incredibly beautiful and powerful thing. A few years ago, our extended family gathered at the County Courthouse on National Adoption Day to welcome my granddaughter, Angelina, and my grandson, Mark, into the family. My daughter, Brittany, and her husband, Matthew, had been fostering to adopt for some time. I'm not sure about the number, but I think they provided a foster home for thirty-one children over a four-year period, so you can imagine our excitement when we got the news that Mark and Angie would be officially joining our family. It was a memorable day for all of us.

As the ceremony began, my daughter- and son-in-law appeared before the court and, after they were sworn in, with the children literally climbing all over them, the state attorney asked them a series of questions. I don't remember her exact words, but it was something like this. "Are you acquainted with these children, their background, situation, personality and health concerns?" "We are," they replied. "Do you understand, and are you willing to accept the responsibility and honor of becoming their parents? Will you faithfully care for them and provide for their physical, emotional, developmental and financial well-being, securing their future?" "We will," they answered again. "Then," the attorney said, "knowing these things and carefully considering the implications of this decision, do you desire to adopt these children as your own, believing it to be in the children's best interests?" "We do," they said happily, and we all broke into applause. It was an incredible day. Adoption is a beautiful, sacrificial thing to do, especially when it's done with the best of intentions, motivated by compassion and compelled by unconditional love. That's what God did for you! You may have decided to follow Jesus but you wouldn't have been able to make that decision if He hadn't first taken the initiative to make you His son or daughter, if He hadn't decided to love you lavishly, extravagantly, generously, if He hadn't chosen you.

My brother, Eric, loves to dig into our family ancestry. I say, "Let sleeping dogs lie!" Why? Because for every interesting tidbit he unearths, he seems to uncover two things I didn't really want to know. For example, my ancestors back in Scotland fought with Robert the Bruce in the battle of Falkirk (think *Braveheart*). They fought with distinction. They fought like warrior poets. It was a long time ago, but it still fills me with pride. It makes me want to paint my face blue, don my kilt and raise the family colors. He also told me we're Sons of the Revolution. Again, that's good, but then I found out that my ancestor fought alongside Benedict Arnold before he became infamous. Not so good. By far, though, the most unsettling thing Eric discovered is that I'm not technically a Warner. Sometime in the late fourteenth century, John Warner, Esquire, of Norfolk County, having no children of his own and no near relation bearing his name, adopted the younger son of his closest friend, Sir James Whetenhale, and left him the family fortune, such as it was. That's when a Whetenhale became a Warner, combining elements of both family crests into a fresh coat of arms. It's fascinating but a little unsettling. I'm actually a Whetenhale by blood and a Warner by…who knows what? Fortunately, I've been learning about my true identity in Christ or I might have drifted for years trying to "find myself." At the very least, I would have sought therapy to get in touch with my inner Whetenhale. "Why, John Warner, why? Why would you do that?" I cried. Just kidding. There are a host of reasons. My ancestor was motivated by a desire to sustain the family name and transfer his wealth. God adopted us, at significant cost to Himself, because He was motivated by perfect love. I mean, there was nothing especially attractive about us or deserving in us to draw out that love, but God loved us, anyway. We can hardly comprehend it, let alone accept it.

As David Jackman wrote, "I suppose it's because God's love is unconditional and limitless that we human beings find it very hard to accept. Many of the Christians I meet have never known a love like that in any other relationship. In childhood, they learned that their parents' approval and love had to be earned by conforming to their dictates and living up to their expectations. And because they could never be good enough, or achieve enough, they were never sure of being accepted."[107] He went on to mention a student he had who called his father to tell him about his success on his exams. When he finished, his father said, "Good, that means we can still be friends." Can you imagine that? "Dad, I got an 'A' on my exams." "Good, that means we can still be friends." That way of thinking — my love, acceptance, and favor depend upon your performance — cuts deeply into the soul. It's easy, then, when you grew up with a mom or dad like that, to transfer the same assumption into your relationship with God, to believe that God is like your parents. Some of you may not even be aware, because of the way you were raised, that when you think about God, your heavenly Father, when you look at Him, you're looking through the cracked and broken lens of your earthly father, mother or some other authority figure. I've met a lot of Christians who have a very hard time receiving love in general, let alone God's extravagant, unconditional, superabundant love. If that's you, you might say to someone else, "God loves you," but you might stumble over the phrase, "God loves me."

God's Delight

Seven centuries before Jesus' arrival, the Father said, "Here is my servant, whom I uphold, my chosen one in whom I delight; I will put my Spirit on Him, and He will bring justice to the nations (Isaiah 42:1)." Jesus was chosen by God, a delight to the Father. The language here points us to someone who is thoroughly loved, thoroughly enjoyed and highly favored, a chosen servant who pleases the Father in everything He says and does. Man, I wanted that. I wanted that for myself. I wanted God to delight in me like God, the Father delights in Jesus. I wanted to be thoroughly loved, thoroughly enjoyed and highly favored, a chosen servant who pleases the Father in everything he says and does. I know that sounds like a lot to ask. I'm *not* Jesus, but Jesus lives in me, so it has to be possible. After all, I'm forgiven, chosen, adopted, containing, belonging and beloved. If I could learn somehow to live authentically, out of my true identity, based on the things that never change, who God says I am, instead of being held captive by the lies of my false self, is it possible that I, too, could experience the love, delight and favor of the Father as a daily, lived reality in my life? Yes, yes, yes!

I'll tell you how I began that journey, out of my false self and into my true identity in Christ, but first, let me ask you again, "What do you think God thinks of when He thinks of you?" In my experience, it is the rarest human being who believes they're a delight to God. More often, we feel like a disappointment. I'm often disappointed in myself. I come away from one conversation or another and think, "Why did I say that? Why did I talk so much? Why wasn't I more affirming? Why didn't we pray together?" Do you ever go back over your conversations and feel bad about what you said? I look at my prayers and often feel inadequate. My first thought in a crisis is not always God. As you look at the various areas of your life, do you have an internal sense of being pleasing to God? Would you say that He delights in you, that He's pleased with you? I'm asking because I think everyone sometimes feels that there's not only something wrong with what they do, there's something fundamentally wrong with who they are! Even if I do absolutely nothing wrong, there's still this occasional sense of shame inside me regarding who I am. The feeling often isn't only that I do wrong, but that I am wrong — self-centered instead of Christ-centered. Do you know what I mean? Have you ever felt that way?

Do you ever inflate your own importance, magnify your gifts, ma-nipulate or even make up stories to make yourself look good? Do you ever excuse your own sins while ghosting others for things that are much smaller by comparison? Can you look at your life and own the fact that you're often lackadaisical when dealing with your own sins, but ruthless when dealing with the mistakes and weaknesses of others? I know this may be one of those things that's easier to see in others than in yourself, but do you see it? I see it in me sometimes. And my experience of being wrong — not just doing wrong — my experience of shame causes me to want to cover up. This happens to all of us. We want to cover up. We want to hide. We create false selves and masks through which we relate to God and the world. Which brings me back to the question: What is it going to take for you and I to please God? What is it going to take for God to look at our lives and say about us what He says about Jesus?

Is it possible that we could ever go to God without a mask, as we truly are, with our actual feelings, flaws and sins and still be His delight? We try so hard to be pleasing to God, but nothing seems to work. We have a temporary sense of being okay, but then we fall back into a greater sense of shame and guilt. Who does God delight in? God loves His Son. He's completely and thoroughly pleased with Jesus. What is the secret of you and I being pleasing to God? How do we win His favor and enjoy His delight? The secret is this: As you are connected to Jesus; hidden in Jesus; as you look to Jesus by faith; trust Jesus; cling to Jesus; yield to Jesus; follow Jesus; as you're attached to Jesus, you share in His favor.

An Underwear Story

Jesus gives us our identity. He enables us to lay down all the false selves we've so meticulously built for ourselves and embrace our true identity. It reminds me of something a friend of mine said at a meeting several years ago. He was standing in a group of leaders, engaged in casual conversation, and one leader happened to mention, multiple times in the space of a couple of minutes, that he had several thousand followers on YouTube. He dropped that little piece of information into the conversation three or four times without taking a breath, prompting my mischievous friend to ask, "Did you stitch that into your underwear?" "Pardon me?" the leader replied. "Did you stitch that into your underwear?" my friend repeated with a wry smile. "I'm asking because you've mentioned your YouTube following four times now in the last five minutes. I just wondered if that's who you think you are."

I cringed when I heard the story. That could easily have been me. I don't have thousands of followers on YouTube or anywhere else for that matter, but I did have, for years, a carefully crafted false self that I propped up by regularly touting my achievements. It also reminded me of something from my distant past. Before my mom sent me off to kindergarten in 1966, she sewed labels with my name on them into practically everything I owned. It was a common practice at the time and for good reason. Sewing a label into a coat or book bag which are easily lost makes sense. But my mom sewed my name and phone number into my pants, shirts, socks, sweaters, even my underwear. What did she think we were doing in kindergarten? It was only half a day! How many clothes can a boy lose in half a day? How many kids are going to steal the shirt right off your back, let alone your underwear? She tagged me in as many places as she could think of, even stitching my name and phone number into the Superband Waistband of my Fruit of the Looms. Call it force of habit. I have two brothers, one older and one younger, both fairly close in age. When we were younger, my mom got into the habit of tagging our clothes so she could tell them apart when they came through the laundry. For the first six or seven years of my life, I rarely wore a piece of clothing that didn't have my name or initials stitched into some inconspicuous place.

It goes, of course, to the question of identity. Who do you think you are? Are you, as some believe, the sum total of your life experiences — your roles, titles, gifts and abilities, achievements and accomplishments? Is that who you are? Are you looking to those things for a sense of identity, worth and value — to define you, validate you? Have you stitched them into your underwear? What are you wearing next to your skin? What skin are you in?

A few Christmases ago, I woke up to find a present on the end of my bed. Dianne has often done little things like that for me over the years, but this one was special. When I opened it, it was a three-pack of my favorite underwear. "You're giving me underwear?" I asked, a bit surprised. Grinning, she replied, "Take a closer look." I opened the package, pulled out the first pair and then I noticed it, stitched into the waistband were the words, "Forgiven, Chosen." I pulled out the next pair. "Adopted, Containing." I pulled out the third pair, "Belonging, Beloved." Forgiven, chosen, adopted, containing, belonging, beloved! "I didn't want you to forget your true identity," she said, "so I stitched it into your underwear." Isn't that phenomenal? I'm wearing a pair right now!

Seeing the Difference

Jesus in us roots us in our true identity. As David Benner wrote, "There is no true life apart from relationship to God. Therefore, there can be no true self apart from this relationship. The foundation of our identity resides in our life-giving relationship with the Source of life. Any identity that exists apart from this relationship is an illusion."[108] Okay. I think I know what he means. Your true identity emerges from your relationship with God. Everything else is just an illusion, a construct, a disguise. Benner goes on to offer a simple chart to help you recognize the difference (See below).[109]

The False Self	The True Self
Security and significance achieved by what we have, what we can do and what others think of us	Security and significance achieved by being deeply loved by God
Happiness sought in autonomy from God and in attachments	Fulfillment found in surrender to God and living our vocation
Identity is our idealized self (who we want others to think we are)	Identity is who we are — and are becoming — in Christ
Achieved by means of pretense and practice	Received as a gift with gratitude and surrender
Maintained by effort and control	Maintained by grace
Embraces illusion as a means of attempting to become a god	Embraces reality as the place of meeting and being transformed by God

Surely, you can see the difference. I couldn't. I mean, I can *now,* but I couldn't then. My security and significance were largely based on what I had, what I could do, and what others thought of me. My pursuit of happiness was more about doing what I wanted instead of complete dependence upon God. My identity was rooted in the me I wanted to be, the image I projected and the story I told myself about myself. I lived this way for years, bending over backwards to maintain the illusion until I finally came apart. I'm grateful that it happened, grateful that God, in His mercy, awakened me from my reverie. But what now? How do you change a lifelong habit? How do you stop living the illusion and start living out of your true identity, who God says you are? How do you separate from your own strength and ultimately find your identity in Christ?

Prayer of Recollection

As I wrestled with what God was revealing to me, growing in self-awareness, I was introduced to the *Prayer of Recollection.*[110] What a wonderful tool! *The Prayer of Recollection* quickly became a staple of my time with God. I prayed it every day for years, using it as a launch point for long conversations. Even now, ten years later, it's still a regular part of my spiritual life. Why? Because there are things I need to remember that I forget, things I need to remind myself of so I don't fall into the same hole, walk the same well-worn path or drift back into the illusion of my false self. *The Prayer of Recollection* is a helpful tool for those who want to leave a left-column life, living apart from God, for a right-column life, living in total dependence upon God (see Benner's chart).

The prayer has three parts. "The first part helps you name your limitations as a finite person while also affirming that this is not the end of the story."[111] The second part is a declaration that God is more than enough and reminds you of His loving involvement in your life. In the third part, you immerse yourself in what God says about you, laying aside your false identity while embracing the truth. It's simple but effective — a tool, a soul-training exercise, a means to a deeper, more intimate love relationship with Jesus, a gateway to deeper dependence upon God. It took me a while to get comfortable with it but, over time, I was able to memorize the movements so I could pray it with my eyes closed, allowing the truth to permeate my soul. Here are the *Three Affirmations of Recollection*. As you pray this prayer, you might begin as I do. Dear, dear Father…

1. I am a finite human being, and apart from you I can do nothing. But your grace is made manifest in my weakness and I can do all things through Christ who gives me strength (John 15:5; 2 Corinthians 12:9; Philippians 4:13).

2. I affirm today that the Lord is my Shepherd [Father, Friend, Creator, Savior], I will want for nothing (Psalm 23:1). Note: Choose a title of God to carry with you that communicates to you God's tender care and loving involvement in your life. This declaration became such an important part of my journey out of my false self. So much so, I wrote a brief reflection on who God is to me. It's not exhaustive, but you might find it helpful. It goes like this: "You are the Father who loves me, the Shepherd who guides me, the Savior who rescues me, the Friend who stands beside me. You are the Lover who pursues me, the Master who takes ownership of me, the Redeemer who ransomed me and the Lord who lovingly rules and reigns over me. You are the Provider who sustains me, the Deliverer who frees me, the Companion who goes with me, the Judge who pardons me and the Creator who isn't finished with me." Choose one title and make it the theme of your day. Carry it with you. Repeat it to yourself.

3. I name, embrace and celebrate my soul's true identity as one forgiven, chosen, adopted, containing, belonging and beloved. Because you forgave me, chose me and adopted me, I contain you, I belong to you and I am loved. These are the things that never change! At the same time, I let go of all the roles and titles (pastor, president, director, CPA, therapist, father, mother, musician…) that can be a source of identity, worth and value for me apart from who I am in Christ. I lay them all down and choose to live today out of my true self, as a dearly loved child of God. <u>Note</u>: Take your time. I often spend several minutes in prayer meditating on the fact that I'm forgiven and all that that entails. I'm chosen and just how special that is. I'm adopted, a co-heir with Christ, a child of God, etc. You want to make room to allow the truth to soak into your soul. If you do, if you spend time with it, it will become a part of you and, as Jesus said, "you'll recover your life (Matthew 11:28 MSG)."

Finally, take a few moments to be still and ruminate on the truths that God loves you with an everlasting-nothing-can-separate-you-from-His-love love. He is with you, within you. You are a new creation, a one-of-a-kind masterpiece of God created anew and afresh in Christ Jesus.[112]

It's a great prayer, a helpful soul-training exercise, but it's not magic. The fact that I prayed it every day for years was not what ultimately enabled me to walk out of my false self into my true identity in Christ. It's where I started. I want to underline that. I prayed it every day because I needed to be reminded of who I am to Him and who He is to me. I prayed it because I needed to confess my weakness as a finite human being and declare my need for God. I prayed it because I needed a way to reject my false self like one might rebuke a demon and step more fully into the truth of my true identity. As I did that, as I practiced the truth, over and over, I changed. It was slow, almost imperceptible at first. I'd spent so many years in the shallow end of the pool. My false self — built on roles, titles and achievements — was deeply entrenched within me. There were so many lies I'd come to believe about myself, God and others. I've talked about some of that — believing it all depended upon me, wondering why God wasn't doing what I wanted, doubting His goodness at times, feeling unlovable. These things, and so many others, once unearthed by the patient prompting of the Holy Spirit, needed to come out. I filled journal after journal during my time in the *Ignatian Exercises,* and for many years thereafter, bringing my wounds to the feet of the wounded One, asking Him to heal me so I might live as His Beloved. It's a process, a difficult-at-times but glorious process, identifying the lies and asking God to replace them with the truth. But I'm making progress. I'm a work in progress, a masterpiece in the making…just like you. Are you ready to take this journey with Jesus? Are you willing to let Him unearth the lies so you can be free to live as His Beloved?

This is where a TV infomercial might say, "But wait, there's more!" Would you like to know the more there is?

seven

You can Live Freely and Lightly

"Keep company with me and you'll learn to live freely and lightly."
~ Matthew 11:30 (MSG)

"Choose evermore rather to have less than more. Seek ever the lower place
and to be under all. Desire ever to pray that the will of God be all and
wholly done. So such a one enters the land of peace and quiet."[113]
~ Thomas à Kempis

My first ever fishing trip was unforgettable, but not in that wistfully glorious, falling in love, Nat King Cole sort of way. I was eight years old, an ordinary boy living happily in a small, predictable world that included our house, backyard, school and church. Those were the days, and that was my life until my dad slipped quietly into my room, early one Saturday morning, to wake me. It was the first day of trout season and I'll never forget it because it also happened to be my birthday. Mom had breakfast on the table when my brothers and I came stumbling down the stairs, the tantalizing scent of pancakes, maple syrup, and bacon drawing us to the kitchen at the back of the house. When we had eaten our fill, my mom produced a birthday cake with eight candles. It was, then, time to open presents. Do you know how weird it is to open birthday presents at four o'clock in the morning? It was still dark out! "Tear into that paper, son," my dad said eagerly. "We need to get on the road. The early bird catches the worm." Nodding sleepily, I opened the first present, and it was a fishing pole, rod, and reel. I opened the next one, and it was a tackle box with lots of...*tackle* in it — hooks, bobbers, sinkers, and salmon eggs. I opened the third present, and it was a little brown fishing vest and matching hat, just my size. I remember it like it was yesterday. Why is that birthday so memorable? There were no toys or, at least, no toys I wanted to play with.

Piling into the car, we drove until the pavement turned to dirt then pulling off the road, we parked in the woods, collected our gear and walked down a seemingly endless, overgrown path until we came to Elk Creek and my Dad's favorite fishing hole. As the sun stubbornly gathered itself and made an appearance, my older brother, Dave, opened his tackle box and dutifully set about baiting his hook while I chattered incessantly, threw stones in the water and ran up and down the bank. My Dad, with the patience of Job, whispered a torrent of well-practiced mini-correctives, trying desperately to regain my attention and get me under control. "Okay," he said urgently, handing me my pole once he got my line in the water, "it's time to settle down and fish." "Stop running. Leave those stones alone. Quiet, you're scaring the fish." "I'm scaring the fish?" I inquired, bemused that fish could be scared and thinking of a thousand ways to do it. Who knew fishing could be so stimulating? That's when the fun began.

Dave hit the button on his reel, threw the baited hook over his shoulder and, with a snap of the wrist, sent it flying toward the water. At that very moment, the bobber on my line suddenly disappeared, the weight of the fish on the other end nearly liberating the pole from my hand. Surprised, I started screaming just as Dave's hook came flying forward, catching my dad by the ear. The hook, lodged in the soft tissue of my dad's left earlobe, grabbed hold and wouldn't let go. The confused earthworm Dave used as bait became a kind of odd, dangling earring as my dad stumbled toward the water in pain. Unaware he had dad on the other end of the line, Dave was so excited, he instinctively started reeling him in. See if you can picture the scene: Me screaming for help, holding desperately to my new fishing pole while a man-sized rainbow trout dragged me down the slippery bank toward the water. Dave, reeling in what he thought was a whopper, a fish so big it would have set a record in those parts if only my dad had been willing to be weighed and measured. And my poor dad, pulled painfully forward and then backward against his will, held fast by a hook that was determined to leave a mark, confused by what was happening to him, with blood streaming down his neck, his two sons oblivious to what had befallen him. It had to feel a bit like being locked in a phone booth with a nest of angry bees.

What he did next is the stuff of legend. And, in situations like this, it's what you do next that matters. Lifting his hand to determine the source of his pain, my dad grabbed hold of Dave's line, right behind his left ear, and jerked the pole out of his hands. He then ran into the water, following my line while dragging my brother's pole behind him. I was agog, my mouth hanging open in amazement, as my dad grabbed my fish with his bare hands and threw it twenty-five feet up into the woods. Watching that fish fly by me that day was captivating, a spectacle to say the least. I don't know how the fish felt about it, but I can tell you he looked just as surprised as I was. And it was huge! Delighted with my first "catch," Dave and I danced around it while my dad pulled out a pair of wire cutters and calmly removed the hook from his ear.

The Free and Light Life

This is the story that came to mind as I sat down to write this chapter. It reminds me that the free and light life Jesus promised us, at the end of Matthew 11, is not a life free of difficulty, setbacks, disappointments, trauma and sorrow. Jesus Himself said, "In this world you will have trouble (John 16:33)." But, in the same verse, He also promised us peace — peace in the unpredictable moments of life, peace in the unexpected, peace in our confusion, peace when we're in pain, peace regardless of our circumstances. Let me take you back to Jesus' invitation. "Are you tired? Worn out? Burned out on religion?" Jesus says, "Come to me. Get away with me and you'll recover your life. I'll show you how to take a real rest. Walk with me and work with me — watch how I do it. Learn the unforced rhythms of grace. I won't lay anything heavy or ill-fitting on you. Keep company with me and you'll learn to live freely and lightly (Matthew 11:28-30 MSG)."

This has been the biggest struggle of my life. I've struggled at times to come to Him. I've struggled to regularly get away with Him, to make time for Him. I've struggled to walk with Him, often running ahead or lagging behind. I've struggled to work *with* Him. I've worked *for* Him plenty of times, but not always *with* Him. I've struggled to learn the unforced rhythms of grace, more often pushing, straining, trying to make things happen instead of simply resting in Him. I've struggled to keep company with Him. Truth be told, for years, I wasn't even sure what that meant or how to go about it. For most of my life as a Christian, as a pastor, the promise of the free and light life eluded me. It all came to a head that day in my office, as I described in chapter 1. I was in crisis. I had no idea what exactly had its hooks in me but I was in pain just like my Dad — pulled back and forth by I knew not what, held fast by strings so fine as to be imperceptible but so strong they might as well have been chains. Something had to change and, thankfully, it did. By now, you know a bit of the story.

What you don't know is all I learned, what I'm still learning, about living freely and lightly. What more can be said about the life Jesus said we could have? First…

1. *The free and light life is the abundant life.* It's the opposite of the trying, striving, self-reliant, success-driven, highly competitive, painfully ambitious, driven, often anxious life. It's a life lived in response to Jesus' gentle invitation to come to Him, walk with Him, work with Him and watch Him. It's a life marked by peace and rest. It's a life where it's enough to just be with Jesus without always having to do for Jesus. It's a life spent attending to His presence, resting in His extravagant love, living out of your true identity, and responding to God in love, motivated by love, as one who knows himself to be "holy and dearly loved (Colossians 3:12)." It's the abundant life Jesus promised us (John 10:10).

2. *The free and light life is a process.* It's about moving toward Him, not away from Him, regularly naming and forsaking your old way of life with its hard yoke and heavy burden for the easy yoke and light burden Jesus offers you. You *learn* to live freely and lightly. If you're determined to leave the shallows, if you long for deeper water, if that is your heart's desire, you will make progress, you are making progress, it just takes time. It takes time to "cultivate the habits and disciplines to learn to swim in deeper waters."[114] Our natural tendency will always be to work for God, not with Him, to take matters into our own hands, to crave His attention — "Watch me, Jesus" — instead of watching Him. It takes time to unlearn your old way of life so you can learn to live the Jesus way.

3. *The free and light life is a gift.* You're meant to float along on the unforced rhythms of His grace, enjoying His favor regardless of your circumstances. It's an unforced rhythm of grace, not works.

You start your life with Christ by grace (Ephesians 2:8), you continue in grace — every day is a gift — and its grace upon grace from there (John 1:16). Grace means *gift*. Your relationship with Jesus is a gift. It's meant to be effortless, easy, and spontaneous, like smooth jazz. You're meant to float on the unforced rhythms. It's about feeling the music, about variations on a theme. It involves riffs and licks, melodies and countermelodies, harmony and dissonance. The free and light life requires you to be flexible to see where the music might take you. It invites you to ad lib so long as you stay on key.

I know a bit about jazz. I've been a big fan most of my life. I played trumpet in a jazz band in high school with people who actually knew what they were doing. As a result, I know the difference between those who study the music, rehearse the music and perform the music and those who feel it. Playing all the right notes the right way, at the right time, with the right volume and intonation, isn't a bad thing. It's where we all start and there's a measure of satisfaction in playing your part, in a job well done. The downside is that it's possible, when you embrace this kind of life — the doing right and being right life — to put undue pressure on yourself, thinking it all depends on you. It's also possible to hit all the right notes and somehow miss the melody of your love relationship with Jesus, the pure joy of a life lived in close proximity to Him, the transcendent song of the Singer who invites you to join the chorus. Your experience might differ from mine, but my life in the shallows was predictable and ultimately unsatisfying. I was studying Jesus, teaching about Jesus, working for Jesus, singing about Jesus. I was in the Jesus business when I could have been enjoying Him. The free and light life is a gift. It's meant to be enjoyed. He means to be bring you joy.

4.   *The free and light life is life with Jesus.* It's about learning to keep company with Him. The phrase "keep company" has been a part of the English language for some time and we use it in a variety of ways. We say, "At least John has his dog to keep him company," which is sweet and sad. We say, "I kept my uncle company for a few hours. He gets very lonely," which is kind. We say, "John and Stephanie are keeping company", which used to mean they were courting or stepping out together, but now might mean they have people locked in cages in their basement. You never know. We also say, "The people you keep company with will determine, in large part, who or what you will become five years from now." And it's true. Questions like, "Who are you spending time with? Who holds sway over you? Who are your influencers, your counselors, your models and mentors?" are things we should ask ourselves regularly.

To "keep company" with someone is, by definition, to spend time with them for the sake of companionship. Far more than a mingle, when you keep company with someone, it implies a growing association, a connection beyond acquaintance. Companionship is so important to us, so a part of what it means to be human, we have a plethora of words and phrases that basically mean the same thing. When two or more people are keeping company with one another, we say they're "rubbing shoulders together" or "rubbing elbows", which is an odd and vaguely creepy way to say they're close. We say they "run around, pal around and hang out together" or are as "thick as thieves," a reference to shared secrets or the fact, perhaps, that thieves make fantastic friends.

When I think of companionship, I think of my wife, Dianne, who is the dearest friend I've ever had. I think of my parents who we're joined at the hip for over forty-eight years. I think of the countless times in the 1970s, when my mom and dad would invite friends over on a Friday night. My Mom always referred to our guests as "company." "We're having company tonight," she'd say. "You boys will have to amuse yourselves." We'd eat dinner as a family then, after dinner, my Dad's second cousin, Judd, and his fun-loving wife, Edna, would show up and the four of them would play cards, drink coffee, and laugh their way into the night. I have wonderful memories of those times, watching my parents enjoy and entertain their friends. I would often leave my room and linger around the table in the kitchen. I just wanted to be part of it. I was also hoping to get my share of Mom's chocolate no-bake cookies.

I always knew we were going to have company because my mom would make up a big batch of chocolate no-bake cookies and put them in the refrigerator. It's been a running joke between us for most of my adult life. I'd open the refrigerator door, see the cookies laid out invitingly on multiple cookie sheets and I'd say, "Mom, can I have a cookie?" And invariably she would reply, "No, those are for company." "Company?" I'd say. "All of them? There's fifty no-bakes in there and there are four of you. Are you trying to induce a sugar coma?" To which she would reply, "Never you mind. Touch them and die." Or something like that. It was a threat, that much I remember.

Keeping company with someone is about companionship, and companionship is a beautiful thing. Would you like to be a companion of Jesus? Do you desire to move beyond mere acquaintance, beyond general familiarity to real intimacy? What would it be like to walk with Him, eat with Him, talk with Him, pray with Him, to sit at His feet and just be with Him? Jesus invites you into just such a life. He offers you intimacy, companionship, and friendship. Think about it. You could be an intimate of Jesus, a trusted confidant, a bosom friend, if you learn to keep company with Him. That's what He's talking about in Matthew 11:28-30. That's what awaits you just beyond the buoys, in the deep end of the pool. You can enjoy His presence. You can find lasting peace and rest. You can walk with Him, work with Him, and watch Him. You can learn the unforced rhythms of grace. You can live freely and lightly. Does that interest you? Are you curious? Are you ready to take the next step?

A Dog-paddler's Guide

Learning to live freely and lightly is not as hard as it seems. You have help. God uses everything and wastes nothing. Your time in the shallow end of the pool has not been fruitless, far from it. What you've learned about God, yourself, and others will serve you well as you move forward. Your shallow water skills are transferable, building blocks for the next adventure. The only thing standing in the way between your current experience of God and the life Jesus said you could have is your lack of desire. Do you want to go deeper? Do you want more of God? Are you content with your relationship with Jesus, content with your prayer life, content with your ability to discern the will of God, content with your experience of His presence? Are you at peace in all circumstances, at rest in turmoil? Are you freer than you used to be? I want to address this issue of freedom. I want to talk about the things that get their hooks in us and impede our progress. Before I do, let me remind you of what I did and what I learned in the process. I'm a dog-paddler and this, you might say, is a dog-paddler's guide to a deeper life. First, let me encourage you to…

1. *Abandon your trying life and start training.* Take the time, as Vanstone wrote, "to cultivate the habits and disciplines to learn

to swim in deeper waters."[115] But keep it simple. Remember to do what you can, not what you can't. Something is better than nothing. Five minutes spent in quiet contemplation, meditating on the Word of God, is better than nothing at all. Even our meager efforts to keep company with Him are a delight to Him. He delights in you! Practice, practice, practice, but give yourself grace, grace, grace. And…

2. *Trade your driven life for a life lived in response to God.* Let Him draw you, at His pace, in His time, from one thing to the next, one season to the next. Ask Him questions. God loves it when we ask Him questions. One of my favorite questions is, "Father, what are we working on today? What do you want to do in me?" Or, "If I saw me as clearly as you do, what would I celebrate and what would I want to change?" Then, respond to Him. Yield to Him. Follow His lead. Then…

3. *Be open, walk slowly, bow often.* Things began to change for me when I asked God for the grace to find Him in all things. "Increase my awareness of you," I would pray, and He did. Over time, I got into the habit of inviting Him to join me in whatever I was doing, in the mundane, ordinary things of life. It was a soul-training exercise, a spiritual practice. "Will you join me, Father, as I enjoy this meal or take this walk or make this call?" He so wants to be included. He wants to be included in every aspect of your life. The more I practiced in this way, inviting Him into everything, the more aware of Him I became. Then…

4. *Root your life in God's extravagant love.* Say it to yourself, over and over again, "God likes me, God loves me and God loves

loving me." This was the tipping point for me. When I finally surrendered to love, allowing myself to be loved with perfect love by the God who *is* love, when I moved from knowing to loving, courtship to commitment, from a performance-oriented life with God, full of duty and obligation, to a freely and lightly life with God, supported, upheld, carried along by His "absolutely unconditional, unlimited and unimaginably extravagant"[116] love, it changed everything. You have to let God love you, receive His love, respond to His love. It's all about love! Finally…

5. *Embrace your true identity.* The three-step process I explained in the last chapter of daily (a) confessing my limitations, (b) expressing my complete dependence upon God and (c) letting go of all the finite sources of identity, worth and value to live out of my true self, the things that never change, who God says I am, has been so liberating. When I fall short and confess my sins, I know that I'm forgiven. When others ignore me, I'm reminded that God chose me. When I'm worried about the future, I know my future is secure. I'm a co-heir with Christ. I've been adopted into God's family. When I wonder if God is with me, I need look no further than my own soul. He has taken up residence within. When I'm rejected, excluded, passed over, left out, that is not the end of the story. I belong to God and nothing can change that. When others insult me and persecute me, I can rest in God's unchanging love. This is my true identity, the anchor of my soul.

This is my story, my journey and, as I said in chapter 1, I have a long way to go. Am I living freely and lightly? Yes, I'm happy to say, sometimes if not most of the time. I'm still learning. That's the exciting part. I haven't arrived. There's so much more to explore, more to discover, so much to look forward to — deeper levels of intimacy with God, a deeper understanding of self and others, more love, joy, peace, patience, kindness, goodness, faithfulness, gentleness and deeper levels of self-control. The water I've explored thus far, just beyond the buoys, only increases my desire for more. For years, when I was teaching the Bible, I would say to folks, "There's so much more," without really knowing the more there was. Now that I've taken this step out of the shallow end of the pool, I *know* there's more. I've experience the more. And there's still way more, more than I can possibly imagine. God has more for me and so much more for you.

That said, the five steps I detail above are not boxes you check or pages you turn or buttons you push. It's about *learning* to walk this way. As I've said, there are no shortcuts to a life with God and there's no reason to rush the process. As Vanstone wrote, "If we are to love God with all our heart, soul, mind and strength, then we need the kind of sustained learning that leads us to into the deep end of the pool."[117] It requires, as author, Eugene Peterson, noted, "a long obedience in the same direction."[118] I've been walking this way for ten years now and it hasn't been easy. In some ways, these ten years have been among the most difficult years of my life. I've suffered abuse, been falsely accused, and mistreated by folks I thought were friends. I've suffered loss, experienced grief and nearly came apart physically and emotionally in the wake of the pandemic with all the turmoil, angst and division, the halving of the church and all the uncertainty. Through it all, I came to see that my circumstances were the proving ground of all that God was teaching me. And He was with me, as present in the midst as I have ever experienced Him. As I practiced my faith — inviting Him in, attending to His presence — and sought to live out of my true identity, rooted in God's unimaginably extravagant love, I eventually found peace regardless of my circumstances and with peace, joy.

So let me tell you, wherever you find yourself right now, God has you exactly where He wants you. If you've read this far, you've already answered the question of desire. You *want* more of God. You want to escape the noise and learn to float on the unforced rhythms of His grace. You want to feel loved by God, the object of His affection, living as one highly favored. You may not be in crisis, like I was when I started, but you can feel the longing rising within you. That's how it starts — the journey out of the shallows into the deep end of the pool.

A Caution

As you determine to walk toward God, not away from Him — living out of your true identity, rooted and grounded in God's perfect love — you need to know that Satan hates what you're doing. He will war against it. You're changing and because you're changing, the strategies of the enemy are changing as well. Along with his usual tactics — sowing doubt, stoking fear, throwing up obstacles, tempting you to sin — he might now present himself to you as something good, as a choice between two good things (i.e. a promotion at work and time with your family). The brilliant military commander always makes adjustments. He becomes craftier, cleverer, making use of Trojan horses — all sorts of evil camouflaged as good. He means to ensnare you, impede your progress, steal your joy, destroy your life with God. Jesus Himself warned about wolves in sheep's clothing (Matthew 7:15) and the Apostle Paul said that the prince of darkness often masquerades as an angel of light (2 Corinthians 11:14). So, by way of application, allow me to highlight two less obvious points of attack. First, Satan often uses...

> 1. *The things we think we need to be happy.* Another way to describe them would be unhealthy attachments or destructive desires. These are the things that often get their hooks in us. An attachment forms when you cling to the false belief that something or someone is necessary for your happiness. These attachments happen naturally, through the course of life, often as a response to life circumstances or experiences. Here's how it works.

First comes contact with something or someone that gives you pleasure. It could be a good thing, an innocent thing — a new relationship, the birth of a child, a leisure activity, the job of your dreams. Then comes the desire to hold on to that something or someone that gives you pleasure and never let it go. You need it. Your happiness depends upon it. Much like Golem in *The Lord of the Rings*, you can't imagine life without it. "We wants it, we needs it. Must have the precious."[119] This often leads to the conviction that you won't be happy without this person or thing, that it's essential to your happiness. Suddenly, almost imperceptibly, you've crossed over in your heart and mind, equating the pleasure this person or thing brings you with happiness. It's subtle, I know, but that's how the enemy often ensnares us. It's how he gets his hooks in us.

"One way you can tell if a natural desire is becoming an unhealthy attachment is when it starts to take you over so you begin to make choices fueled entirely by the desire to get what you want or the fear of losing what you already have."[120] Are you making decisions fueled entirely by your desire to get what you want or the fear of losing what you have? I'm pushing on this because it's such a blind spot for many believers. What do you think you need to be happy? What are your core desires? Ask yourself.

Do I need to be in control?
Do I need to be right?
Do I need to be liked?
Do I need to rescue, help or serve others?
Do I need to be understood and appreciated?
Do I need to be perfect?
Do I need to be comfortable?

Do I need to be healthy and pain free?

Do I need financial security?

These subtle desires express an unhealthy attachment that Satan may be using to subvert your love relationship with God. If this is what you think you need to be happy, you'll never be happy! You'll make decisions based on your need to be in control or your need to be liked or your need to be comfortable. Do you see how these unhealthy attachments can take over your life? The question you should ask is, "What core desire am I trying to fulfill with these finite, temporal sources?" Are you seeking attention, affection, control, security, belonging, significance, or power? God is supposed to be the sole source of your happiness. True satisfaction, true contentment, is found in Christ and Christ alone. The question that emerges, as you long for the more I spoke about earlier, is the question, "Is God enough? Is intimacy with God enough?" Because that is what you will find just beyond the buoys, more of God, a life with God. Is that enough for you? A. W. Tozer warned against pursuing "God and…"[121] If you decide to walk this way, leaving the friendly confines of the shallows to pursue the more, you must want God for Himself. Satan uses the things we think we need to be happy and…

2. *The things that own us.* "It is not what we own that we must discard, but that which owns us."[122] Again, an unhealthy attachment is "anything that takes away your freedom to freely respond to God."[123] So it's not what you own, it's what owns you. Consider Abraham, in the Old Testament. It's possible to have everything and possess nothing, to own everything and not be owned by anything. In my journey with Jesus, I had to wrestle with some tough questions. I'll put them to you as they were put to me. "Look

at your life: your use of time, resources, your relationships, your daily life and ask yourself…

What consumes my thoughts and plans?
What holds my allegiance?
Who or what tell me who I am?
What gives me security and comfort?
What makes me feel whole and complete?
Who/what meets my deepest needs?"[124]

These are hard questions. It's hard to face the fact that someone or something other than God consumes your thoughts and plans, holds your allegiance, meets your deepest needs and tells you who you really are? It's hard when you realize that you've been planted in the wrong soil, that your roots go down deep into something other than God's perfect love. Satan doesn't want you to ask these questions. He wants to keep you attached, hooked, in bondage, to something that takes away your freedom to freely respond to God and step into all He has for you.

Here's another question. Can you imagine the joy you would feel if you removed the hook from your ear, if you finally broke free from the things you think you need to be happy and the things that own you? Wouldn't that be wonderful? How is it done?

The Mind of Christ

Besides what I've already shared about practicing your faith, responding to God, attending to His presence, resting in His love and living out of your true identity, let me add another suggestion. Breaking free from unhealthy attachments is made easier when you adopt the mind of Christ. What was Jesus' attitude toward things? How did He respond to the praise and criticism of others? How concerned was He with His own security and comfort? How did He respond to suffering? What consumed His thoughts and plans? If the Apostle Paul encouraged us to have the same attitude as Jesus (Philippians 2:5-8), what was His attitude? While we can't answer these questions definitively, the Bible offers us several clues. For example, Jesus said…

- "Foxes have holes and birds of the air have nests, but the Son of Man has no place to lay His head (Matthew 8:20)."

- "My food is to do the will of Him who sent me (John 4:34)."

- "I do not accept glory [or praise] from human beings (John 5:41)…"

- "I seek not to please myself but Him who sent me (John 5:30)."

- "Yet not as I will, but as you [God] will (Matthew 26:39)."

What was Jesus' attitude? How did He feel about the things we think we need to be happy? He was indifferent, detached. You might say He held the non-essential loosely. It's not that He didn't care about people or relationships or creature comforts, it's just that those things didn't consume His thoughts and plans. They were not what made Him feel whole or complete; they did not define who He was. As a result, He was free, free to say "yes" to God, the Father. He wasn't fueled by the desire to get what He wanted or the fear of losing what He had. He was free, the freest man who ever lived. He walked through life unencumbered, with a broad smile and a light touch. Jesus lived freely and lightly.

And it's not just Jesus. Mary, His mother, also practiced this indifference or holy detachment. She and Joseph had their lives all planned out when, suddenly, God broke in, uninvited, and upset their apple cart with news of a baby and not just any baby. In the end, Mary says essentially the same thing Jesus would say in the Garden of Gethsemane thirty-three years later, "Not my will but yours be done (Mark 14:36; Luke 1:36)." We see something similar in the Apostle Paul. He writes, "I know what it is to be in need, and I know what it is to have plenty. I have learned the secret of being content in any and every situation, whether well fed or hungry, whether living in plenty or in want. I can do all things through Him who gives me strength (Philippians 4:12-13)." He wasn't driven by his desire for things or the fear of losing what he had. He was content, indifferent to his circumstances.

How do we get there?

I believe indifference to the things we think we need to be happy, to our wants and desires, is a by-product of owning who God is and who we are as the beloved of God. As we own, in an ever-deepening way, God's unconditional love for us and our unshakeable worth, value and significance as His dearly loved children, our felt need for the approval of others, the entice-ments of this world — power, riches, popularity, possessions — will grow weaker and weaker and our ability to be indifferent to all but the triune God will grow stronger. It all comes back to perfect love. If you're rooted and grounded in perfect love and you embrace your true identity as a child of God, "the things of this world will grow strangely dim," as the hymn writer put it, "in the light of His glory and grace."[125]

Think about it for a moment. "What if you didn't care? I mean, really didn't care about what people said or thought about you? What if your sense of identity, worth, and value were all grounded in the actions and words of Jesus? What if you truly believed, with absolute certainty, that God loves you, delights in you, even likes and enjoys you, and that will never change? Would you live differently? Would you live Jesus more fully? Would you feel free to be yourself, a one-of-a-kind masterpiece created by God in Christ Jesus? Would you be free to own all you are with your gifts, abilities, quirks and struggles without pride or hiding or condemnation but with an acceptance flowing from your deep belief that nothing can separate you from the unconditional love of God? What if you believed, really believed God was for you and not against you, that you are truly a child of God and that God is actively loving you into this moment and the next — not out of some self-imposed divine duty but because God loves loving you? Would you be more willing to love others, the marginalized, your friends, family, sisters and brothers in Christ, returning blessing for cursing, loving without strings attached?"[126] This is something to hold before the Lord and let Him search your heart.

Prayer of Detachment

I'd also encourage you to pray this brief prayer of detachment. A simple soul-training exercise, it's been a tremendous help to me in my quest to live freely and lightly. It's adapted from a sixteenth century prayer by Peter Faber. It reads,

> I ask you, Lord,
> To remove anything that separates me from you,
> And you from me.
> Remove anything that stands in the way of my
> Seeing you, hearing you, experiencing you, enjoying you, reverencing you
> And being mindful of you.
> Help me know you, trust you, love you and rest in your love for me,
> Always conscious of your caring love and involvement in my life,
> Earnestly seeking to be present with the One who is ever-present with me.[127]

The More

I want to share one final story. Last summer, my daughter-in-law invited Dianne and I to join her and the kids for an afternoon at their local pool. It was a beautiful day, an azure-blue, cloudless sky keeping watch alongside a gaggle of ever-vigilant lifeguards barely out of puberty. With the temperature hovering in the mid-90s, most folks were huddled under an awning that stretched the length of the pool on one side, sunglasses making those who were monitoring things indistinguishable from those taking an afternoon snooze. Several things immediately caught my attention. There was one enormous pool, shaped like a square, where ninety-nine percent of the folks were congregating, and a much smaller pool which was largely empty. The larger pool, ankle deep on one end and not more than five feet deep on the other, was home to a variety of aquatic delights. Colorful over-sized mushrooms provided shelter from the sun and a refreshing, never-ending curtain of rain, cascading down from the rim of each mushroom, added to the excitement. Kid-sized dolphins, whales and sea turtles squirted water from their snouts and blow holes while a horde of sun-tanned children rode their backs — jumping, splashing and shouting with delight.

We took the only loungers available to us, out from under the crowded awning, in the full view of an angry sun. It was hot. I could already feel the sweat dampening my brow as I hastily slathered myself with sunscreen. I needed to get out of the *Fry Daddy* and into the water as quickly as possible. Pulling on a ball cap, I grabbed my grandson's hand and joined the revelers in the shallow end of the larger pool. For the next hour, I chased, carried and followed Elly and Theo from one mushroom to the next, clambering and splashing over dolphins and sea turtles as they played with me and others. I settled mini-arguments, pulled more than one kid to his feet when they'd gotten a mouthful and served as a weigh station, out of the tumult, where they could cling to my shoulders when they'd had enough.

Eventually, Elly asked me to toss her. I knew immediately what she meant. She loves to fly, as we call it. She learned how to do it by practicing with her father. Putting one foot in his cupped hands and steading herself with her hands on his shoulders, she would bounce up and down for a count of three and he would launch her into the air like she was shot out of a cannon. Eventually, she learned to tuck her legs and perform a full rotation right before splashdown. She loves it. Her brother, Theo, loves it. Their older cousins love it, too. They'll do it endlessly if you let them for as long as you can stand it. Twice my son's age, with less than half his muscle mass, asking Papa to launch you is not the same thrill ride. It's definitely a young man's game.

That day, with my son at work, I did the best I could and an odd thing happened. As I was tossing my grandkids, one after the other, knowing I would need traction later in the day, several other kids about their size, watching the party at a distance, just couldn't help themselves. Suddenly, I was tossing half the kids in the pool. Total strangers were lining up to be thrown into the air while their parents watched from afar, happy they weren't me. Eventually, I had had enough. I was played out and floated over to the edge of the pool for a breather, five or six of the kids hanging around my neck, begging me to do it "one more time." As my daughter-in-law rescued me, letting the kids know Papa needed a rest, I closed my eyes and tried to relax while the kids moved on to the next amusement.

Several minutes later, catching my second wind, I looked around for my grandchildren. Elly was in among the mushrooms, talking excitedly with some friends, but Theo, the three-year-old, was nowhere to be seen. With Dianne and my daughter-in-law engaged in conversation behind me, playing with the baby, I wasn't exactly alarmed. I knew they were paying attention, so I asked them, "Where's Theo?" "He's over there," his mother said casually. Following her gaze, I couldn't believe my eyes. My three-year-old grandson was climbing out of the *other* pool. Do you remember the other pool, the smaller one? I mentioned it earlier. It was flanked by a diving platform that rose some fifteen feet in the air. I'd seen some teenagers bouncing up and down on the diving board earlier, daring each other to go higher before cannon balling into the water. They were gathered there now, egging on my grandson, encouraging him as he slowly climbed the ladder and, with a look of pure joy on his face, walked out onto that diving board and started jumping up and down. "Are you seeing this?" I asked my wife. "He's fine," his mother said reassuringly. "He does it all the time." "He does it all the time?" I asked incredulously. "How deep is that pool?" "It's like twenty feet deep?" she guessed.

Just at that moment, Theo was airborne, and I realized I was holding my breath in fear. It seemed really dangerous, dangerous for a full-grown adult, let alone a child. I, personally, wouldn't go anywhere near that thing, even in my prime. The climb was too high; the board was too thin and the pool was far too deep. "Sure, it *looks* like fun," I would tell myself. "It's all fun and games until somebody gets hurt." That's when I realized I was content in the shallows, a lifelong shallow-dweller, carefully applying my shallow-water skills, the life of the shallow water party. "Look at this crowd," I could have shouted to him. "We've got dolphins and sea turtles over here, basketball hoops and weeping mushrooms. If you want to fly, you can fly over here, in the shallows, where it's safe, where I can keep an eye on you." And he could have replied, "That's good, Papa, but there's more. There's so much more."

Do you know the more there is? If you've decided to respond to Jesus, to the longing He's put inside you, to His invitation to move from knowing to loving, so much more awaits you. Will you take the next step? Will you venture out beyond the buoys? Will you join Him in the deep end of the pool?

going deeper

The following is a short list of resources that have helped deepen my journey with Jesus. I pray they might be as helpful to you as they were and are to me. I've arranged them by subject in no particular order as a supplement to the exercises and prayers I've already shared in the telling of my story.

- Exploring Spiritual Practices: Alongside Richard Foster's classic, *The Celebration of Discipline: The Path to Spiritual Growth*, no book has helped me understand and engage spiritual practices more practically than Adele Ahlberg Calhoun's *Spiritual Disciplines Handbook: Practices that Transform Us*. If you want to open yourself to God, lay down your false self, hear God's Word or simply learn to pray, Adele offers a list of practices to choose from, with simple explanations and a host of suggestions.

- Practicing Silence and Solitude: There's no better way to practice the presence of God than engaging in the twin, soul-training exercises of silence and solitude. In that regard, Ruth Haley Barton's book, *Invitation to Silence and Solitude: Experiencing God's Transforming Presence,* is a wonderfully helpful guide.

- Meditating on Scripture: Latin for "sacred reading," *Lectio Divina* is an ancient spiritual practice that deepens your time in the Word and encourages you to listen for the voice of God. I've seen this practice described in a variety of ways, but I remember it best using the Five R's: Ready, Read, Reflect, Respond and Rest. For a fuller explanation and forty days of guided meditations, I have loved using *Meeting God in Scripture: A Hands-On Guide to Lectio Divina* by Jan Johnson.

- <u>Resting in the Father's Love</u>: For a thorough treatment on God's extravagant, unimaginable love for you and how this truth can become a lived reality in your life, I have two recommendations. The first is a book by David Benner entitled *Surrender to Love: Discovering the Heart of Christian Spirituality*. The second is *Connecting: Rediscovering Life-Giving Love with God* by R. Thomas Ashbrook. These books filled in a number of gaps in my understanding and helped me find a home in the God who is Love.

- <u>Deepening Desire</u>: *Living in Christ's Presence: Final Words on Heaven and the Kingdom of God* by Dallas Willard, mentioned in Chapter 2, has served as a catalyst, deepening my desire for more of God. I've listened to the audio version multiple times and still find it captivating. I pray it will inspire your pursuit of God as much as it has mine.

- <u>Engaging the Ignatian Exercises</u>: If you're drawn, in this season of your life, to a more concentrated time of sustained learning at the feet of Jesus, I'd encourage you to prayerfully consider the Ignatian Exercises. It was, as I've said, an immersive, life-changing, and transformative experience for me. Larry Warner's book, *Journey with Jesus: Discovering the Spiritual Exercises of Saint Ignatius,* is incredibly accessible and comprehensive.

- <u>Finding a Spiritual Director</u>: Like so many other things that originated in the church, the world has co-opted the ministry of spiritual direction. A simple Google search for qualified spiritual directors uncovers a cornucopia of New Age spiritualists and self-appointed gurus, many of whom are practicing with no reference whatsoever to God and His Word. What is the earnest follower of Jesus to do? How do you find a Christ-centered spiritual director or listener that you can trust? I would recommend *Grafted Life Ministries* (www.graftedlife.org) and the *Evangelical Spiritual Directors Association*. Every one of their members has to agree with a doctrinal statement, complete an approved spiritual direction training program, and concur with a code of ethics in their spiritual direction work.

- <u>Walking with God with Others</u>: The opportunity to grow in community — walking with others — while pursuing a deeper, more intimate love relationship with Jesus is a rare gift. So much of what passes for community leaves us feeling reticent to share openly. You're more likely to say the right thing than the real thing. My experience leading *Life with God* groups has changed all that. I've never walked in such close community with others while engaging my relationship with God on such a deep level. *Life with God: A Journey of Relationship* was developed by Debbie Swindoll, the Executive Director of *Grafted Life Ministries*. There are six workbooks in total, all rooted in Scripture. The first two — *The Genesis of Relationship* and *The History of the Heart* — are foundational to the rest of the series. Dianne and I, along with our team of trained facilitators, have walked with more than one hundred and fifty people using this material over the last five years. So many lives have been changed. I can't recommend it more highly. For more information or to find a group near you, go to www.graft-edlife.org. You can also inquire about upcoming online cohorts led by our team at www.markvictorwarner.com.

There are countless other books and resources that have blessed my journey with Jesus, far too many to name. I'm grateful for them all but especially grateful for those God has used to reawaken my desire for the more Jesus said we could have.

gratitudes

As I've processed my journey aloud in countless sermons and hundreds of conversations over the last ten years, I've been blessed to be surrounded by a multitude of gifted listeners who offered wisdom, asked really good questions, prayed for me and encouraged me along the way. I've also had the incalculable benefit of drafting off a host of authors, thinkers, pastors, leaders and other, less known, followers of Jesus who have gone before me, profoundly shaping my understanding of what it means to live freely and lightly. Many are referenced in the pages of this book. In truth, after more than forty years in ministry — with all the books I've read and all the sermons I've listened to — it's hard sometimes to know where they end and I begin. I've done my best to give credit where credit is due. Where I might have failed, I beg your forgiveness. I'm grateful for your work and your willingness to share it with others. You've had a profound impact on my life.

Though I can't possibly name everyone who's blessed me in this season, I want to acknowledge those whose contributions have been especially memorable. First, to all the wonderful folks — past and present — at Vineyard Community Church in Overland Park, Kansas, thank you for taking me and my family in all those years ago. It's been a privilege and delight to walk through life with you. You've inspired me in ways words cannot express, and I'm grateful. To Tom Ashbrook, my dear friend and mentor, your godly wisdom and investment in my life have made a lasting difference. I'm so glad to have found you. To Larry Warner, it's been an adventure. From that first cryptic email through countless Zoom calls, thank you for walking with me through thick and thin. To my children, Alexis, Cameron, Brittany and Savannah, you're so dear to me. I'm blessed to be your dad, proud of you and your families, and eternally grateful for a lifetime of fabulous sermon illustrations. To my mom and dad, Luke and Lou Warner, and my dear brothers, Dave and Eric, I love you. It's a joy to share pieces of our shared life with others. And to Dianne, my dearest, not a word of this book would have made it to print without your tender care, constant prayers, and a lifetime of encouragement. I see the evidence that God likes me, God loves me and God loves loving me in every moment we've spent together. You are a gift to me.

about the author

Mark Warner is an author, speaker, storyteller, and coach. He's served as a senior pastor for over forty years, helping congregations in crisis recover their footing and return to health. He's also ministered alongside his fellow pastors as an Area Leader, a Regional Leader and as the Director of Development for the Vineyard Pilgrimage, a ministry of Vineyard USA.

It was during his time at the Pilgrimage that Mark did extensive research into how Christians grow, exploring ways the church can partner with the Holy Spirit to help believers discover a more meaningful life with God. That research gave birth to the Pilgrim Pathway, a roadmap for pastors and churches who long to help their congregations escape the spiritual shallows and go deeper. Trained as a spiritual director, Mark's blog on the deeper life explores a variety of topics related to Christian Spiritual Formation and spiritual growth. He lives with his wife, Dianne, and a little dog named Milo, in Overland Park, Kansas.

For additional resources and information visit:
www.markvictorwarner.com.

endnotes

1. https://greenleafbookgroup.com/learning-center/book-creation/distinguishing-between-a-foreword-a-preface-and-an-introduction
2. *The Gift of Being Yourself* by David Benner, p. 49.
3. As cited in the training *Becoming a Transforming Church* by Ruth Haley Barton, p. 1.
4. As spoken by Baptist Evangelist Vance Havener in chapel at Toccoa Falls College, 1981.
5. As cited in the training *Becoming a Transforming Church* by Ruth Haley Barton, p. 1.
6. As cited in https://www.goodreads.com/quotes/35269-i-have-so-much-to-do-that-i-shall-spend
7. *Liturgy of the Ordinary* by Tish Harrison Warren, p. 34.
8. As cited in the training *Becoming a Transforming Church* by Ruth Haley Barton, p. 1.
9. James 3:17 (NLT).
10. From The Empire Strikes Back, 1980.
11. *Journey with Jesus* by Larry Warner, p. 40.
12. Ibid, p. 41.
13. *Mudhouse Sabbath* by Lauren F. Winner, p. xi.
14. James 1:22.
15. *The Good and Beautiful God* by James Bryan Smith, p. 26-7.
16. Ibid.
17. *Living in Christ's Presence* by Dallas Willard, p. 140.
18. *Soul Keeping* by John Ortberg, p. 22.
19. *Living in Christ's Presence* by Dallas Willard, p. 141.
20. Dictionary.com.

21.   1 Samuel 3:9-10.

22.   Luke 22:42.

23.   *Living in Christ's Presence* by Dallas Willard, p. 141-2.

24.   *Journey with Jesus* by Larry Warner, p. 32.

25.   *When the Soul Listens* by Jan Johnson, p. 9-10.

26.   Dallas Willard, widely quoted.

27.   Look Down, *Les Misérables*, the musical, original lyrics by Alain Boublil and Jean-Marc Natel, adapted by Herbert Kretzmer, an English lyricist, 1980.

28.   *Invitation to Silence and Solitude* by Ruth Haley Barton, p. 99.

29.   Philippians 1:17.

30.   Philippians 2:3.

31.   Matthew 4:19.

32.   Matthew 9:9.

33.   As cited in *Invitation to Silence and Solitude* by Ruth Haley Barton, p. 55.

34.   Ibid.

35.   Ibid.

36.   Ibid.

37.   Luke 10:41.

38.   *Vincent's Word Studies*, Matthew 11:29.

39.   "Breathe," a training by Larry Warner, p. 3.

40.   NASB.

41.   MSG.

42.   *Life Without Lack* by Dallas Willard, p. 199.

43.   As cited in The NIV Study Bible, 2 Samuel 15:14.

44.   The word here is literally "cease."

45.   As noted in The NIV Study Bible, Mark 2:27.

46.   As cited in *From Stressed to Blessed,* a message by Rick Warren, 2014.

47.   As enumerated in "Breathe," a training by Larry Warner, p. 3-4.

48.   Ibid.

49.   As cited in *From Stressed to Blessed,* a message by Rick Warren, 2014.

50.   *The Spiritual Life* by Evelyn Underhill, p. 59.

51.   From *Jabberwocky* by Lewis Carroll.

52.   Hebrews 13:2.

53.   *The Pursuit of God* by A.W. Tozer, p. 57.

54. *When the Soul Listens: Finding Rest and Direction in Contemplative Prayer* by Jan Johnson, 2017.

55. Matthew 1:23.

56. Paul Stevens, as cited in *The Gift of Being Yourself* by David Benner, p. 41.

57. These thoughts on loneliness as homesickness for God inspired by a sermon by Rich Nathan entitled *The Best Mental Health Advice Ever*, Vineyard-Columbus, 2008.

58. https://www.goodreads.com/book/show/12447.You_Can_t_Go_Home_Again

59. *The Gift of Being Yourself* by David Benner, p. 41.

60. *Journey with Jesus* by Larry Warner, p. 98.

61. Ibid.

62. *Discernment, God's Will and Living Jesus* by Larry Warner, p. 82-3.

63. https://www.loyolapress.com/catholic-resources/ignatian-spirituality/finding-god-in-all-things/

64. *Discernment, God's Will and Living Jesus* by Larry Warner. p. 87-91

65. *Living in Christ's Presence* by Dallas Willard, p. 144.

66. *Discernment, God's Will and Living Jesus* by Larry Warner. p. 87-91.

67. Ibid, p. 87.

68. *Backyard Pilgrim: Forty Days at Godspeed* by Matt Canlis.

69. *Discernment, God's Will & Living Jesus* by Larry Warner, p. 88.

70. Ibid.

71. Ibid, p. 89.

72. *Invitation to Silence and Solitude* by Ruth Haley Barton, p. 44.

73. Ibid, p. 74.

74. *Discernment, God's Will & Living Jesus* by Larry Warner, p. 88.

75. *Invitation to Silence and Solitude* by Ruth Haley Barton, p. 35.

76. *The Gift of Being Yourself* by David Benner, p. 49.

77. From a training compiled by Larry Warner entitled, God Loves You!, p. 3

78. *Life of the Beloved* by Henri J.M. Nouwen, p. 30.

79. *Journey with Jesus* by Larry Warner, p. 58.

80. *The Gift of Being Yourself* by David Benner, p. 47.

81. Ibid, p. 46.

82. *Connected: Rediscovering Life-Giving Love with God* by R. Thomas Ashbrook, p. 36.

83. *Journey with Jesus* by Larry Warner, p. 61.

84. Ibid.

85. New International Bible Commentary, note.

86. *Surrender to Love* by David G. Benner, p. 61.

87. I'm grateful to David Benner for this image and awakening this memory in me, *Surrender to Love*, p. 60-1.

88. Larry Warner at the Vineyard USA Midwest South Regional Retreat, 2015.

89. Widely attributed to Dallas Willard.

90. Daniel 3:1.

91. *Do You Love Me?* By Debbie Swindoll, p. 85.

92. *The Genesis of Relationship* by Debbie Swindoll, p. 74.

93. *Born Again* by Charles Colson.

94. From a message by Rich Nathan on John 15 entitled, *Greater Love*, 2009.

95. https://deeperchristianquotes.com/abide-in-christ-jc-ryle/

96. *Experiencing God: The Three Stages of Prayer* by Thomas Green.

97. *The Problem of Pain* by C.S. Lewis, https://www.goodreads.com/quotes/tag/masterpiece.

98. Psalm 139:14.

99. *The Confessions of St. Augustine* by Augustine of Hippo, p. 7, paraphrased.

100. As cited in an article entitled, "The Future of the Church is Analog, not Digital," Christianity Today, September 2016.

101. *The Gift of Being Yourself* by David G. Benner, p. 47.

102. NIV Study Bible, note.

103. Pierre Teilhard de Chardin, SJ, excerpted from *Hearts on Fire*.

104. John 1:3.

105. https://www.moma.org/collection/works/80220

106. *The Call* by Os Guinness, p. 45.

107. *The Message of John's Letters* by David Jackman, p. 83.

108. *The Gift of Being Yourself* by David Benner, p. 83.

109. Ibid, p. 84.

110. As compiled by Larry Warner, www.b-ing.org.

111. Ibid.

112. Ibid.

113. *The Imitation of Christ* by Thomas à Kempis, Book 3, chapter 23.

114. W.H. Vanstone, as cited in the training *Becoming a Transforming Church* by Ruth Haley Barton, p. 1.

115. As cited in the training, *Becoming a Transforming Church* by Ruth Haley Barton, p. 1.

116. *The Gift of Being Yourself* by David Benner, p. 49.

117. As cited in the training, *Becoming a Transforming Church* by Ruth Haley Barton, p. 1.

118. *A Long Obedience in the Same Direction: Discipleship in an Instant Society* by Eugene Peterson, 2020.

119. *The Lord of the Rings: The Two Towers* by J.R.R. Tolkien, film directed by Peter Jackson, 2002.

120. As cited in a training on *Disordered Attachments* by Larry Warner, p. 2.

121. *The Pursuit of God* by A.W. Tozer, p. 97.

122. From a training by Larry Warner entitled, *Additional Week of Exercises on Indifference*, p. 2.

123. *Journey with Jesus* by Larry Warner, p. 301.

124. From a training by Larry Warner entitled, *Additional Week of Exercises on Indifference*, p. 2.

125. *Turn your Eyes Upon Jesus* by Helen H. Lemmel, 1922.

126. Adapted from *I Wonder* by Larry Warner, www.b-ing.org.

127. Based on a prayer by Peter Faber SJ, 1506-46, with additions by Mark Victor Warner.

All the

NOISE

is in the

SHALLOW END

of the

POOL

A Dog-paddler's Journey to a Deeper Life

MARK VICTOR WARNER

SOLI DEO GLORIA
PRESS

All the Noise is in the Shallow End of the Pool
A Dog-paddler's Journey to a Deeper Life

Published by Gatekeeper Press
7853 Gunn Hwy., Suite 209
Tampa, FL 33626
www.GatekeeperPress.com

While the stories in this book are true, some names and identifying information may have been changed or combined to protect the privacy of individuals.

Library of Congress Control Number: 2024947805

ISBN (hardcover): 9781662957178
ISBN (paperback): 9781662957185
eISBN: 9781662957192